PHILOSOPHY AS DRAMATIC THEORY

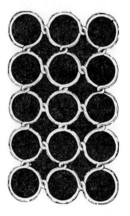

JULIÁN MARÍAS

PHILOSOPHY
AS
DRAMATIC
THEORY

Translated from the Spanish by
James Parsons

THE PENNSYLVANIA STATE
UNIVERSITY PRESS
University Park and London

International Standard Book Number: 0–271–00100–3
Library of Congress Catalog Card Number: 72–84669
Copyright © 1971 by The Pennsylvania State University
All Rights Reserved
Printed in the United States of America
Designed by Marilyn E. Shobaken

CONTENTS

PREFACE

This book, which you now hold in your hands, is not listed among my works in Spanish. Is it a new book? No—it was not written recently, and all its contents have been published in Spanish before. It is a collection of essays that have appeared in various periodicals; many have been included in different books with other titles. But as a book, it exists only in English; as a book, it is entirely new.

We might say that, while I have not just now written it to be published in English, I have *composed* it. Books of essays by an author are not generally translated into other languages; unitary books with a single theme are preferred. Collections of articles, of whatever length, seem to have less value and, at any rate, to be of less interest. But it does happen that some of the best writings of an author are often short pieces. Such writings achieve greater intensity, more literary brilliance, a keener precision; there are no inert elements in them, no dead weight, no areas of lesser tension without inspiration. The good Homer naps with more difficulty in short writings. In the authors whose complete works I am acquainted with—those I read in their original languages—I find that my preference is always for a few essays and articles, along with some books.

I believed it might be worth while for readers of English to have available a few short writings from among those that seem to me most personal, that reflect with unusual intensity my way of confronting a theme, of thinking, and of writing. Thus I have brought together fourteen philosophical essays from among those that are most "my own" in order to make this book out of them.

Now that it is completed, I find with some surprise that
the result is not a "collection" but a book—one more book,
with its own personality. I would even call it a systematic
book; the reason for this is given in the title. If philosophy
is—as I believe is proved in this volume—dramatic theory,
if philosophical theory has a dramatic structure, if it is
something that happens, that has a subject, that happens
to somebody (to the author and no less to the reader),
something that has its *argumento* or "plot," then philosophy, when it is living and in *status nascens*, when it is
not erudition or disputation, has all the characteristics of
human life.

And human life is "what we do and what happens to us";
it is on the one hand a *dramatic* reality and a *systematic*
reality on the other. It is something that happens and at
the same time a unitary operation that I perform, because
of something and for the sake of something, in consideration of the whole of the reality I find in my surroundings.
This systematic character of life is the real reason why
philosophy is systematic, even though the philosopher may
not try to be or even wish to be. I have said many times
that the philosopher is a system-maker *malgré lui*.

The essays that compose this volume have all been
written by the same person and during the same period of
time, that is, within the same situation. When, from time
to time, a philosophical question is raised in them, the texture of that drama which is human life is discovered in its
truth and with it the systematic character of reality as it
appears from this perspective. The themes of these essays
also represent facets or dimensions in which the reality
that surrounds us and requires us to philosophize has been
discovered (*alétheia*): their literary style, the temper of
the interpretation, the combination of their images and
metaphors, the *metaphorical* system that discovers and
illuminates this same reality and which is the correlate of

the *conceptual* system with which an attempt is made to take possession of it.

Upon being brought together, these essays begin to influence one another. They reciprocally interpret and comment on one another, prolong what each of them says, perhaps even talk among themselves, and confront one another as forms that produce a single consequence. Thus, beyond what each of them separately has to say, their combination brings into play the drama that is philosophy. And since philosophy, far from being an impersonal kind of knowing, is always a personal matter (and a philosophical book that many people are going to read is transpersonal), these pages have come to be a confession or confidential report about what their author has most genuinely tried to be. In the plurality of their facets these pages resemble most of all perhaps a portrait by Picasso.

Julián Marías

CHAPTER ONE

LITERARY GENRES
IN PHILOSOPHY

I believe that one of the principal difficulties, if not the most important one, that the philosophy of our time encounters relates to its literary genres. It has become customary to speak, all too precipitously, about the literary genres into which philosophy is "poured." Some time ago, in a study on "the novel as a method of knowledge," [1] I observed that this trivial image is dangerous because it supposes a relation between philosophy and its literary genres analogous to that existing between a liquid and its container—that is, the prior existence of both and their independence of one another. The reality is quite different. Philosophy is expressed—and for this reason is fully made real—within a definite literary genre; and it must be emphasized that prior to this expression it did not exist except in a precarious way or, rather, only as intention and attempt. Philosophy is thus intrinsically bound to the literary genre, not into which it is poured, but, we would do better to say, in which it is *incarnated*.

What happens is that philosophy usually resorts to certain prevailing literary forms, which are then adapted for better or worse to its own internal requirements. Only rarely has philosophy invented its own literary forms— not so much because of a lack of imagination on the part of creating philosophers but because they have been subjected to social pressures. In a certain sense the frequent inauthenticity of literary expressions in philosophy has been a defensive measure—a *burladero*, we might say, a not inappropriate term from the bullring—in order to hide its radical originality, its incredibility, its scandalous nature. This matter is so radical that it begins, as was to be expected, with the very name of philosophy.[2] Philosophical writing is, if one considers it closely, something unheard of. In order to keep it from being too much so, the writing itself tends to be something ordinary and acceptable. But at what cost? This question is decisive because it leads to the problem of "accomplishment" or the realization of philosophy. What I mean is that it raises as an issue to what extent philosophy has become what at each moment it had to be, or to what extent it has been frustrated. A reconstruction of the history of philosophy from this point of view would be of the greatest interest. But since a history of philosophy in the full meaning of this term is impossible today and for the foreseeable future, it is thus best to go on attempting a series of partial and one-sided microscopic analyses of that extremely complex reality, the history of philosophy, making them as radical as possible. One such analysis would be concerned with the issue I have just drawn attention to; another, with what I call the "biography of philosophy"—that is, the history of what is called philosophizing, of what this has successively turned out to be.[3]

It is necessary to note that the act of reading almost always obscures the singularity of literary genres. Let me explain. The reader in whatever epoch—for example, our own —reads all philosophical texts in the same way, that is, from the point of view of what *he* understands by philosophy. In any literary form he looks for those elements that satisfy what he normally expects from a work of philosophy, and he disregards the others, or he relegates them to a secondary level, even though they may have been the most important thing about the work from the point of view of its author. For example, he "prosifies" the pre-Socratic poem or he tries to extract from the Platonic dialogue the doctrinal theses that are expressed and formulated within it. Only to a historical gaze that is perceptive and practiced, such as is beginning to exist in our own times, are the texts of the past available in their proper and original form. In order to cite the clearest and most extreme example of the lack of this historical vision, consider the formal reduction of philosophy that occurs in all those works that attempt a Scholastic exposition of its subject matter or, even more to the point, the manner of utilizing and discussing a philosophical work that is to be found in any book of this orientation. The attention of the reader is directed exclusively to the theses that from its own point of view are "relevant," and all the rest are automatically left out. In other words, this approach deprives the original philosophical text of its form and projects upon it a scheme that is foreign to it— in this way, and as a consequence, imposing upon it a "literary genre" it never had. Thus, if to a philosophical work its literary incarnation is essential, this manner of reading is a radical adulteration of its contents. A partisan of this way of reading might argue that, for the historical or sociological understanding and evaluation of the text in question, it is possible to proceed in this way. But the only thing important to him remains the truth or falsity of that text, and thus its reduction to a thesis, to pronouncements, or to statements (and I use this plurality of terms because an analogous attitude is commonly expressed from a variety of systematic dispensations). In the face of such an attitude, one ought to counter that the truth is not in any way in-dependent of literary genres nor indifferent to them. Cer-tainly this is recognized by the Catholic Church when it points out that the truth or inerrancy of the Scriptures is not "homogeneous," but that each book possesses the truth appropriate to its genre. To believe that what is important in the poem of Parmenides is only the thesis, 'being is one,' and that the journey in the chariot is irrelevant, or that what is "philosophical" in Plato's *Phaedrus* is the definition of the soul as that which is *autokíneton* (or what moves by itself) and that one may disregard the myth of the winged horses, is to ignore what Parmenides and Plato have thought and, incidentally, the very meaning of the word "truth." In an old essay of mine, written during my adolescence, I showed how the sense of the ontological argument depends essentially upon this forgotten "fool" or *insipiens* whom everyone overlooks in order to examine whether Saint Anselm's process of reasoning "comes to a conclusion" or not, without stopping to consider where it really *begins* and thus, especially, what it deals with.[4]

All this reveals at one and the same time the scope and the difficulty of our theme. The *scope*, because the understanding of any philosophy is conditioned by the clarity with which its literary genre is taken into consideration. This problem is certainly not limited to works from the past, but affects our own time; that is, we cannot wholly understand contemporary philosophy without being aware of this condition, and, what is more serious, any philosophy that leaves this theme unclarified will possess an inevitable component of somnambulism and inauthenticity. And *difficulty,* because we are required to do strenuous violence to our mental habits in order to make the literary genres of the philosophy of the past appear before us in all their original singularity. This is true to such an extent that we do not yet know with scientific certainty which those genres have been and, even less, exactly of what each has consisted.

Now, first of all, what have been the literary genres in philosophy up to the present time? Even though we are restricting ourselves to Western philosophy (a consideration of Oriental philosophy would not only extend the problem but complicate it with other, prior, questions and divert us from our course), the reply is not easy. For we run the risk of contemplating those literary genres from the outside and of giving attention to certain of their schematic characteristics that might not be decisive at all. For example, the *Theaetetus* and the *Three Dialogues Between Hylas and Philonous* are conversations between several speakers; does this fact allow us to maintain that they belong to the same literary genre? Will we be able to classify the *Confessions* of Saint Augustine and the *Discourse on Method* within the same genre in view of the fact that both books are auto-biographical? The characteristic of "treatise" is common to the *Nicomachean Ethics,* the *Ethics* of Spinoza, and Hegel's *Science of Logic;* does this common characteristic authorize us to consider these works identical as far as literary genre is concerned? All these questions arise even without taking into account the need to distinguish between original genres and imitations of them. But even that distinction is not suf-ficient, since, after having made it, it is not enough that we leave the imitations out of consideration, for we have to confront the fact, not at all trivial, that at certain moments in history the literary genre chosen by philosophy might be nothing less than an *imitation.*

I would like to make it clear that I do not intend to study the problem in general terms here, but only insofar as it bears upon the difficulties of philosophy in the twentieth century. For that reason, there is no need to expect a rigorous or exhaustive enumeration of literary genres in philosophy; it will suffice to point out, in approximately chronological order, a series of clearly distinguishable forms that, solely by being enunciated, will clarify the nature of our concrete problem:

1. The pre-Socratic poem
2. Pre-Socratic prose [5]
3. *Logos* or Sophist discourse

4. The Socratic-Platonic dialogue
5. The Aristotelian *pragmateía* or *akróasis*
6. The Stoic dissertation [6]
7. The Christian meditation (Saint Augustine, Saint Bernard)
8. Scholastic commentary (Islamic, Judaic, Christian)
9. *Quaestio*
10. *Summa*
11. Autobiography (Descartes)
12. Treatise
13. Essay [7]
14. System as a literary genre (German idealism).

From this point on we see the beginning, not of change, for we have already seen how extensive the variation has been, but of the crisis of literary genres. And in a very concrete way, because what has begun is the history of a series of *temptations*. I will explain.

German idealism, especially with Hegel and Schelling, signifies the triumph of the university in European society. Above all, after the founding of the University of Berlin, this university radiates its influence in an extraordinary way over Prussia, over all of Germany, and subsequently over almost the whole of Europe. And this irradiation is mainly philosophical. In this way the philosopher is converted into a *professor*. (The philosophy of the nineteenth century will not be understood if one does not observe how extensively it is determined, in its contents and in its values, by the predominance of the university professor; the pejorative *Kathederphilosophie*, which came into circulation at that time, expresses the reaction of a minority to that dominance.) The consequence was not long in appearing: the literary genres of philosophy were automatically menaced by the temptation that emanated from teaching. This is not the first time this has happened, certainly, and I will return to this theme in a little while. But it is necessary to point out that in other epochs very different forms of teaching were involved. What is decisive is that teaching is always a secondary and derived reality, presupposing the existence of the philosophy that is to be taught. Pedagogical procedures pour an already given content into literary forms that are philosophically inauthentic. This was the first temptation, which dominated almost the whole of the nineteenth century and has not yet come to an end.

The second, which interferes with the first, is that of science. The rise of science to dominance approximately coincides with the final phase of German idealism and is one of the causes of its dissolution. Philosophy tries to get into step with science, it tries to become a science ("a passing attack of modesty," Ortega has called this), and the writing of philosophy does not wish to be out of tune. Philosophy appears as a scientific discipline among the others, occupying its corresponding place in university programs and publishers' catalogues. It has become a specialty, a *Fach*, whose peculiarity resides solely in its themes and in its doctrinal contents. The idea that a book of philosophy might be different, as a book, from a book of history, psychology, or biology would have seemed the height of impertinence.

And, actually, it was only the impertinent ones who dared to think such thoughts. Who were they? The *déclassés*, the exiles from philosophy, the nonconformists—in other words, those who were not university professors or, if they were, held lower positions: Maine de Biran, Kierkegaard, Schopenhauer, Nietzsche. Comte resembles these others in some ways too, although only in part, since he was excessively dominated by the prevailing scientific tendencies— except at the end, when his magnificent *Système de politique positive* scandalized his faithful and dense *Littré*, more papist than the Pope, more comtean than Comte himself—

and because, although he was not a professor, he ardently desired to be one.

Here begins the third temptation: literature. And then new things are tried out: intimate diaries, different ways of exhibiting one's inwardness, romantic passion, aphorisms. And the stupendous titles, all of them literary: *Either/Or; The Concept of Dread; Treatise on Despair; The Instant; Philosophical Fragments; Concluding Unscientific* (note it well, "unscientific") *Postscript to the Philosophical Fragments; The World as Will and Idea; Human, All Too Human; Thus Spake Zarathustra; Beyond Good and Evil.*

There is no doubt that this literary influence was fruitful and brought back to philosophy what we may call an internal form—inadequate, in the long run inauthentic, but when all is said and done a form nonetheless. Out of the moderation of that literary impulse by the prevailing scientific temper, forms were born that vacillated greatly in terms of literary genre but were quite enjoyable, such as those of Dilthey, James, and Bergson. If we compare them with Wundt, Spencer, or Brunschvieg, it will soon be seen how great the danger was and that the literary temptation, for all its risks, was a first-aid bandage applied to the torn artery through which, at a steady rate, philosophy was bleeding to death.

And with this we arrive at our own times, where the crisis has grown increasingly acute, to the point that, in my judgment, what is today mainly responsible for holding back the development of philosophy, what interrupts the maturation of thoughts in all other respects clamoring for expression, is the perplexity that reigns concerning the question of literary genres. But before asking ourselves why our times are plagued with such special difficulties and what their characteristics are, it seems proper to raise another question, one more general and radical: What is it that literary genres in philosophy are responding to, and what determines them?

The first thing that has to be considered is, naturally, what one wishes to say. I am not, of course, referring to the concrete doctrinal content of each philosophy (since if that were the case the literary genres would coincide with existing philosophies), but to whatever it is that the statement means to the philosopher and, secondarily, to the reader. Let us leave the pre-Socratics to one side; since philosophy began with them, the problem of their literary genres was submerged in another problem earlier, and more profound: that of their genre of "thinking" and, even more, of their genre of human doing. If the Platonic dialogue is compared with a medieval commentary, the difference between them is immediately evident. In the first case what Plato says is *what he is seeing*—more exactly, what he expresses is his vision itself, since philosophy is unable to expound itself, as he says in Letter VII. The medieval commentary—for example, a commentary on Aristotle, whether by Averroes or Saint Thomas—tries to voice a philosophy that is itself present, existing and already made, to reveal it and, possibly, to refine and complete it. The Christian *meditatio* relates an itinerary, personally traveled by the philosopher but—and this is essential—repeatable in principle by the reader, whose role is that of participating in it and thereby returning to it on his own. If from here we go on to the English essay of the seventeenth century, what it tries to relate is the result of a particular investigation on some chosen theme, and it is written in such a manner that the results and the procedure are communicated at one and the same time. Note the significant form of the titles—"An Essay *concerning* . . ."—or the arbitrary prolixity of Berkeley's *Siris*. In the system of German idealism what is said has to be the key to what is real in all its fullness, just as it is made real and present in the mind of the philosopher, and this necessity conditions the literary genres and is reflected in the titles. Consider the parallelism in the three Kantian *Critiques*, Fichte's reiteration of the *same* purpose in the successive versions of his *Theory of Science*, and the culmination of Hegel's *History of Philosophy* in a *Resultat* that brings it to a close and is nothing other than Hegel in person. Although a detailed analysis of what each and every one of the literary genres of philosophy has signified is a tempting project, as few others are, the preceding allusions ought to be enough simply to clarify what it is we are talking about.

In the second place, the literary genre is conditioned by the reader. To whom is the book of philosophy directed, and what does it require of him? This twofold question is indivisible. The material fact that these books have been printed since the end of the fourteenth century radically alters the situation and, consequently, brings about repercussions in all the literary genres. Of course it is true that following the introduction of printing the same kinds of books were cultivated as before, but this occurred for the same reason that early automobiles look extraordinarily like horse-drawn carriages: everything in history is delayed. Yet from the time that the internal combustion engine was invented, the automobile was already there; and from the time of Gutenberg, the structure of the ancient and medieval book had been left behind. The manifestation of this fact was only a matter of time. The Sophist discourse was not written down; or more exactly, it probably was, but only so that it could be read aloud or recited. The Scholastic *quaestio* was in principle meant to be used by a group of students. The books of Leibnitz, Clarke, or Locke were sent out to a far-flung audience of readers belonging to an international minority: the scholars, *die Gelehrten, les savants*—the audience, for example, of *Acta eruditorum*. If we examine two kinds of books that are intrinsically tied to teaching, such as the *akróasis* of Aristotle and the *Lehrbuch* of the German professor of 1880, we see that in a certain sense they are exactly opposed to one another. Aristotle's book rises out of the teaching process and is the *result* of teaching, of what we might call a "classroom investigation." The German manual is devised *for* teaching, and if we had to place it within one of those categories that thirty years ago were wittily called "regional ontologies," we would have to say that it exists only in the world of academic objects.

But knowing how many and who the readers of philosophical books are is not sufficient; it is still necessary to know what each of these books intends to do with its readers. And the differences are not insignificant. The poem of Parmenides proposes leading the reader to the ultimate nature of what is real, unveiling the radical condition of what there is and which consists of consistency or being; the dissertation of Seneca does not lead toward anything at all similar, but tends to pour security and contentment over the soul of the reader, to comfort him in his passage through life. If the first is the violation of reality by the intelligence of man, the second is a supply of provisions for a journey. Could any two things be more dissimilar? While Aristotle proposes finding out *why* all things are as they are, Descartes tells the story of his own life in order to reveal his inescapable shipwreck, which is the condition for reaching solid land from which the whole of creation is miraculously going to deliver up its secret and, along with it, its powers and resources. It would not be difficult to extract out of each literary genre of the philosophical past its ultimate aspiration.

All this, however, is not yet enough. The most important thing is still missing, the very basis of the literary genre, surely the most difficult thing of all to discover: who determines the genre. The delimitation of a certain intellectual realm, of a determined portion of the *globus intellectualis*, or, rather, the decision about the point of view from which this realm is going to be presented and, above all, about the "motion of the mind" that the philosophical book is going to follow—what does all this depend on? Perhaps on the limitation of the philosopher's horizon, at least in all archaic thinking. Perhaps on some prevailing extraphilosophical tendency—concern for religion, science, or his own prestige —that presses upon him. Picture the situation of Saint Augustine as he writes, *Deum et animam scire cupio;* or of Averroes confronted with Aristotle; or of Auguste Comte, bedazzled by the natural science of his time. It is also possible that the genre may be determined by social pressures, for example, by a certain manner of living intellectually or of teaching—which explains the medieval *Summae.* Or perhaps by the philosopher's will alone, as a creator imposing the structure of his own thoughts upon what is real—not upon speculation about reality. Or (let us not disregard this) perhaps simple publishing demands: the requirement that a book be sufficiently attractive to interest a few thousand readers and, thus, a publisher; or sufficiently pedantic to excite the committee of judges of some foundation and garner a fellowship or a subvention for its publication or the election of its author to membership in an Academy.

Only if all these matters are made sufficiently clear will we be able to know what we must be guided by with respect to the literary genres of philosophy. But these considerations would require a book, and not a very short or easy one. For the present I am not going to attempt any such hair-splitting and seductive undertaking. I simply wish to try to make clear what the perplexity is that dominates present-day philosophy on this point. Perhaps, upon discovering what the difficulties are, it might be possible to determine which path we are required to take, in what sense certain literary genres impose themselves upon us or, at least, suggest themselves.

If we cast a glance over the panorama of Western philosophical production during the twentieth century, and especially during the past thirty years,* we find evident abnormalities in what relates to literary genres. For reasons of simplicity I shall not refer to any but the greatest names, in whom the situation manifests itself with particular purity and clarity. The difficulties appear as well, and for more compelling reasons, in those forms of philosophy that have less authenticity or have an imperfect command of philosophical themes and resources of expression.

It will be necessary to distinguish, within the contemporary philosophical bibliography, four groups of authors and books. First, those who, finding themselves attached to a tradition out of the past that they accept as valid, assume the problem to be solved and revert to inherited literary genres. Second, those who deal with very precise questions, marginal with respect to the philosophical problem as such and related to the natural sciences; they maintain their adherence to the forms of "scientific" exposition used over the past fifty years in many disciplines—and among them are writers on symbolic logic or logistics and the majority of phenomenologists to the extent that they carry out specialized studies. Third, those who, because of their very deep immersion in the function of teaching, are content with the traditional "treatise," regardless of whatever innovations they might introduce into its contents—for example, Nicolai Hartmann. Fourth, those who have taken philosophy itself to be a problem and who are, for this reason, at once creative and fully contemporary. Naturally

* [Marías was writing in 1953—Trans.]

it is this fourth group that interests us, since here the problem of literary genres is actually presented.

Well, the difficulty that the most representative philosophers of our time have in preparing their points of view is obvious. Remember the vicissitudes encountered by phenomenology as soon as it had reached its definitive forms. Husserl's *Logical Investigations* is hardly even a book. It is a series of special studies, though with a convergent purpose, of whose deficiencies as a "piece of writing" Husserl was fully aware, as he made known in the second edition. Regarding the theory of phenomenology, it should not be forgotten that Husserl during his lifetime published only the first volume of his *Ideas,* that there was in it an evident indecision concerning the form his books were to take (just as there is in the posthumous *Erfahrung und Urteil*), and, above all, that the forty-five thousand shorthand pages comprising the Husserl Archives as a post mortem legacy are the most striking testimony to the impossibility of reducing a philosophical doctrine to accomplished books.

If from Husserl we go on to Max Scheler, we find that, in spite of his great gifts as a writer (in a sense too as a teacher, but only in one sense and not one that matters here), it is a fact that he did not leave a single satisfactory book. Only to the degree that he poured his thought into traditional forms (as in his *Ethics*) or that he formulated it fragmentarily in brilliant essays (*The Principle of Resentment in Morality, Repentance and Rebirth*)—only to that extent did he arrive at literary normalcy. And if you want an example of what a literarily frustrated book of philosophy is like, there is *On the Eternal in Man.*

With regard to Heidegger, things are even more complicated. There can be no doubt that Heidegger is a formidable writer, of amazing literary and, especially, poetic talents. However, if we take the word "book" seriously, Heidegger has only written one half of a book—the first part of *Sein und Zeit.* Since then he has written only brief pamphlets, an investigation with a formalist structure dictated by the theme (*Kant and the Problem of Metaphysics*), and recently *An Introduction to Metaphysics,* which is not a book but a series of connected investigations (on whose dust jacket, beneath the announcement of a new edition of *Sein und Zeit,* the promised second volume is abandoned: "*ein zweiter Band erscheint nicht*").

And if we make what we can of this half-book, the conclusion is not very reassuring. In it Heidegger has carried out the formidable labor of renovating language, but in structure—that is, as a literary genre in the strict sense—*Sein und Zeit* adheres to the usual form of investigation, more or less scholarly, of the phenomenological school. Perhaps its initial publication in Husserl's *Jahrbuch,* as well as its development from university courses, were influential in shaping it, but the important fact is that there is very little innovation in it from this point of view. On the other hand, although Heidegger's originality might be expected to include his mode of expression, it cannot be said that this has been realized. The constant violence he brings to bear upon the German language, his resolute way of arriving at etymologies, the excessive dependence of his philosophy upon the language in which it is written—to the point that his work is strictly not translatable (the enormous and intelligent effort that the translation into Spanish by José Gaos represents is conclusive proof that it is not possible to translate *Sein und Zeit*)—all this makes of Heidegger probably the most visible and the most critical example of the crisis of literary genres.

In a different way something similar has happened with Jaspers. To begin with, the excessive dimensions of his book *Philosophie* were alarming. The eleven hundred enormous pages of the *first* volume of his *Philosophische Logik* deprive this work of the character of a book and make of it an undeniable literary monstrosity. At a time when the old German treatise in the manner of Lipps or Sigwart or Vaihinger seems intolerable, the hypertrophy in the writings of this great thinker demonstrates his incapacity to carry the communicative realization of his philosophy to a happy conclusion, that is, to write a book that might contain it and revive it again in the reader.

Are we not, perhaps, dealing with a certain literary density among Germans? But if we go to the country of literature, to France, the situation is not substantially different. In the first place, the academic fact that an important part of French philosophical production is incorporated in doctoral theses nullifies three fourths of the literary talent of the French. The French theses are usually sound, useful, and even admirable; what they are not is books.[8] And the enormous effort they require consumes, in many cases, the major part of their authors' capabilities, upon which the topical mold of the academic dissertation is forever stamped. But not all are theses. What happens with the free writers of philosophy in France, with the books that are written without hobbles and that draw upon the entire creative talent?

We leave out of account those authors whose writings, even though they are not theses, are "instruction manuals," but in the best sense of the term: Gilson, Lavalle, Le Senne, Gouhier, etc. We have two examples of independent philosophers who are not, or hardly not, professors and, in addition, are writers, even great writers, genuine *hommes de lettres:* Marcel and Sartre. And we find that the first of them has not up to the present written a single *book* of philosophy. The *Metaphysical Journal* lacks structure; the other books are collections of articles, except for *The Mystery of Being.* And this, which is the best, is a course (two series of Gifford Lectures) in which the structure imposed by the lessons provides a channel for Marcel's sinuous, sharp, suggestive meditation, faithful to all the aspects and discontinuities of what is real, but up to now never incarnated in an adequate literary expression. At least unless we believe that this expression is found in his works for the theater; but this is a delicate question, about which I will have a word to say later on.[9] With regard to Sartre, his only *book* of philosophy, *Being and Nothingness,* although full of passages that reveal a genuine literary talent, is excessively long, labored, sometimes deadly, and, above all, without form as the book it is. *Being and Nothingness* might be taken precisely as an example of what a book of philosophy cannot be in the middle of the twentieth century, since it is (I repeat, as the book it is, apart from its doctrine) absolutely unjustified. And the philosophy of the present day imposes upon itself the inescapable obligation of justifying itself completely and of justifying its public image, its existence as *utterance,* in a very special way, since our sensibilities are beginning to find it indecent to hurl a piece of writing at the head of the reader the way somebody might throw a stone.

Looking next at British and American thought, we find the following. First, the most important philosophers are those already dead or very old—Dewey, Santayana, Alexander, Whitehead, or the octogenarian Russell,* all of whom belong to generations that are no longer *present.* Second, the best of recent British and American thought are very concrete investigations, especially on logical or epistemological themes, from which one cannot expect innovations in literary genre. Third, the renewal that, as I see it, is beginning to take place in the United States in the idea of what a book is has not had any effects in philosophy. Two reasons explain this: one, the relatively marginal position of philosophy in this country and, consequently, the predominance of innovation in other disciplines; the

* [Now a nonagenarian—Trans.]

other, the fact that this impulse, which I believe to be healthy and fecund, is obstructed by the routines of the committees that control the reviews, publishing houses, and universities and in many cases by the simple-minded use of the scholarly apparatus (the untimely inheritance of a German vice) as a means of evaluating, for purposes of publication or advancement, works that one does not wish to read or that one does not understand. Thus, for all these reasons, the situation is no better in the English language.

And in Spain? In spite of the fact that the volume of philosophical production is much less than in any of the other countries that have been mentioned, we have to stop and think, because we find, along with an extreme case of preoccupation with literary genres, creative efforts that are very advanced and original.

The case of Unamuno is especially clear. The fact that I have studied him in detail in other writings of mine [10] makes it possible for me to be very brief here. At the end of the last century and during the early years of this one, the problem was posed in an extremely acute way in Spain on account of the lack of an immediate philosophical tradition. Neither Balmes nor the Krausists offered any possibility of an adequate literary version of a philosophical thought. On the contrary, they appeared like two reefs that had to be avoided. Unamuno unquestionably represents what I have called the literary temptation, but to such a high degree that it surpasses itself and comes out as something else altogether. For, it is not that Unamuno presents a philosophy in literary costume, but that, by virtue of this temptation and of his irrationalism, he *renounces* the task of philosophizing. But since, on the other hand, he moved within the inexorable problematicity of philosophy, he wrote books on a subject we might call "negated philosophy." Such a book is *The Tragic Sense of Life in Men and Peoples* (here the complete title is required), which is presented only as "poetry or phantasmagoria, mythology in any case," in spite of the fact that in this book, in 1913, many ideas are to be found that today we read with increasing frequency in books of philosophy.

This book by Unamuno, it must be said, is irritating. For many years the quite frequent expressions of silly admiration for its defects, for its frivolities, and for its histrionics, along with the failure to understand it and making of this failure a virtue (not only in the author but in the reader as well), caused me to feel a certain aversion toward it. But after having said this, it must be added that the book is supremely alluring and that on this account it fulfills one of the most important of the conditions that will be demanded of future literary genres of philosophy. Considering when it was published, and in spite of its inadmissible errors, carelessness, and simple-mindedness, it is magnificent and full of extraordinarily fecund divinations.

But Unamuno's great creation is of course neither more nor less than a literary genre, to which I have given the name of "existential or personal novel," a genre with an essential value from the perspective of philosophical knowledge of human life. But it is not necessary for me to say anything more about this here, since this is precisely the central theme of the books of mine previously mentioned and because the problem that interests me at the moment is that of the genres of philosophy in a strict sense.

And with this we come to Ortega. The preoccupation he has shown in all his work for the problems of expression is quite well known. Ortega has probably never written a line without raising the question in his own mind of what he was going to say, of whether he had to say it, to whom and in what way. In addition, he was one of the most profound writers there has ever been in our language or in any other language, and he bestows all his fundamental character upon this preoccupation. But I must explain this phrase, "one of the most profound writers." I mean that for him, to be a writer was not merely an activity or function, nor even a question of talent or vocation, but his own deepest and most inward condition. For this reason, when he began to write he placed his integrity as a person at stake, from the somatic factor to the vital program of each hour. That is why, replying once to an attack from a politician who had reproached him for the delight he took in being a thinker and a man of letters, he replied that this is what he fundamentally was and that what the politician had taken to be "a colorful necktie" he had put on "turns out to be," Ortega said, "my own spinal column showing through" (I quote from memory).

Thus, Ortega's philosophy signifies renovation *a radice* of the modes of utterance in philosophy. Not only do the newspaper article and the essay undergo transformation at his hands, but his innovations reach to the sentence itself and to the meaning of the use of words, to what I have called "the *logos* or utterance of vital reason." [11] Recall the program of "salvations" at the beginning of his first book, *Meditaciones del Quijote* (1914): * ". . . given a fact—a man, a book, a painting, a landscape, a wrong, a pain—to carry it by the shortest route to the fullness of its meaning. To arrange things of all kinds that life, in its perennial undertow, throws at our feet like the weary residue of a shipwreck, in a setting such that from them the sun gives forth innumerable reflections." Unite this with the structure of that "utterance of vital reason," and you will have what I believe to be the most promising point of departure

---

* [Translated into English as *Meditations on Quixote*, with an introduction by Julián Marías (New York, 1961), but without all the extensive, erudite, and illuminating notes that Marías contributed to the latest Spanish edition of this work (Río Piedras, Puerto Rico, 1957); it is as if a publisher were to bring out an edition of the *Shulchan Aruch* without the commentary of Moses Isserles— Trans.]

from which to arrive at a literary genre adequate to the philosophy of our time.

Only the point of departure, it is true. Because, if things are considered in all strictness, up to the present time Ortega has not published a single *book* of philosophy. His work to date is composed of brief essays and studies (those that make up *El Espectador, History as a System, Ideas y creencias, Ensimismamiento y alteración, Apuntes sobre el pensamiento,* etc.) or of incomplete books. Thus, his *Meditations on Quixote* contains only the preliminary meditation and the first. *The Modern Theme* is nothing but the development of a university lecture, followed by several relatively autonomous appendixes. *Invertebrate Spain* and *The Revolt of the Masses* (aside from the fact that, although philosophical books, they are not formally about philosophy) are inconclusive—the final chapter of *The Revolt of the Masses,* remember, bears the title, "We arrive at the real question." Ortega's longest book, *En torno a Galileo,* which is probably the best and most important of all his works, is a course of twelve university lectures (which I heard in 1933) and, furthermore, does not contain anything but the introduction to the theme.[12] That is to say, in none of these cases is the architecture of a book fully realized, and thus their author has never given us his own personal version of the literary genre corresponding to his philosophy, even though this question is central and decisive, not secondary, within that philosophy. For this reason, this aspect must be taken into account in any interpretation of Ortega's thought and of the trajectory of his life.

In Zubiri too we do not find the problem solved, nor anything like it. His only book, *Naturaleza, Historia, Dios* (1944),* with a very revealing title,[13] is only a book *a posteriori,* made up of essays written at different times. Be-

---

* [Since Marías wrote this, Zubiri has published *Sobre la esencia* (Madrid, 1963)—Trans.]

cause Zubiri's public activity since then seems to have been reduced to his courses (long courses of thirty-some lectures, long and extremely dense, each of them), his persistent silence as a writer seems to me significant. It is said—by Zubiri himself, among others—that he has difficulty in writing; but this has to be properly understood. Zubiri is an excellent writer, of sober, nervous, splendid rhetoric; his words, sure and precise, flow easily. His difficulties, then, will at least not be awkwardness or lack of fluency and will have to be discovered elsewhere. Perhaps with respect to the function of naming? Perhaps with regard to the structure of his exposition, that is, precisely in relation to literary genre? This seems quite plausible, and would be one more case confirming the difficulty in which all the philosophy of our epoch is to be found submerged, extending even to the most creative and most talented of those who cultivate it.[14] And now we must ask with some precision, having seen that this difficulty really is occuring, why is it so?

Why is the problem of literary genres so acute in our time? The reasons that explain this are not few. It may be that there are too many of them, not only in relation to the problem of elucidating them, but also with respect to understanding the phenomenon they explain. For, among their multitude whatever hierarchy there may be is rendered indistinct, and making up one's mind between them becomes impossible. I will try to gather them into three groups: (1) those that refer to the intense variation within philosophy during what has passed of this century, (2) those relating to the social situation of philosophy during these decades, (3) those that arise from the very idea of philosophy and from the most profound of its aspirations.

For the present, it must be said that contemporary philosophy is suffering from a grave discontinuity. At this juncture in history, the fact that philosophy has found a relation to its most profound traditions, in so far as the pre-Socratics have never been so close as they are today, does not make a bit of difference. I refer to the circumstance that, on more superficial levels, the philosophy of the twentieth century represents a break with that which dominated the preceding century. And this means that today there is no *prevailing* philosophy. In some measure (though this is not the occasion to determine exactly in what measure), there is a certain prevalence *of philosophy*, but not of any definite philosophy. On the contrary, what is essential in this "prevailing" philosophy is its own problematicity and its search for itself. More than at any but the most occasional times in history, philosophy has again become *zetouméne epistéme*, as Aristotle very rightly baptized it. Therefore, it is not possible even to dream that the occupation of the philosopher might be *to expound* a philosophy. And the consequence is that he finds himself without any inherited outlines. In other words, when the philosopher has to fulfill his publication requirements and sits down to write, he does not find that his book is already largely written by his social circumstance (this is exactly what it would mean for there to be a prevailing literary genre), but he finds it necessary, not simply to write it (that is, to fill out its contents), but *to invent* it. Where to begin?—this is the first doubt that assails the author.

Since the philosophy of the past is not genuinely current, there is nothing that the philosopher can do but innovate. It is not that he wants to do this or that he finds it interesting, but that he has no choice. Because, even in the hypothetical and most unlikely case of his being able to adhere to some philosophy out of the past, if this adherence is to be philosophical and not a caprice, a mania, or an imposition, he would have to *arrive at it* and justify it philosophically, and the present philosophy that he would have to bring into play in order to make the past philosophy his own would necessarily be innovating. (If this is lacking, the attachment to a past philosophy, regardless of how much seriousness it may simulate, is pure frivolity or a decision in consideration of other interests, which naturally has nothing to do with philosophy.)

This enforced innovation characterizes everything, from the most significant to the most picayune. It affects, and in a fundamental way, even language. To name something new or a new aspect of something that is not new is to suppose the appropriate word to be lacking. Thus what has no name has to be named, and in the face of this situation there can be but two solutions (other than silence, of course): neologism and metaphor. Ortega, for example, has chosen this latter course; Heidegger, the former. But lately it seems that Heidegger is inclining toward the metaphoric solution, and in his latest writings we read that "man is the shepherd of being" (*der Hirt des Seins*) and that language is "the dwelling place of being" (*das Haus des Seins*)—illuminating expressions, about which it will not be possible to say that they are not metaphors.

Not only is all this happening, but during these years a profound alteration has been taking place in the *themes* of philosophy as such. The philosopher of the past thirty years speaks constantly about things that philosophy never talked about before, or only rarely—and then usually without being understood.[15] We find philosophers speaking, no longer about anguish (which has been trivialized), but about discontent, sacrifice, self-envisagement, fidelity, vital projects, prevalence, choice, nothingness, authenticity, interpretation, death, things to be done, the situation, engagement, intentionality, vocation, circumstance, care, and even, in some instances, of the sexual organs. What is to be done with the traditional "chapters" of a book of philosophy? How are these themes to be housed in them? Nothing is more clarifying than the comparison of the subject index in a philosophical work of the past century with that of a present-day work. One sees to what extent new realities have been discovered and how philosophy has changed course a full ninety degrees. Is it possible to believe that books like those written seventy years ago might shelter a thought, but not books today—with not only different content, but of such dissimilar inspiration?

With regard to the social situation of philosophy, we have to go back to what was said a while ago: that there is a certain prevalence of philosophy but that no definite philosophy prevails. This means, in other words, that *credit* is conceded to philosophy but that this has to be converted into currency in each instance. In almost all the countries of Europe and Latin America—to a lesser degree in the United States—philosophy has ceased being an exclusively scholarly matter. Philosophy today interests a considerable number of readers, who buy up relatively extensive printings of philosophical writings. Now, this expansion of the public automatically influences the author through the attention concentrated on him. Whether he wishes to or not, he has to consider the fact that his book is going to be read by many persons, who are going to express their opinions about it. This leads him, for example, to take a position regarding the intelligibility of his writings. It must be obvious that I am not saying that he is forcibly led to be clear—at times, strictly the contrary, but in this case with a deliberate and cultivated obscurity that is aware of itself as such.

If to this the crisis of the university be added—extremely serious in some countries, existing in all—it turns out that teaching, the most "normal" form of philosophical communication during the past century, has become problematical.

Naturally there are important differences between countries. Without going further afield, the conditions of publication are different in many ways. In countries like Spain, where printing is not very expensive and a philosophical public of considerable volume exists, the publication of a philosophical work of some attractiveness and intellectual quality is easy (it is understood that I am speaking about private and independent publication, not about public institutions). In other European countries the printing of a book of philosophy is not as easy and certain unless it can count on definite professional or publishing connections, but, on the other hand, a much more widespread circulation and, consequently, an audience that is qualitatively and quantitatively heterogeneous are in some cases possible and foreseeable. In the United States the situation is very different and oscillates between two opposite extremes. In the first place, the cost of printing and the comparatively restricted number of buyers make the publication of a philosophical work by a commercial publishing house difficult, and it is relegated to the foundations or the university presses. However, it is improbable that those institutions would undertake the publication of a book not narrowly bound to their own concerns and that did not comply with a very limited and *external* canon of scholarship, and if one wants to count on the public as the economic support of a work, one has to go to the other extreme. Thus, in the second place, the enormous popularity of the "pocket book," run off by the hundreds of thousands of copies at 25 or 35 cents each, something that is possible only if the book is uncommonly easy to read or if it is commanded by the immense fame and prestige of the author (Dewey, Whitehead, Ortega, Toynbee).[16]

The philosopher, apart from what he is going to say, thus finds himself confronting the fact that he is speaking to people other than those who have made up his traditional audience. At the same time, the expectations that this public has regarding him are quite varied. The attitude the philosopher takes toward these expectations, however, is not important. Let us suppose that he is irritated by them and decides to disappoint them; this obliges him, in the same way as if he were to satisfy them, to take them into account. The one thing he cannot do is ignore them. He writes his book, therefore, as a function of these expectations, of the claims that this public makes upon him. And this naturally conditions the literary genre of his writings, because these expectations are always the consequence of a collaboration between the writer and the invisible chorus of his readers.

Although all this is extremely important, what is decisive is the idea that philosophy has of itself, what it is trying to say today, when and how a man feels that he is justified before others, and above all to himself, in dedicating his life to this strange and always problematical task that we have known for the past twenty-five centuries by the name of philosophy—or, said more precisely, to a task that we call by this name because it comes to us, through those twenty-five centuries and through innumerable variations, from the task to which half a dozen men devoted themselves on the shores of Asia Minor.

We have to return to a point we left upstream. We have to look now at how the question is raised in our time concerning what it is that determines the literary genres, what or who it is that defines them. In those epochs during which the social situation of philosophy has been clear, that is, when philosophy has possessed a fundamental social reality, it is the society that has decided the literary forms of thought. With regard to these effects (although only with regard to these effects), it is unimportant whether we are dealing with *the society* in a strict sense, that is, with the whole of historical society, or with that partial and abstract "society" which is the "world" of the clerics, the enlightened, the intellectuals, or however you may wish to call them. This last is what happened, for instance, with the Scholasticism of the twelfth, thirteenth, and fourteenth centuries and (across a gap) with Humanism at the end of the fifteenth and the first half of the sixteenth century; the first, with the *philosophie* of the eighteenth century and the university philosophy of the nineteenth. The Thomist idea, which I have quoted so many times before, of a *scientia demonstrativa, quae est veritatis determinativa,* as opposed to a dialectical science, directed toward the *discovery* of truth,[17] was born in an intellectual situation defined by the existence of rival claims pretending to be true and between which one had to decide, and this situation conditioned the literary genres: the *quaestio,* with its pattern of two series of contrasted opinions (*Videtur . . . Sed contra . . .*) and the discrimination between them (*Respondeo . . .*). And all the forms of instruction in the medieval university explained the articulation of the *quaestiones* in *tractatus, summae, quodlibeta,* etc. The literary genre in which the first treatise of metaphysics that, properly speaking, ever existed—the *Disputationes metaphysicae* of Suárez—was expressed, was conditioned by the situation of thought at the end of the sixteenth century, in which there was room only for the solutions of the two great contemporaries: to innovate as Giordano Bruno did, or do what Suárez did, which I have called "rethinking the tradition to take account of things." [18]

Today there is no social form of philosophy that is able to impose its genres; nor is pedagogy capable of doing this. No doubt books do exist in whose form that conception of the science professed by Don Fulgencio Entreambosmares, the character in Unamuno's *Amor y pedagogia,* is realized: "to catalogue the universe so as to return it to God all in order." But it is not likely that present-day philosophy will take that path.

Even the division of philosophy into disciplines, which for a long time exercised a decisive influence on its forms, is without vitality. This division seems more and more problematical and arbitrary, less certainly based on philosophy's real texture, more inclined to scholarly falsification and to pure convention.

It seems that the literary genres of contemporary philosophy are abandoned to the inspiration or to the simple discretion of their authors. And, in fact, this is what is happening to some degree—under the protection of the irrationalism that dominates vast areas of contemporary thought. According to this idea, it would be the free will of the philosopher that would decide the genre in which his work is to be realized. This situation, in a very curious way, might go back to resemble that of the idealists at the beginning of the nineteenth century, although what was then done in the name of rationalism and system, would be done now in the name of the irrational and the imagination. This similarity is not capricious nor simply accidental, and is derived from the profound connections of a good part of contemporary thought with romanticism. The success achieved by the "temper"—not, of course, by the doctrines —of Kierkegaard is excellent proof of this.

But the present-day irrationalist philosopher suffers from *mauvaise conscience*, because he knows at heart, as I have pointed out in another place, that irrationalism today is the same as anachronism. He knows that his irrationalism is laziness, incapacity, or pose. He knows that he *cannot be* an irrationalist, because to live is to have to give account about reality, to have to give reasons for reality.* In other words, arbitrariness implies falsehood.

However, one cannot be a rationalist either—even less,

* [Marías writes *dar razón*, an expression meaning "to give information," but which in the literal sense of its words would mean "to give reason"—Trans.]

since the irrationalists of the last century were right in relation to the rationalists, although they are not right today because something completely different is understood by reason. In our times the traditional "system" of philosophy, as a structure of thought imposed on things, is not possible. But, on the other hand, there is evidence that philosophy, whether it wants to be or not, has to be systematic.[19] What was for a long time called system was, instead, *esprit de système*. The genuine system is unavoidable, one that imposes itself on thought, not one that thought imposes upon the real. I have said that the philosopher today is a system builder *malgré lui*.

Upon arriving at this point we begin to see a few things clearly. This entire transit has been necessary in order to outline the problem correctly. And here we have, by the way, an example of a radical need in philosophy: problems cannot be "formulated"; one has to *arrive at them*, that is, to take the steps necessary in order to bring oneself to the point where they really are problems, that is, where nothing can be done except knowing precisely what to guide oneself by with regard to them. If philosophy is systematic, this is so because reality is; and the systematic character of the real reappears in the doctrine. Looking at the question from the point of view of literary genres, this indicates the necessity that the book be determined and defined *by things themselves*.

But this is not as clear as it may seem. Things by themselves would never write a book. What is that concatenation of things that is able to mobilize a thought and flow into the piece of writing? Provisionally there is no other but history. This, yes. Things present themselves to man as *events*, and these have a connection and a movement to which the mind can be directed. It is not by chance, but something perfectly explicable and legitimate, that philosophy, especially during the past couple of decades, has been given over to a historical mode of posing problems. At the moment this is the most that could be done. What has been facetiously called "speaking through the mouth of the classics," searching for the antecedents of one's own doctrine in the past, even more, to present a personal philosophy upon the thread of history [20]—all these have been well-directed but inadequate trial efforts through which it was necessary to pass.

I have, however, said that this is not enough. Because history carries us into the present, and in it we find ourselves with things. What are we to do then? Take literally what I have just said, without by-passing a single element: we find ourselves with things—not, then, things only, but *my encounter* with them. What is decisive is the installation of man among things, and this signifies neither more nor less than a world.

Thus it is the structure of reality just as the philosopher encounters it in living that determines the system of philosophy and, consequently, the architecture of its literary genre. The real connections that I discover in my life are those that condition the coherence of the philosophical writing. The order and the mode of exposition have to correspond to the modes of my actual insertion in the real, of my implantation in the world. We stand at a pole opposed to arbitrariness: the philosophical book is a *venture*. It is the expression of the dynamic vital situation in which its author finds himself.

This means that the book of philosophy will have to be *dramatic* by necessity. From this it follows, aside from the significance that the novel may have for philosophy, that the philosophical book, even the most rigorous theoretical study, must have the dimensions of a novel. For what we are dealing with is not only, as one might be inclined to think, the fact that the book expresses or narrates a kind of adventure but that the book itself *is* the personal adventure of its author.

And this brings us to a final question: the justification of philosophy. It is not possible today to *set out* from philosophy as from something obvious and which presents itself as valid in itself. Why does one have to philosophize? Why do I have to dedicate my life to philosophizing and to writing about it? Above all, why is the reader going to interest himself in it and spend his time reading a book that a philosopher has written? One cannot set out from philosophy: this means that one must *arrive* at it. This is the reason (no, this is not an intellectual or biographical anecdote) that the first *book* of philosophy, in the strict sense of this term, that I have written—and up to now the only one [21] —may be an *Introducción a la filosofía.** Because in this exceptional case one can achieve the appropriate literary genre; it is enough to be inexorably faithful to what is being done. The introduction to philosophy, as I said in 1946,

> is not a "discipline" in the sense of a complex of propositions, but a task or venture. . . .
>
> . . . the introduction has to be rigorously systematic, in the concrete sense that the horizon of its problems is imposed by the very structure of the human life in which they occur, which is a *system*, because any of its elements or ingredients, any of its activities or their forms, implicate the rest, and in this way the apprehension of any one of them necessarily uncovers that general structure of life.
>
> This is [I continued] the peculiarity of the introduction to philosophy and is what defines and justifies its existence as a function and as a literary genre. Thus, its schematic structure has to consist of a *description* of the real situation of the man of our times, which may then serve as a basis and a point of departure for an *analysis* of that situation, in which all its ingredients may be made clear, as well as their function in the life of this concrete man

* [This is the book published in English as *Reason and Life* (see note 19)—Trans.]

who is "one of us" or, better still, *each one of us*. This analysis will reveal the pertainment of *truth* to that repertory of vital functions and the appearance in human life of a horizon of problematicity. The very attempt comprehensively to formulate this situation as it is being experienced reveals a context of *problems* and, at the same time, of methodological and vital *requisites* demanded by the very nature of those problems when one tries to *give information* about them. The result of this investigation will be twofold: on the one hand, to demonstrate the need for philosophy when our situation (habitually trivial) is radicalized and has to justify itself; on the other hand, to discover the authentic, historically conditioned form in which our situation *has* to come into being and, with that, to trace out the precise profile that philosophy has to have within this circumstance.[22]

The introduction to philosophy thus consists of an active dedication to the situation in which the author or the reader find themselves, carried to its authentic radicalness. In it, then, but only through strict fidelity to the real, the *literary genre* and its *justification* are given at one and the same time. For this reason it is necessary to begin here; but history does not end. Imaginative creativity is required in order to come to terms with subsequent levels of this elementary situation. Along that path literary genres are to be found adequate to that dramatic, novelistic, and for that reason alluring, creative and unpredictable venture that we still continue to call philosophy.

NOTES

1. "La novela como método de conocimiento," published by the Universidad Nacional de Colombia in my book *El existencia-lismo en España* (Bogotá, 1953); also to be found in *La Escuela de Madrid* (Buenos Aires, 1959) [*Obras* V].
2. On this matter see Ortega y Gasset, "Stücke aus einer 'Geburt

der Philosophie,'" in the volume in homage to Jaspers, *Offener Horizont;* also, in Spanish, in Ortega y Gasset, *Origen y epílogo de la filosofía* (México, 1960).

3. I have raised this question in several works, brought together under this title in my book *Biografía de la filosofía* (Buenos Aires, 1954) [*Obras* II] [to be published in English translation as *Biography of Philosophy*].

4. *San Anselmo y el insensato* (Madrid, 1944; second edition, 1954) [*Obras* IV]. The Essay that gave its title to this book was first published in 1935.

5. On the difference between the poems and the prose writings of the pre-Socratics, see the study by Ortega cited in note 2.

6. The work of Marcus Aurelius—should we include it among the dissertations, or is it a "meditation"? Recall the oscillations in the tradition regarding its title *Eis Heautón: To His Own Self, Reflections, Meditations, Soliloquies.*

7. In English naturally, since what we are dealing with is a literary genre that was typically British from the time of Bacon. The others, Leibnitz first of all, caught it from the English—and thus the whole of the eighteenth century.

8. The French thesis, the result of ten or fifteen years of work, has usually been an astonishing bundle of paper. In comparison with that conception of the thesis, the German or Spanish thesis was a brief monograph, a preliminary youthful labor of investigation. However, recently theses have been presented in Spanish universities of 500, 700, or 900 folio pages, with the appearance of the French but with nothing more than the traditional preparation of the Spanish thesis—that is, one or two years beyond the completion of the master's degree.

9. On this question, I refer the reader to my previously mentioned study, "La novela como método de conocimiento" (see note 1), to my essay "La obra de Unamuno: un problema de filosofía," published in the same volumes, and to my book *Miguel de Unamuno* (Madrid, 1943) [*Obras* V], translated into English (Harvard University Press, 1966).

10. Beginning in 1938, in the essay and the book, *Miguel de Unamuno,* mentioned in note 9, and in *La Escuela de Madrid.*

11. Cf. the chapter "La razón vital en marcha," in *La Escuela de Madrid.*

12. Few books more completely confirm the ancient aphorism, *Habent sua fata libelli* ["Books have a fate of their own"—Trans.], than this one. Delivered at the University of Madrid in the spring of 1933 in the form in which it is now printed, this course of lectures was published some ten years ago in an abridged form (less than half of its contents) under the title *Esquema de la crisis.* In 1946 it appeared, now complete and with its title *En torno a Galileo,* in volume V of Ortega's *Obras completas.* Thus this book has not yet known *public existence.* Although it is the most important work of its author and the most mature published expression of his thought, it has had neither performance nor resonances, but has remained "im-

pressed" within one of the tomes of his *Obras completas*. It has not been placed before the public and, literally, if the expression be taken in its proper sense, it remains *unpublished*. It is urgent that it be liberated from the gray binding and set free, into the windows of bookstores and into the minds of readers. [This was done in 1956—J.M.]

13. With regard to its structure and rhythm, only Samuel Alexander's *Space, Time, and Deity* (London, 1920) may be compared with it. (I am speaking of course of philosophical books.)

14. The universality of this situation is abnormal, and if there were space it could be shown in thorough detail. To readers of Spanish two examples will be of interest: recall that up to the present Gaos has also not written a *book* [Since Marías wrote this, Gaos has published *De la filosofía* (México, 1962)—Trans.]; with regard to Ferrater Mora, quite penetrating and very talented, quite sincere and authentic (remember his article "Mea culpa"), his work *consists* in one of its dimensions of a struggle with expression and, especially, with literary genres—passionate in *El hombre en la encrucijada*, a valuable and moving effort but inadequate. Morente did not write a single book *sensu stricto*. Zaraguëta represents the culmination of didacticism. Eugenio d'Ors, with such a fine and tranquil literary talent, might be described in this way: Eugenio d'Ors, or the temptation to pampering.

15. In my book *La filosofía del Padre Gratry* (Madrid, 1941) [*Obras* IV], I have shown how during his lifetime many of the philosophical concepts of this thinker were taken to be images of piety.

16. This situation has changed in recent years due to the introduction of high quality *paperbacks*, produced in large printings and at a moderate price (seventy-five cents to two dollars), inundating the market by the thousands. The social and intellectual consequences of this flood of high quality books is bound to be significant. [Note added in 1959—J. M.]

17. *Summa theologiae*, II-II^{ae}, q. 31, art. 2.

18. Cf. "Suárez en la perspectiva de la razón histórica," in *Ensayos de teoría* (Barcelona, 1954) [*Obras* IV].

19. On this subject see my *Introducción a la filosofía* (Madrid, 1947) [*Obras* II]; translated into English as *Reason and Life* (Yale University Press, 1956).

20. To my knowledge the first person to do this in a thoroughgoing way and in a thematic manner was Gratry, just a century ago, in *La connaissance de Dieu*. See my book on Gratry mentioned in note 15.

21. Today I would have to add *La estructura social* (Madrid, 1955) and *Ortega, circunstancia y vocación* (Madrid, 1960); the latter translated into English as *Ortega y Gasset: Circumstance and Vocation* (University of Oklahoma Press, 1970).

22. From *Introducción a la filosofía*, pp. 18–19.

CHAPTER TWO

THE DRAMATIC STRUCTURE OF PHILOSOPHICAL THEORY

. . . und alles, was man weiss, nicht bloss rauschen und
brausen gehört hat, lässt sich in drei Worten sagen.
—Kürnberger (Quoted by Wittgenstein, *Tractatus Logico-
Philosophicus*).

Readers without haste, warned that all just opinion is long
in expression.
—José Ortega y Gasset.

The International Institute of Philosophy is assembled in a
symposion within the framework of an International Congress of Philosophy. The theme chosen on this occasion
could not be more circumstantial, for what is done in these
assemblies is to argue about philosophical themes. This
year, in a reflexive gesture, we turn our gaze upon our
own activity and question the very thing we are doing,
or are going to do: argue. And we ask ourselves about
*philosophical argumentation.** Why? Is it possible that at

---

* [Since Marías's argument in this essay depends essentially on the
use he makes of the etymology of the words *argüir* and *argumento*, I have chosen to translate them in all their appearances as
"argue" and "argument" (along with words, like "argumentation,"
derived from them), even though the use of these words in English will require the reader to keep in mind that the Spanish
words, while equivalent in meaning to the English in the sense of
"to discuss" or "a line of reasoning," hardly at all contain the
meaning that is dominant in English, that of engaging in an

heart we have some reservations about the fruitfulness of our occupation? Each year, at the end of many months of solitary labor, we meet and make an attempt at communication. Strictly speaking, of course, since we write and read, we are always making this attempt at the same time that we meditate in silence. Intellectual life today is not lived in isolation, but in community. However, if we are sincere, we have to confess that things are not entirely satisfactory. When we become intimately acquainted with a form of thought, we see that only rarely is it well understood outside the intellectual sphere in which it originated. Critical reviews of philosophical books, even those published in professional journals and which are supposed to be competent, are frequently superficial or entirely confused. The establishment of hierarchies is very uncertain and in a considerable number of cases is too much influenced by chance or by extraprofessional motives. Probably the two most important events in the field of philosophy during recent years have been the two series of posthumous publication of works by Husserl and Ortega; neither of them has been received in a philosophically adequate way, nor have they had the intellectual consequences that were to have been expected.

Our own immediate experience leaves much to be desired. When we speak at a philosophical meeting, we quite often have the impression that we are not being very well understood and, to a no lesser degree, that we do not quite understand those who discuss with us. What is involved is not disagreement, which is usually fruitful and, when it is genuine, is based on previous comprehension. Rather, what occurs is a dual phenomenon that produces in me a singular

_____

"angry dispute," while a meaning that is now almost completely lost from English is very much present in Spanish, that of the "narrative outline" or "plot" of a literary or theatrical work—Trans.]

discomfort. On the one hand, it is usual to ignore what is *behind* what is said, and thus what is said is isolated from its true context, so that at times something that rests upon a process of reflection of many years' duration and that has been justified at length or included within a whole tradition is taken to be a "sudden flash of wit" or *Einfall*. On the other hand, what is read or heard is "translated" into intellectual formulas that are familiar, and if by chance what is said is something different or independent, the unavoidable result is a misunderstanding. For this reason an effective *dialogue* rarely occurs, and one begins to speak with a discouragement complex, believing that the audience—even those members of it who are most competent and closest to one's own point of view—will not be in possession of the body of doctrines in which what one is going to say is founded and that, therefore, one will have to say many *preliminary* things in order to be correctly understood. And the impression still remains that, with few exceptions, nobody will have enough patience and intellectual capacity to transport himself to a point of view *other* than his own and from there penetrate into the interpretation of what is being propounded.

There are many reasons explaining this disturbing situation. Some of them are social—for example, the excessive number of persons involved in the cultivation of philosophy in the world, the multiplication of books and articles on philosophical themes, the tendency to "manipulate" a vast number of them in an external way, to mention them and quote from them, because of certain academic customs that seem to be simple-minded and could turn out to be dangerous. But other reasons are less external and are related to the content of philosophy itself, to its form, to the very structure of argumentation. When we talk about philosophy, are we really doing this ourselves? Might it not be that we are making use of a notion of what it is to argue

that is derived from historical and intellectual situations
not our own, from an idea of philosophy that we are far
from accepting?

Let me take a brief detour and attack the problem of
argumentation by asking what the structure of philosophical theory is.

It is possible that silence is golden, but in any case speech
(at least the word that interests us here, "argument") is
silver. This metaphor, is it not out of place in a context
that seems to call for exactitude, syllogisms, perhaps theorems with logical symbols? No, I am not being whimsical:
the words "argue," "argument," "argumentation," have the
same root as *argentum* or "argentine," the same root as the
Greek *árgyros* (ἀργυρος) or the adjective *argós* (ἀργὸς).
All these words refer to the same semantic nucleus: ra-
diance, brilliance, whiteness. Silver (*argentum*) is, par excellence, that which glistens, the white and brilliant metal,
whose principal property is *clarity*. The Latin verb *arguo*
means first of all to brighten, to clarify, to illuminate. That
is the original function of argument, or argumentation: to
clarify things, make them glisten, bright, or, what is the
same thing, to make them apparent or manifest—the same
meaning as *alétheia* (ἀλήθεια) or "truth."

Well then, if the mission of argumentation is to brighten
or clarify, to manifest, this means that what we are concerned with is *discovering*. However, the idea traditionally
associated with argumentation is, rather, that of "proof,"
discussion, perhaps demonstration. We see that this is not
the original meaning. If it is possible to speak of demonstration in relation to argument, this is because what is decisive
is enclosed in it: the moment of *showing* or "patency." And
if argumentation is discussion, this is so only on condition

that it comply with the dictum, which may be too optimistic, that "out of discussion comes light."

The reason for this semantic displacement can be found in the fact that argumentation has flourished in a special way at two very distinct turning points in the history of philosophy: Sophism and Scholasticism, especially the latter. Whatever the differences between them (and it is unnecessary to recall that the differences are enormous), they coincide in that for both of them discovery is of only secondary significance. The Sophists affected ignorance of the *alétheia* and let themselves be guided by *dóxa*, by opinion; they were not interested in discovering the truth but in persuading, convincing. Their argumentation is rhetorical and practical; the goal of discussion for them is not to cast light on reality, but rather to trap the adversary and "prove to him" either what is true or what is false, indifferent to whether it be true or false. The Scholastics do have an interest in the truth; not, however, truth in the sense of *alétheia* or discovery, but in the sense of determining the true thesis or opinion from among several proposed (*scientia demonstrativa, quae est veritatis determinativa,* which Saint Thomas contrasted to the dialectic, *quae ordinatur ad inquisitionem inventivam*). Scholasticism, essentially *mediatory*, does not move within the realm of reality but through opinions or judgments: *Videtur . . . Sed contra . . .* To argue is not to brighten, to make clear or manifest what is hidden, but to decide between theses that are placed in contrast.

On the other hand, things acquire a different dimension if we consider the meaning of argumentation in Plato. There is, however, one risk to be avoided: Plato's Socratic dialogues seem to be very close to Sophistic argumentation; in large part they consist of discussions with Sophists and might give the impression that they move within the same sphere of discourse. But this is only a first impression, and an erroneous one. Plato does move among opinions, true, because this is what for the moment he has at hand—the effective point of departure for philosophy. This may be said of all philosophy except the earliest; but even this restriction is not necessary, since original philosophical thought confronted traditional and prevailing beliefs and the removal of these was its own first step. Philosophical ignorance is not merely lack of knowledge, but not knowing *what to be guided by* among things that are insufficiently known. Thus, the Socrates of the Platonic dialogues is not a judge of opinions; he is not going to decide which *among them* is the true one, but to reveal the insufficiency of them all—including his own if he has one—in the interest of acquiring a superior knowledge. The Socratic dialogue consists in the destruction of opinions as such. Socrates, I have sometimes said, is "not in on the secret," and for this reason the Platonic dialectic is of a *real* and philosophical nature. Socrates is not a judge, but a midwife, aiding in the painful birth of the *alétheia,* in the bringing forth * of truth into souls, beginning with his own. This movement through (*diá*) the utterances (*lógoi*) is the *dialogue,* which is argumentation because it is a technique of *bringing out into the light,* of illumination, of clarification, a *maieutics.* In arguing or engaging in argumentation, Plato brightens reality, makes it resplendent, makes it manifest, illuminates it.

In what way? The traditional belief is that Plato is seeking a definition of *horismós* (ὁρισμός) as the object of philosophical knowledge. But things are somewhat more complicated. In the *Phaedrus,* for example, Plato indicates a grave deficiency in the *lógoi* or speeches, in that of Lysias and in that of Socrates himself. What love is has not been

* [In Spanish the common expressions for "to give birth" are *dar a luz* (literally, "to give to the light") and *alumbrar* ("to illuminate")—Trans.]

defined in them, and thus nobody knows what is being discussed; if discussion is to be fruitful, we have to begin by defining it. But this is not a little surprising. For, if what is being asked about is the *tí*, the *what*, then the definition would be the *outcome* of the investigation. How could we begin with it? If the definition is the object sought by means of discourse or discussion, once it is given, all investigation would be superfluous. What Plato does in that dialogue is not only make an objection about method; in it he sets forth a definition of the soul as the *autokíneton*, the self-moving, that which moves itself: "the essence of the soul and the very notion of it consists in this." And then having said this, he relates the *myth* of the winged chariot. That is, the definition, far from being the outcome or object of knowledge, is only its point of departure.

The function of definition is delimitation, to "signal" or mark out the limits of the theme being talked about—that is, to bring into view the reality that interests us, to keep it from escaping or losing its contours, and in this way to make sure we agree about what it is we are investigating. Otherwise, there could be a discrepancy and the confusion of not knowing exactly what is being talked about, as occurs in the dialogues of the Sophists or rhetors. But the definition alone is not able to tell us "how" (οἷον) that reality (for example, the soul or love or the sensible and the intelligible world) is to be investigated. The *logós* or definition does not exhaust the *ousía*; one must set out from a definition and not a mere name (*ónoma*) in order to circumscribe the *ousía*. But effective philosophical knowledge is reached only *later on:* beyond the definition of the soul comes the myth in *Phaedrus*, and following the conceptual definitions in Book VI of *The Republic* comes the myth of the cave in Book VII. That is, the myth is not something to fall back on in the absence of a definition, but something superior, in which genuine philosophical knowledge consists. The argument, setting out from the definition or de-limitation, seeks illumination by way of the myth.

The Platonic myth, which sets out from the determina-tion and intellectual capturing of its theme, is not a pre-philosophical myth. Exhaustive knowledge of the soul is not possible, but the myth tells "how" it is, becoming in this way something like an abbreviation accessible to man (the other would be a divine task). However, the Platonic myth is not primarily nor essentially an allegory; the myth begins precisely where what is allegorical (if it is present) ends. In Greek the word *myth* (μῦθος) means "story," some-thing that happens to somebody and is narrated. This "tell-ing," this narration, is essential. The soul is compared with a wing, and the mission of the wing is to carry heavy things upward. In the myth of *Phaedrus* what is decisive is not the allegorical "similarity" between the soul and the chariot, but the account of the fall and the difficulties the driver has with the two horses. In *The Republic*, the unity of the two worlds, that of the cave and that of genuine reality, rests within the man to whom it *befalls* to be present first in one and then in the other. Thus the narrative, the story, is the life-giving nucleus of the myth and, for this reason, is the decisive element in philosophical knowledge. All the other elements—"proof," "reasoning," "demonstration"— are nothing but resources or artifices for achieving the true end of argumentation, which is to make reality glisten or manifest. And for Plato this comes to pass out of narrating what happens, in the telling of a story.

Theory means vision or contemplation. This signifies that it is the outcome of an action performed by somebody, so that the elimination of the person who sees or understands, and who is the subject of that theory, is a surreptitious amputation of its true reality. Another matter is the question of *who* it is that contemplates. It is possible that to some degree the theory could be made independent of any concrete subject and be referred to a transpersonal one; but in that case this operation will become part of the theory and, consequently, something that *I* have to do. And this "I" is, at the same time, real, concrete, and circumstantial; everything else, though it may be possible and perhaps legitimate, is derived and secondary in relation to that original and radical level.

All thinking, and for profounder reasons all speaking, always occurs with reference to a situation. Nothing exists anything like a *situationsfreier Satz*—even though Bühler does invent something like that. The most that can be admitted is that there may be utterances that are referred to situations so vague and extensive that they could coincide, at least in principle, with any form of human life whatsoever. A mathematical formula presupposes a generic "situation" that is precisely the mathematical attitude—in its most elementary form, the situation that consists of "counting" or "measuring." Thus, every utterance refers to a *context*, which is not to be reduced to other utterances, but which is the total situation within which all of them are given and within which they have meaning. This has to be remembered at all times, especially when trying to decide (something quite frequent in modern philosophy) which propositions, statements, or *Sätze* have meaning and which do not. One would have to look at the credentials—their justification with regard to meaning—of the very doctrines by which the meaning of the rest is being decided; since, if one enters into the question while disregarding the problem of justifying the very thing that is being done, *its* meaningfulness, everything that follows, regardless of how impressive the apparent display of critical keenness may be, will turn out to be ingenuous and *la précaution inutile*. I am not saying that this justification may not be possible (at least at the level at which considerations of this kind usually take place); I am saying only that *if* it is not possible, or as long as it is not done, all the rest is vain and illusory.

This enables us to disclose with some clarity an important characteristic of philosophical theory. It is usual to demand that such theory be *without presuppositions;* but we have to be more precise about the meaning of this *Voraussetzungslosigkeit*. Philosophical theory must justify itself, it has to give the reasons for all its truths. This does not mean, however, that it begins at zero, but that it sets out from a situation defined by multiple claims to knowledge and by certainties that are partial and insufficient and that do not preclude (but may even produce) a *radical uncertainty* which philosophy tries to overcome. In other words, philosophy takes into account the whole of the situation that makes its own presence necessary, including those certainties—which, however, function not as certainties but as realities, that is, as elements or ingredients in this situation. Philosophy does not *derive* its own certainty from them, but it does set out from them. They are its stimuli and its problems.

If this situation be eliminated or forgotten, philosophy loses its radical nature and is deprived of its strength, converted finally into an abstract element of itself. To speak about philosophical *theory* is not the same as speaking about its isolated ingredients, *disjecta membra* of an indivisible whole. When, for example, the propositions that seem to compose a philosophy are analyzed, precisely what it is about them that makes them philosophical is left out.

Argumentation has flourished especially within situations that were (or at least appeared to be) *common* to those who carried on the arguments but who, on the other hand, did not have a clear consciousness of the requisites appropriate to *philosophical* theory, to the point that, looking at things from our own perspective, their condition is uncertain. Sophist doctrine was only φαινομένη σοφια οὖσα δδῦ, apparent wisdom that really was not wisdom; and with regard to Scholasticism we are dealing with an adjective ["Escolástica" is an adjective in Spanish—Trans.] whose substantive is problematical and of which it would be very risky to say that it was "philosophy." This has brought about a state of affairs in which there is an inclination to exclude from consideration the entire situation of the one who is philosophizing (or of those engaged in philosophical argument). But when, as today, this aspect begins to acquire particular importance, we can do nothing less than reflect that upon it depends the very possibility of the existence of efficacious and fruitful argumentation, which would be beyond all equivocation and would not reduce itself to a dialogue among the deaf.

It is certain that philosophical communication has never been at any other time as effective and fruitful as it was in the seventeenth century. Not only were all the philosophers and men of science in close contact with one another, and investigation took place as much in solitude as in society, but a decisive part of the thought of that century was born out of that communication. We are today surprised by the "objections" and "replies" that complete Descartes' *Meditations*, but even more by the correspondence that contains such a substantial portion of the philosophy of the Baroque century. But one does not arrive at this situation by means of a fictitious "leveling of circumstances" (such as occurs in the works of Scholasticism, where all the authorities examined and discussed appear on a single plane, without reference to the distinctive situations that made them possible and gave each of them his concrete significance), but just the contrary: by means of a keenly developed consciousness of the historical and individual situation to which each has come. Perhaps it will be enough to recall that

Francis Bacon made the whole of his philosophy proceed from the theory of the *idola,* which he tried to supersede but not to eliminate, since they are the real conditions of life and of human understanding. The *idola* comprise, not only the condition or nature of man (*idola tribus*), but the reality of the individual man (*idola specus*), and, as if that were not enough, the social and linguistic dimensions of man (*idola fori*) and the historical consequences of his intellectual activity, the fictitious and staged worlds (*mundos fictitios et scenicos*) that he has created in the course of time. This *reliance* of what is external, admitted and apparently valid, upon genuine reality is what explains the very interesting evaluation Bacon makes of Greek philosophy—his disdain for what is professorial and concentrated on discussion, as opposed to the investigation of truth:

> *Erat autem sapientia Graecorum professoria, et in disputationes effusa: quod genus inquisitioni veritatis adversissimum est.*

And within this inferior form Bacon includes not only the Sophists, but the most famous philosophers from Plato and Aristotle on (*utrumque genus professorium erat, et ad disputationem rem deducebat*), and reserves his praise, with singular modernity, for the earliest, the pre-Socratics (with the exception of the "superstitious" Pythagoras), who did not open schools but who with more silence, severity, and simplicity, with less affectation and ostentation, devoted themselves to the quest for truth (*maiore silentio, et severius, et simplicius, id est, minore cum affectione et ostentatione, ad inquisitionem veritatis se contulerunt*).

All this will be even more clear if we consider the beginnings of modern philosophy on the continent. The *Discours de la méthode* of Descartes, who is the writer in whom the *level* that is going to make the philosophy of rationalism possible is effectively achieved, is an *autobiography* in the strictest sense of the word. Descartes talks about himself in full detail, with the utmost simplicity: *ne proposant cet écrit que comme une histoire, ou, si vous l'aimez mieux, que comme un fable*. And this narrative, this story, or (if you wish) this personal drama, represents precisely the new form of philosophical theory that is being inaugurated in Europe and is going to make possible the supersedure of Scholasticism that was announced, but never realized, in all the thought of the Renaissance.

Ten years ago I treated the problem of "literary genres in philosophy" in some detail. This question is closely bound up with that of argumentation. What is decisive is *to whom* the philosophical work is addressed and *what it tries to do* with this whom. Not even the first part of this question is today entirely clear and unequivocal. Those to whom philosophical production is destined are not the same in all countries today, nor in each of these countries have they remained invariable during recent decades. In some cases philosophical writings are "public"—that is, they are directed (at least also directed) to nonprofessional readers. Thus they have to avoid unnecessary technical terminology and, on the other hand, be adequately attractive. In other cases they are directed exclusively to the "technically qualified," to the "philosophers by profession." It might be said that they then are "allowed" another structure and other literary characteristics, but it would be more precise to say that they "must conform" to those specifications—that is, to a form that will gain them admittance to an academic world that has fixed certain standards of "rigor" and "scholarship." In other words, they have to be adjusted to the demands of a different public, although this "public" may be quite small. These demands (and I wish to take advantage of this occasion in order to say this) are usually somewhat simple-minded: in the "technical" publications in which the doctrines of the great philosophers are studied, certain requisites are commonly considered ineludible, among which are some that, obviously, the philosophers who are being studied themselves never observed. And here we come to the unexpected and paradoxical conclusion that, if one of those great thinkers were to present an original manuscript to the editorial committee of one of those journals, this committee would probably reject it, considering it "beneath" the required standard. A book "like" one of the classics would have extreme difficulty in being taken seriously in the academic world. (Strictly speaking, I could very well remove the conditional mood from the two preceding sentences and rewrite them in the present indicative with a few proper names added.) The external and most naïve form of this attitude is to be found in the disdain in which the older (that is, not critical) editions of philosophical works are usually held, in spite of the fact that it is precisely in those editions that these books have *existed* and exercised their influences in the history of philosophy.

The reason for all this is that today the "technical" public is not, as it could be in other times, the infinitesimal number of "philosophers" but the small (though considerable) class of "professionals in philosophy." When I say "philosopher," I am not, of course, referring to the *creators,* who have never been more than a handful of individuals, incapable of forming even the most restricted "public"; I am thinking of those persons for whom philosophy is not the *medium* in which and by which they live, but their way of living, in the sense that they rethink philosophical doctrines from within and make of them a genuine reality of their own intellectual life, but they do not need to be "creators" ("re-creators," yes), and the philosophy they possess is always their own, appropriate to themselves, although not original, since it has been appropriated.

Philosophy today has reached a state of excessive *social* displacement: it has too much external importance—professional, educational, editorial, and economic—and this conditions all the forms of production and communication. For this reason it is not clear to whom one who writes philosophy is addressing himself; this depends on the language in which he is writing, on his position in society, and, above all, on what it is he is trying to do.

Here we are touching on the second part of the question previously formulated: what the philosophical work proposes doing with its readers. "The poem of Parmenides (I have said on another occasion) proposes leading the reader to the ultimate nature of what is real, unveiling the radical condition of what there is and which consists of consistency or being; the dissertation of Seneca does not lead toward anything at all similar, but tends to pour security and contentment over the soul of the reader, to comfort him in his passage through life. If the first is the violation of reality by the intelligence of man, the second is a supply of provisions for a journey. Could any two things be more dissimilar? While Aristotle proposes finding out *why* all things are as they are, Descartes tells the story of his own life in order to reveal his inescapable intellectual shipwreck, which is the condition for reaching solid land from which the whole of creation is going to deliver up its secret and, along with it, its powers and resources. It would not be difficult to extract out of each literary genre of the philosophical past its ultimate aspiration."

And those of the present? This too could be done, though it has not been done. And, if we are sincere, we will have to confess that we have very vague and confused ideas about this. We take it for granted that there is no problem, that the aspiration of all those who write philosophy is the same and that what it is is commonly recognized. Both these assumptions are erroneous, and from this circumstance arises that difficulty of mutual comprehension that frequently renders all argumentation sterile.

When a philosophical work coming from a distant intellectual circle is read or the words of its author are heard, what is at stake is not that "what he says" will not be understood, but rather that there will be no comprehension of "what he wants to say"—what he is talking *about* and *for*, why he is saying what he does say. For a long time I have believed that the greatest difficulty that present-day philosophy comes up against is that relating to its literary genres: the traditional ones turn out to be inadequate and inauthentic; we must innovate, but nobody knows very much about how. All this ends up by producing a strange paralysis in many of the most sensitive and responsible thinkers of our times. Some of them devote the best part of their talent and efforts to demonstrating that nothing now being done is admissible, or that at least it is not philosophy. But we wait in vain for them to tell us something that would let us think of them as philosophers and not simply as the basilisks of philosophy. But, above all, the presuppositions on the basis of which they disqualify the philosophy of the past and present are the least evident of all things, and the theses in which they carry out that critical operation might be subjected to a similar analysis, from the same or from a different point of view.

I have just spoken the key word: *presupposition.* The difficulty of philosophical argumentation at the present time consists, above all, in the absence of common assumptions. If by argumentation "discussion" is understood, the matter will be obvious; if, as is more exact, the technique of bringing reality to birth, of illuminating reality or making it manifest—in a word, of discovery—is understood, then it is even more evident. Conduct a simple experiment: compare the alphabetical index of themes or subjects of a few books, representative of what is today understood by philosophy; take four or five books whose authors may be found among us—a philosopher from Oxford, a Scholastic from Louvain, an existentialist from Paris, a thinker from Heidelberg or Tübingen, from Yale or Berkeley, from Madrid, from Rome, or from Mexico. The differences are astounding. It is not so much that they express distinct opinions, that they think different things about the same themes; it is the themes themselves that are diverse, and when they seem to coincide, that is when the divergence turns out to be greatest, because the function they fulfill in each system makes of the apparent community an equivocation.

How to overcome this situation? Perhaps it may be desirable (I am not certain about this) that the philosophy of an epoch have common assumptions. In any case, it is not in our hands that things be this way. We have to resign ourselves to the fact that the situation in which it has become our turn to live, to philosophize, and to argue is not like that at all. In my judgment, the path to take to achieve effective communication and comprehension (without, of course, excluding disagreement) would be twofold: on the one hand, to be aware that, in spite of everything, there *are* "certain" common assumptions and to separate them clearly from the total complex; on the other hand, explicitly to accept that partial diversity and to *set out from it*. I will try to explain myself.

Normally one begins with an attitude of confidence in the possibility of communication: one supposes that philosophical words and writings are understood, at least in principle, without difficulty. When this becomes more problematical, the doctrines of others are automatically and almost spontaneously deformed through trying to press them into the molds with which they have the greatest affinity. There is a third moment when the evidence that this is not possible imposes itself, and then it is admitted that there are various, relatively incommunicable "areas": for example, "Anglo-Saxon" thought and "continental" thought (in which Hispanic American thought is usually included); some add, as a third area, "Soviet" thought. It is then supposed that there are common presuppositions "within" each of these areas and that, as a consequence, at least within them argumentation and comprehension are possible. Between one area and another, however, it would be necessary to "translate" things on account of the lack of a common philosophical language.

But this is not a true picture, except to a very tenuous degree—only if things are viewed so vaguely that all cats seem gray. There is no such thing as a homogeneous and coherent "continental" thought; English and American thought cannot be lumped together, nor is communication easy within the primary spheres of this "area" of thought. With regard to "Soviet" thought, perhaps there may be a greater community of assumptions, but it is doubtful whether this affinity has a *philosophical* basis and, consequently, whether one may, strictly speaking and without equivocation, apply this adjective to that form of thought.

I believe that the community of assumptions would have to be sought by descending to that subsoil which is made up of the assumptions themselves. In other words, more than a convergence of doctrines and ideologies, we have to look for the convergence of things. Reality itself has a structure, which is imposed upon *all* thought if it gets close enough to reality not to let it escape and does not replace it with constructions. This does not mean that doctrines have to coincide as they approach reality; to believe this was the error of rationalism. Reality is multiple, *mehrseitig*, many-sided, and is inexhaustible; thought apprehends and discovers it, but always in a way that foreshortens it from a definite perspective. Thus, *coincidence* is neither necessary nor would it be likely; but *concordance*, yes, which is the consequence of reference to the same reality. And that is enough to make comprehension and communication possible. Each of the different philosophies should make an attempt to "renounce" its own presuppositions, that is, to analyze them, to make them the object of an investigation from its own point of view—while not disregarding what Ortega called "pre-philosophy," which is, as he rightly saw, nothing but the basis and the very nerve tissue of each philosophy. The only path for philosophy is for it to take its own claims and its demand for *getting at the root of things* seriously, that is, as something requiring performance.

Along this path, once having clarified the partial community of presuppositions imposed by reality and having made maximum use of them, this operation might be completed with what is complementary: accepting diversity and setting out from it. How? This brings us to the central theme of these notes.

Everything that man does is circumstantial, as is his life in its entirety. Everything is done in view of a precise circumstance in which one finds oneself, in view of an ambition, also circumstantial, that one wishes to realize. A *philosophical* doctrine, if it is philosophical, is responding to a human need to orient oneself, to know what to guide oneself by in relation to reality. It is, thus, a reality that forms part of *the* reality; it is conditioned by this reality and at the same time modifies it. A philosophical theory has a systematic character, not because philosophy wishes it, as happened with the German idealists, but because the reality that is human life is itself systematic. The present-day philosopher is a system-builder *malgré lui*. The connections existing in what is real (including the philosopher's own life) are what determine those of theory. For this reason a logical "concatenation" is not enough, since the vital structure is not simply a chain; but what is required is a *vivification*, a discovery of the ties to reality of the kind that do actually appear—that is, in life, not in a mere abstract or intentional consideration. Thus, a philosophical theory needs an *argument:* the vital "why" and "what for" of the one who is thinking. Only out of that argument will the function of the elements of any dramatic structure be discovered, and this is what pertains to the theory, if it be viewed within its true circumstantial condition, as something that emerges from a definite vital situation.

The argument of the theory is its *real*, not merely logical, justification. Philosophy has to disclose its own necessity; I would say its *inevitability*—if one could live without it, why get involved in it? Only if the situation in which a man finds himself leads him to the need to philosophize in order to live a human life, in order to know what to be guided by with respect to reality and, thereby, decide what to do at each moment—only then will it be justified. Philosophical theory is in this way a taking possession of *a* human situation, which in some measure will perhaps be *the* human situation, and its formulation and articulation in the baring of the internal movement of that situation, since each situation is intrinsically dynamic (a "unique" situation is a contradiction in terms). For this reason, philosophical theory is *intrinsically* dramatic; and insofar as it may not be, this means that it has been divested of its reality, that it is abstract, because it has been abstracted away from its circumstantial condition.

Well now, human life is the only known reality that may be truly intelligible, since it is the very phenomenon of meaning. We understand some particular thing when we observe its functioning within life itself, when we precisely know its "argument." Thus argumentation consists, as the etymology of the word suggests, in brightening or polishing, clarifying or making manifest. When we look at a theory as something that a man does, as something he has had to think in order to know what to be guided by and in order to be able to live in a certain situation, we transmigrate to this situation and from it, virtually in possession of it, we are able to understand that theory. Each human situation is irreducible, and from this flows the radical solitude of which life consists. This condition extends to thought, insofar as it is a vital reality, and this is why all expression is frustrated, all comprehension deficient. But, although each man has his own circumstance, it is no less certain that these are *communicable:* thus there is a common "world," even though it is not primary and radical, but something that is already theory and interpretation.

The only way of reaching it, we now see, is to be faithful to the circumstance in which one is, and this means to transmigrate to that of one's neighbor, to accept it in what it has of *other* and is irreducible, and that requires the comprehension of the argument of his life, from which he is able to argue. Only then does my neighbor become relatively transparent; only then do I *see* why he thinks what he does think and understand what is thought. By imaginatively recreating the thread of his theory, following its dramatic structure, the flow of events that is his life, I place myself within his point of view. But this is a manner of speaking: transmigration of this sort is illusory, because even supposing that I did succeed in transporting myself into his situation, I could not abandon my own—that is, I would be in a situation that would be *at one and the same time* his and mine, and thus neither of the two, but a third situation to which I had come and from which I would see reality in a distinct third way. That is what the clarification called *argumentation* consists of, and it is only possible if we attempt those imaginary transmigrations—the only trips that justify our taking these others that carry us from one continent to another. It would not be proper for me to cross the Atlantic, going from old Spain to the lands of New Spain, if I were not disposed to transport myself into the point of view from which my friends and companions in this humble and proud task that is called philosophy look at reality, if I were not capable of interesting myself in those essential and sober dramas that philosophical theories are.

NOTE

In the text there are allusions to some of my writings, in which I have treated in greater detail and from other perspectives some of the questions dealt with here. They are the following:

Introducción a la filosofía (Madrid, 1947) [*Obras* II]; translated into English as *Reason and Life* (Yale University Press, 1956).

Biografía de la filosofía (Buenos Aires, 1954) [*Obras* II].

Idea de la metafísica (Buenos Aires, 1954) [*Obras* II]. ["The Idea of Metaphysics" in *Contemporary Spanish Philosophy*, ed. by A. R. Caponigri (University of Notre Dame Press, 1967).]

"Los géneros literarios en filosofía," in *Ensayos de teoría* (Barcelona, 1954) [*Obras* IV]; translated in this volume as "Literary Genres in Philosophy."

"Comentario por Julián Marías a *Meditaciones del Quijote* de José Ortega y Gasset" (Río Piedras, Puerto Rico, 1957).

Ortega, vol. 1: *Circunstancia y vocación* (Madrid, 1960); translated into English as *Ortega y Gasset: Circumstance and Vocation* (University of Oklahoma Press, 1970).

CHAPTER THREE

WHAT IS PHILOSOPHY?

In August 1955, Heidegger went to France for the first time in his life. When he arrived at the Chateau de Cerisy in Normandy, he carried in his lively and penetrating eyes— the eyes of an astute man, as in the poem by Antonio Machado—a reflection of the Paris he had just seen. Scrutinizing eyes, of the kind that have gone most deeply into the real, within the bronzed face of a country dweller, perhaps a German forest guard, always watchful through the thick underbrush and along the paths lost in it that perhaps do not lead anywhere—his *Holzwege*. On the third day he abandoned his city suit and put back on the jacket he usually wears, a mountaineer's jacket of greenish gray with green flaps over the pockets. He felt more himself; it helped him overcome his shyness, his emotional country timidity. "I am timid," he said with a smile when bidding us goodbye, "because I come from country people, *ich komme aus den Bauern.*"

Martin Heidegger came to engage in dialogue with a group of people, most of them not Germans. An attempt at communication—the great problem of his philosophy, as Gabriel Marcel has stressed—turning upon the very question in which all those present were personally involved: "What is philosophy?" The idea was not, as Heidegger himself said, to try to reach some definite conclusions, a *Protokoll*, but to unite our voices in a kind of consonance, in a dialogue where what mattered was *die Zustimmung*. In opening the discussion Heidegger formulated his orienting

principles: (1) The most stupid questions are the best.
(2) To forget everything. (3) To try in this colloquium
not to argue, not to reason, but to open one's eyes and ears.

Obviously holding his emotions in check, Heidegger
evoked the years of his own intellectual formation, from
1906 to 1914, the most stimulating in Germany—years of
the translation of Kierkegaard into German, of the complete printing of Nietzsche's *Der Wille zur Macht*, of Husserl's publication of his essay *Philosophie als strenge Wis-
senschaft*. "From the time I was seventeen," Heidegger recalled, "I have been concerned with Aristotle." And he
talked about the aged Brentano and of Trendelenberg, who
had brought Aristotle, "the father of this kind of thinking,"
back by the hand.

An inaugural lecture, discussions, other lectures from
other points of view; but above all, three seminars directed
by Heidegger: one on a text taken from Kant, another on a
text from Hegel, the third on a poem by Hölderlin.
Heidegger, supreme professor—as Aristotle and Hegel were
too. There is nothing discreditable in that; it is nothing but
fate, *"Schicksal,"* as he liked to say. Heidegger, perhaps
not a very widely read man—but how deep and tenacious
a reader of his ancient Greeks, of his German idealists, of
his Hölderlin! Consider the almost childlike delight with
which he is absorbed in those writings. What a marvelous
devotion to the task of revealing them, taking them apart
and seeing what they are like from within! Heidegger's
workshop! What profound intellectual pleasure it is to
enter into it and pass the hours as time stands still within
it (no matter that the seminar might begin promptly at
teatime and be extended until sundown), watching him at
work, as he operates the mechanisms, turning them loose
and then readjusting their initial courses, tinkering with all
the parts, happy when somebody points out to him the

decisive bolt, the precise link, or moves the appropriate lever. Intoxicated in his labor, forgetful of everything and of everybody, absorbed in his vision, listening to the voice of being and to the voice of his familiar, beloved, and profound classics, unable to transmigrate, marvelously creative and simple, limited by his own greatness, "monster in his labyrinth."

And now Heidegger has published his inaugural lecture from those dialogues at Cerisy: *Was ist das—die Philosophie?* He asked some of us, apart from the discussions that followed, to express our points of view or our disagreements in brief independent lectures. This was done by Marcel, Ricoeur, Goldmann, and myself. I preferred to separate myself from what Heidegger had said and to raise the question just as I see it, within our minimal Spanish philosophical tradition. Now that Heidegger's text has been published, I think that to translate what I read at Cerisy into Spanish is justified. The reader who follows my work consistently—if there is any such reader—will find ideas that have already been formulated in previous works of mine (cited at the end of this essay). In any case, I consider it worthwhile to reach yet another reverberation from the dialogue with Heidegger.

When we talk about philosophy, we speak first of all of a noun, of a Greek noun: *philosophía.* This carries us, then, into a tradition, which is that of Greece *and* of the West. Philosophy has in fact been talked about for some twenty-five centuries: there is a continuity within *one and the same* human activity or at least within a series of activities that contain common elements and that are responses to an equivalent or analogous situation. However, on the other

hand, since philosophy is something that *has to be done,**
this means that it is not made or finished, but is something
to be made, a chore or a task—which is to say that we have
to make *another* philosophy, different from those that have
preceded us. There is, then, behind us a whole series of
relations of *otherness,* whose system is the history of philosophy. Our own situation is strictly the inverse of that of
the pre-Socratics: they had to create philosophy because
they did not have it; we have to create it because we encounter it in our tradition, because what already exists does
not serve our needs and we have to make another, precisely
our own. (If we did not have to make *another* philosophy,
we would not have *to make* philosophy at all, since this
would already be made. To make a philosophy when one
is not making another is literally "to be making what is
made.")

The name philosophy does not mean very much. Something similar occurs with the noun *metaphysics.* "Metaphysics" (I have insisted on this elementary and significant
detail several times) is not one Greek word but four: *tà
metà tà physikà.* The Latin word *metaphysica* is, in its turn,
not a translation but a simple fusion and transliteration. The
noun *metaphysica* means nothing in Latin and nothing interesting in Greek. Its function is, rather, rhetorical and
poetic: it is a word borrowed from another language, which
is not first of all a signification or *Bedeutung* but a quite
mysterious sign to which a quite vague meaning is attributed
—"what there is *beyond physics* or beyond nature." That
is, the name *metaphysics* holds out hope but does not de-
clare either its limits or what its requirements are, and this

* [The Spanish word *hacer,* used here and through the subsequent
sentences, may have as its English equivalent either "to make" or
"to do," and I have used whichever of these words seemed most
appropriate in each circumstance, sometimes even going so far as
to translate *hacer* as "to create" when this seemed inescapable—
Trans.]

is the reason for the exceptional fate of this word and—I might dare to say—of its interest and its value. One might speak in much the same way about the name philosophy, a rather late designation of a certain Greek activity (suspect and disquieting for a long time) that turned out to be necessary, at least for some men in a very concrete situation in ancient times.

If what is called philosophy has some function in human life, it is necessary to discover its origin and its justification in a human need that previously had been satisfied by some *homologous* reality to which philosophy stands in the relation of *surrogate*. If we had time, I believe it would be interesting to study the idea of *moîra* from this point of view; for a long time I have believed myself to have encountered in this idea a pretheoretical *análogon* to physics, as well as the function of the oracles. To cite something precise, I will recall that in the *Theogony* (v. 27–28), the Muses say:

> We know how to speak many lies similar to true things;
> but we know, when we want to, how to proclaim truths.

There is a dual contrast in Hesiod: *pseúdea* is opposed on the one hand to *étyma*, genuine or *authentic* things, and on the other hand to *alethéa*, truths that are spoken or declared, revealed or discovered. This passage in Hesiod coincides almost exactly with a verse of the *Odyssey* (XIX, 203) in which Ulysses says, "many lies similar to true things" (*pseúdea pollà légon etymoisin homoîa*), that is, likely or verisimilar (*verus* [= "true"] + *similar*). And the Muses are in Hesiod *artiépeiai*, "truthful" or, better, "inclined to the exact word"; they speak in a way that is precise and adequate.

Aristotle talks about the *sophía* that men have sought *dià tò pheúgein tèn ágnoian* in order to flee from ignorance or to make it flee, in order to know what to be guided by, in order to escape from that perplexity and even *vertigo* of which Plato speaks in Letter VII. To know what to be guided by . . . But here we have to ask: with regard to what?

When things are present, man makes vital use of them in very diverse ways; when they are not present, they raise problems. But we have to remember that there are three quite different ways of nonpresence:

(1) When the thing I need, which is necessary to me, or which I simply desire, is not within the space or the time in which I find myself. I recall things that I was able to have at hand at other times, or perhaps I imagine possible situations in which it would be necessary to have things that at present do not exist. The complex of human reactions to this form of nonpresence is what might be called *technics*.

(2) Another form of not having things at hand is failure or frustration. I begin (this is essential) by having the things; later on I no longer have them or I have them in a way that is precarious or deficient, which changes the situation. I go on walking in tranquility and suddenly the ground sinks away under my feet or, at least, becomes insecure. I was looking at the things (no more than installed in that vision, not even thinking about it), and now I am in darkness because the sun has set and put out the light that made things bright for me. The man with whom I was talking has remained unmoved, has turned deaf, makes no response whatsoever. And I do not know what to be guided by. This is *thaumázein*, astonishment or strangeness: I am outside my previous situation; I have become strange and, as Aristotle says, *I do nothing*. Simply to say this is not to say enough: I do nothing because I am not in possession of my situation and, instead of pursuing the action to which I was committed, I initiate *another* (in principle entirely different from the previous one, and it is for that reason that I can say I do nothing, understanding by this "nothing of

what I was doing"), another action that consists of asking myself what has happened, what is my new situation, how is it possible for this to have befallen that thing. In other words, what *is* that thing? No longer am I concerned with the thing itself but become preoccupied with its *being,* in the sense of its consistency. And this is the origin of that form of thought we call *knowledge* or, if you wish, *science.* (To this *pre-occupation* with being corresponds the characteristic of *pre-thing* that pertains to the being of the thing.)

(3) But there is a third, more radical form of nonpresence, of "not being here." This is that of what is latent. What is latent declares and at the same time negates its presence. We are in a forest, it is still daylight, we see clearly; but night is *imminent.* Where is the night? Nowhere, of course; but it follows us, we take it into account, we behave in relation to it. While I am living, my death has no reality at all, it is nowhere, I can do nothing *with* it; but it waits for me, I do not know where, I do not know when, but I take it into account. The future is what is latent par excellence, and I have no other way of living except precisely in consideration of the future, in anticipation of it. And that which is most distant is God himself, whom "nobody has ever seen" (*Deum nemo vidit unquam*), but without whom I do not know what to be guided by—by which I mean that I absolutely do not know what to be guided by if I do not know what to be guided by with respect to God.

This third form of nonpresence leads me to the requirement that I consider the *totality* of my life and of my circumstances. That which is latent *about* my life surrounds and envelops it, gives it a horizon, in this way conferring upon it its unity and its character of totality. My attitude in the face of what is latent, in its entirety, has to be for that reason total, radical. *Thought* is not now technical or cognitive or scientific; it has to become radical and ultimate. But on this account, it is not yet decided whether what is involved here is, strictly speaking, *knowledge* (in the rigorous sense that Ortega gives to this word in his *Apuntes sobre el pensamiento*) or some other form of thought, whether what is going to be born is philosophy or something else.

At the beginning, in fact, man can do nothing to reach the latent ground of things; it is that latent ground itself that has to reveal itself in one form or another. To the degree that a man has faith in the flashing revelations of the real—in the oracles, divinations, and so on—he is oriented and he knows what to be guided by. But when, after a multitude of historical experiences, of attempts and of failures, of contacts with other systems of belief, that faith is shattered, then uncertainty ensues. Remember the passage in Herodotus referring to the "examination of the oracles" by Croesus and the passages in Xenophon in the *Anabasis* about the conflict between the evidences of reason and man's orientation by means of sacrifices. But there is a moment in which a new *belief* begins to rise up: the belief that all things are "at bottom" the same, that one is not derived from another by generation, but that there is a certain *consistency—eón, ón*—about which one is able to ask questions.

The situation reverses itself: now it is no longer a matter of passively waiting for the revelation—of the oracle, for example—but, rather, of addressing oneself to reality and obliging it to respond. It is man himself who is able to *unveil* reality. Here is a two-way path: from what is latent to what is manifest, and from what is revealed and manifest to the latent and hidden reality. In other words, there is a *method*. The truth is now not what is *said* truthfully to man; it is what man himself *does* with things, that is, what he discovers in them. What is involved is a way of finding out, a *verification* or *verum facere*—"truth making." And what man makes out of things is an interpretation letting him know what to be guided by with respect to them, and in this way he makes his life in the midst of them and with them, in his circumstance or world.

Now, the name of the most widely recognized interpretation of reality, the name of what has been the foundation of Western philosophy during the course of twenty-five centuries, is *being*. So now the radical problem is raised of what to guide oneself by with respect to reality itself, underneath and beyond all interpretations (and underneath and beyond being too), at the same time giving an account of all of them. And to raise this problem is equivalent, in my opinion to posing the question that has brought us together here: What is philosophy?

NOTES

1. On the interpretation of truth as *alétheia* or *apokálypsis*, discovery, unveiling, see José Ortega y Gasset, *Meditaciones del Quijote* (Madrid, 1914); in English translation, *Meditations on Quixote* (New York, 1961).
2. On the passages from Hesiod and the *Odyssey*, as well as on the word *metaphysics*, see Julián Marías, *Idea de la metafísica* (Buenos Aires, 1954); in English translation in *Contemporary Spanish Philosophy*, edited by A. Robert Caponigni (University of Notre Dame Press, 1967), pp. 325–370.
3. On the origins of philosophy, *Biografía de la filosofía* (Buenos Aires, 1954) and especially *Introducción a la filosofía* (Madrid, 1947); in English translation, *Reason and Life* (Yale University Press, 1956)—where the reader will find an interpretation of the *moîra* and reflections on the relation between reality and being. On this point also see the article "Realidad y ser en la filosofía española," *La Nación* (Buenos Aires, 7 August 1955), and compare *Filosofía actual y existencialismo en España* (Madrid, 1955).
4. I have added a few phrases (within parentheses) to the text read at Cerisy on the first of September 1955.

CHAPTER FOUR

PRESENT TENDENCIES IN KNOWLEDGE AND THE HORIZON OF PHILOSOPHY

This is the text of a lecture given at the University of Valladolid—the city of my birth, full of fond memories, although I lived there only five years. It is one in a series of lectures in which that University wished to examine the nature of the advanced knowledge of our times. It has always been necessary for science to turn its gaze upon itself and to see itself as an aggregate and as an objective. At the present time such examinations must be frequent, since the risk is being run of taking the past for the present—at times, deceitfully, for the future. The reader will find in the text that follows some ideas I have expressed on other occasions, in other contexts, for different purposes—in any case, quite a number of years ago. They now appear with a renewed and more urgent presence.

In speaking of the tendencies of knowledge I would like to emphasize the last two words of this phrase: the tendencies *of knowledge*, of knowledge itself. This is not the same thing as the styles or inclinations of those who cultivate knowledge. Thus I am going to refer much more to the objective demands of philosophical knowledge than to the tendencies, proclivities, or the simple fashions that appear in the philosophy of our time.

In other words, what I am interested in clarifying in a precise way is *what must one know* when one wishes to know in the radical sense of that word: to know what to be guided by, to know what to think about things, to know what to do. When this is done at a radical level, it is precisely what is called *philosophy*.

There are some philosophical positions, from former times and again in our own, characterized by renunciation in relation to knowing or by the renunciation of certain ways of knowing that are considered ultimate and which, at times, are declared inaccessible, impossible, or, on occasion, uninteresting. In my judgment the attitude of renunciation in relation to knowing is always contrary to the essence of philosophy. Philosophy consists precisely in the opposite attitude, in not renouncing any state of knowledge; philosophy grows in the face of difficulty and tries again and again. In any case, it renounces some plot or dimension of knowledge only if it can be shown or demonstrated that this knowledge is impossible, that it is inaccessible; and not even then does it give up but, rather, goes on trying in other ways. At the end of the eighteenth century Kant posed the problem of the possibility of metaphysics and in a certain sense his solution was negative: metaphysics within the limits of pure speculative reason appeared to be impossible. And yet this apparent renunciation by Kant of metaphysical knowledge was nothing but a way of opening a new door to philosophy: first, from the point of view of practical reason; in the second place, as the initiation of the whole of German idealism, from Fichte to Hegel. Kant's apparent renunciation was, strictly speaking, nothing but the taking of a new position from which to create metaphysics in a more radical sense. It is enough to recall the interpretation that Kantianism has received during recent decades, especially beginning with Heidegger's book *Kant und das Problem der Metaphysik* (1929) and even before that in Ortega's essays "Kant—Reflexiones de centenario" (1924) and "Filosofía pura—Anejo a mi folleto Kant" (1928), in which an attempt is made to discover the metaphysical dimension in Kantian thought no longer in the *Critique of Practical Reason* but in the *Critique of Pure Reason.*

In speaking of the present directions in philosophical knowledge, I would say that all are legitimate to the degree in which they do what they do, to the degree in which they do what they propose doing, whatever they may be. On the other hand, they are not legitimate to the degree in which they pretend to determine what must be done and, especially, what must not be done or is uninteresting. In recent years, in Spain and in other places as well, it has frequently been said that certain aspects, certain portions, certain aims of knowledge *are not interesting.* For example, not many years ago a curious "disqualification" of metaphysics was in process of being initiated. There are people who say that metaphysics is uninteresting or, rather, that it is impossible or composed of statements without meaning. This idea, which is presented as something new, is, as a matter of fact, to go back to thinking what was thought in almost the whole of Europe beginning around 1880. Thus the first thing that is done now is to give back the word "metaphysics" in a surreptitious way the meaning it had at about that time, forgetting that this word has a long history and forgetting the decisive steps that have been taken during the last forty or fifty years, steps that affect not so much the concrete contents of metaphysics but very significantly do affect the idea we have of what metaphysics is.

From a different point of view, there is an initial objection to be made to all those orientations in philosophy that pretend to decide whether or not certain statements have meaning, and this is: those orientations would, before doing anything else, have to justify themselves in their entirety and, in order to do this, to take a step backward and concern themselves for what Ortega called "prephilosophy"—that is, the ground on which all philosophical doctrines rest and which, in the last analysis, forms a part of each of them. When philosophy is radical, it has to include its own prephilosophy and justify it.

It will be said: How is this possible? Philosophy has sometimes been defined as a discipline that has no presuppositions, what the Germans call, in a word that is much too long, *Voraussetzunglosigkeit*, "absence of presuppositions." If philosophy is a radical way of knowing, not founded on any other knowledge, evidently it cannot have any presuppositions, in the sense that it is not able to derive its certainty from any prior knowledge, anterior to it, but has to justify the whole of its contents and demonstrate thereby the validity of everything it affirms. But here one must ask: Does this mean that philosophy begins at zero, that it can begin at zero? Evidently not; that would be utopian. Philosophy sets out, as all human activities do, from a *situation*. The idea, defended by the great theoretician of language Karl Bühler in his otherwise admirable *Theory of Language*,* that there are statements unrelated to any situation (*situationsfrei*) seems to me erroneous. There are no utterances unrelated to any situation, not even the most abstract statements, including those belonging to sciences that do not deal with real but with ideal objects— mathematics, for example. The simple statement "Two and two are four" pertains to a vital situation which is *counting*, quite different from that of a man who is walking through the countryside or swimming or eating or dreaming. This means that, even though the situation may be enormously general and could be extended to practically

---

* [Julián Marías translated Bühler's *Sprachtheorie* into Spanish— Trans.]

all human situations or might be able in principle to form part of or be an element in *every* situation, no utterance will ever be "unrelated to a situation." And this is analogous to the way in which human realities are historical and never intemporal, that they are never "constant" although they may well be "enduring"—that is, there are determining factors in human history in the concrete sense that they begin and end and affect man in a phase of history that is sometimes very brief, while other determining factors may accompany man through the entire course of history, so that in principle they might extend from Adam to the Last Judgment without, on that account, ceasing to be historical. They would not be a constituent of man in an unmediated way but consequential to historical reality, and thus historically acquired, even though they might endure from the beginning of history to the end.

Every statement, every utterance is related to a situation, however vague, generic, and permanent this might be. And there is one concrete situation that embraces the whole of human life, and this is language. Every statement sets out from a prior situation that is the language we speak, and language already represents a primary interpretation of reality. The language in which we are installed, its phonetic system, its system of grammar, its vocabulary—all this, in and of itself, already constitutes an interpretation of the real. To speak Spanish is not the same thing as to speak English, nor German the same as Greek; and I do not say Hebrew or Chinese or any other language outside the Indo-European family of languages, within which there are considerable resemblances.

Language is thus the first interpretation of reality and that first *installation* in which we find ourselves and from which our intelligence functions in order to comprehend things. This means that philosophy is already borne on a language, that it derives from a language in the same way that the characteristic expression of an individual is derived from a biological inheritance. The characteristic expression of each of us consists of certain modulations, variations, or indentations that each of us performs starting from the biological reality we have inherited, with the physiognomic traits we have received from our parents and grandparents, to which we add our own personal expression. In an analogous way every scientific, literary, or philosophical interpretation starts with the body of the language and, precisely by virtue of a literary style, whether written or spoken, proceeds to produce those personal modulations upon it. It would be chimerical to try to imagine a philosophy that did not begin with a language and that was not, for that reason, related to a prior situation. But this, as we shall soon see, does not mean that language may be the "final authority," nor that philosophy can be reduced to the analysis of language.

Furthermore, philosophy has never set out from ignorance but from knowledge, from the knowledge of many things, from a complex of certainties that are insufficient and in conflict. And it is precisely those certainties, since they are insufficient or because they contradict one another or leave gaps or fissures in our vision of the world, that force us to philosophize. Philosophical statements, from the time of the pre-Socratics to our own day, have never taken the form "A is B" but, rather, "A is not B, but C"—that is, the first thing philosophy has done is remove, eliminate a certain thesis (for example, a *dóxa*, an opinion, a socially dominant belief, in any case an erroneous or insufficient interpretation of reality) in order to replace it with another of its own, profounder, more radical, truer. "A is not B, but C": this is the traditional form in which philosophy has historically occurred.

Then what happens with the radical nature of philosophy? What becomes of the absence of presuppositions?

What happens is that philosophy, which sets out from a language and a multitude of certainties, does not derive its own certainty from them but has to go back over them precisely in order to *justify* them. It sets out from them, not from zero, but it has to go backward (philosophy is always a trail of comings and goings, it is always a priori *and* a posteriori) in order to justify them or, rather, to demonstrate their lack of justification, to correct them, to replace them.

If this is forgotten, philosophy loses its radical nature, and then it turns out that the theses of philosophy, the statements of philosophy are not, properly speaking, *philosophical* statements at all; they are statements or theses about reality, but as isolated parts or *disjecta membra* of a philosophy, and lacking from them is precisely what it is that makes something philosophical. No statement whatsoever, no matter how theoretical it may be, is in and of itself a philosophical statement. In order for a statement to become philosophical it is necessary for it to be sustained by a whole philosophy, and this means by that radical process by virtue of which philosophy sets out from certainties and goes back over them in order to justify them. Philosophy always *has* a "prephilosophy" at its back, but it *consists* in going backward and justifying, taking over, and raising up that "prephilosophy" into philosophy, for it cannot be left abandoned at the door. Thus it is philosophy that, in the last analysis, decides about all its presuppositions (certainties and language) and not the other way around.

If what is decisive is philosophy itself and not mere "statements," since these by themselves cannot be philosophical, then we are led to ask about the characteristics of philosophical theory. I believe that philosophical theory has to refuse formulas whenever possible. It is well known that philosophy is frequently expressed in formulas and that there has been a tendency in some philosophical currents, in other times and in our own, to convert philosophy into a system of formulas, which are defined by an exceedingly precise terminology. However, this seems to me dangerous for philosophy for one very clear reason.

The conventional way of naming a reality (Ortega saw this quite clearly many years ago) is with a "term," which is the contrary of a "word." A *term* is something I define, to which I attribute a fixed meaning in a conventional way. But a word is exactly the contrary: something that nobody has agreed upon or defined. The words I am using belong to the Spanish language; none of us has invented them or stipulated what their meanings are to be, and for this reason we understand one another, since these words exist before we do. And this is what occurs in language in general.

Yet when a philosophy is composed primarily of terms, it is able to produce the illusion that reality is being taken in hand, but such is not the case: the philosopher is simply manipulating terms and combining them. I have always been impressed with what is told about the great philosopher Francisco Suárez, who tried several times to get into the Society of Jesus but without success. Why? Because he did not understand a thing; he was a very bad student. Finally there was a teacher more patient or more intelligent than the others and he decided to give Suárez one last chance, and that was how he got into the Society of Jesus. I ask myself why Suárez was so dense, why he did not understand anything. Probably it was because he *tried* to understand and was not fond of what was in the sixteenth century called *leer por cartapacios*, "to read by taking notes and memorizing them." Evidently the majority of the professors and students handled the terms and formulas of Scholasticism very well and made up syllogisms on demand. Suárez, it seems, understood nothing; the others, of course, did not understand anything either, but Suárez tried to understand. He was not content with rolling his tongue around terms; he was not capable of blindly operating those precious syllogisms that the students of Alcalá and Salamanca, Paris and Coimbra, strung together like parrots. Suárez, so it seems, tried to do more: to understand. And since he did not understand, he failed the examination several times. Later on it turned out that he was capable of understanding quite a few things, but in a very different sense, from the point of view of reality, not by means of mere formulas, not by means of terms.

The formulas of philosophy must be reduced to the minimum, and their function must be the reverse of that they have usually had. The only acceptable ones are those I once called "germinal formulas," by which I mean those that acquire a new and concrete meaning in the mind of everyone who uses them and that are, for that reason, capable of becoming the germ of new thoughts—the contrary, thus, of those formulas that are passively received and that have to be transmitted intact and unchanged, to such a degree that the people who think according to them give the impression of behaving like those slightly unbalanced persons who walk along the street trying to avoid stepping on the cracks between the tiles of the sidewalk.

The proof of a doctrine, the supreme proof of a theory, is precisely that one may *walk through* it. This is less frequent than might be supposed and is the characteristic of creative thought. When a philosopher is able to walk through his own doctrine (by which I mean that he is able to go back and forth in all directions), when from it he is able to confront a new question, to receive an objection and to reply, not with prefabricated formulas, but by having recourse to the whole body of his discipline and lodging this new reality which is the question within it—then it can be said that what is involved is really a philosophical theory. This characteristic that I call *transience* * seems to me fundamental, since a theory, and above all a philosophical theory, is something that lives, and lives creatively, as language does. Language is there, it is a common wealth that we find around us and from which we set out in order to speak; but each person uses it creatively. I choose some words and not others out of our vocabulary; within the customary ways of Spanish pronunciation I speak in a certain way, placing more emphasis on some phrases than on others and on certain words in the phrase; I construct with the freedom that is permitted me by Spanish syntax—and all this indicates that I, like all those who speak, use language creatively, inventively. Theory, I repeat, lives the way language does; it is not applied like a code of laws. When this does happen, it is an indication that what is involved is a dead theory or, at most, the skeleton of a theory. Don't forget that theory is *theoría*, which in Greek means "vision," "contemplation"; and the verb *theoreîn* does not mean anything but "see." Theory is, neither more nor less, a vision of reality; and this means, in all strictness, that theory is characterized by *visuality*. When a philosopher does not see what he is saying, what he may be saying is not worth while. When you are reading a philosopher and have the impression that you are seeing, that he is seeing, and that he makes you see what he is saying, go on reading; if not, my advice is that you not waste too much time with him. Furthermore, this is what the word meaning "truth" is in Greek, *alétheia:* patency, manifestation, discovery, or (better) unveiling. Concepts are valueless in themselves; they are simply instruments that let us discover—*alétheia*—what was in front of our eyes without being seen.

* [Perhaps in this context this word should be spelled *transcience;* the Spanish, however, is simply *de tránsito,* meaning "in transit" or "transient" and related to the verb *transitar,* "to walk (or pass or drive) through"—Trans.]

Concepts serve to illuminate reality; their function is illumination. Etymology is frequently a powerful aid in philosophical thought, as long as one does not abuse it and remains conscious of its unusual or exceptional character. And I say this because the etymological view of a language is an artificial view; language is not used etymologically. However, once in a while one must descend to the subsoil of a language in order to look for the origins of a word. Some years ago I observed that the words "argue," "argument," "argumentation," which are much used by philosophers, have the same root as the word *argentum*, "silver"— *árgyros* in Greek. Silver is the white metal, the radiant metal, the metal that shines; and argument, arguing is what makes things shine or glisten. To argue is to make things brilliant, glistening, or radiant; and if silence is golden, philosophical argumentation is at least like silver.

This *visual* condition of philosophy, this function of philosophy to make reality glitter and be manifest is frequently replaced by other things: at times by erudition, at times by terminology, on occasion by regulations, perhaps by interminable dialectical processes, resembling an inertial system, in which nobody knows what is being talked about.

Philosophical theory, on account of this condition that I have just pointed out and as an unexpected consequence of it, is simple and complex, both at once. Why? If theory is contemplation, philosophical theory has to possess at one and the same time the simplicity of vision and the complexity of the reality that is viewed. Vision is always simple (though it may not be *simplex mentis inspectio*) because it is a unitary and embracing action: the unity of the act of *looking*. But when I look, what do I see? A reality, and this means a *concrete* reality, and this possesses a complexity that is in principle infinite. When traditional philosophy insisted that it is not possible to define the individual, it had in mind this characteristic of infinite complexity of the real.

Vision is thus inexhaustible; it begins and never ends or, it would be better to say, it is reborn out of itself; it consists of continuity and cannot be reduced to formulas. It is true of course that vision needs and utilizes formulas, but the formulas of philosophical theory have no other function than to propel vision once again off into a different direction. If an image is desired, I would compare formulas to the successive charges of a rocket that make it go on advancing. The mission of a philosophical formula reduces itself to sending vision off again in a new direction, and this means literally that philosophy can never *remain* within its formulas.

In addition, philosophy has as its aspiration discovering truths and *justifying* them. The mechanism of justification is essential to philosophy, and for this reason all unjustified philosophy, all unverifiable philosophy is to that degree something that is not philosophy. Some time ago I proposed an excessively concise definition of philosophy that does, however, unless I am mistaken, genuinely contain most of its essential characteristics: *philosophy is responsible vision*. It is vision that is responsive to reality and responsive to itself, vision that justifies itself at each moment, not gratuitous but continuously justified.

And this imposes a consequence from which it is difficult to escape. A philosophy that consists in visuality and in the justification of itself, which thereby has a clear and verifiable meaning, is necessarily *categorical*. At least during the time that I remain within its perspective—that is, while I have not achieved another, more inclusive perspective that would account for the first at the same time that it explained its insufficiency, that would see that it is insufficient and integrate it into a superior one. Until I have done this, all philosophy that is authentically philosophical theory is categorical, by which I mean that one has to take it or leave it; and philosophically not to take it means to show that it is erroneous, that things are not the way that philosophy reveals them or discovers them to be. For this reason, what one cannot do with a philosophy that has these characteristics is ignore it, forget it, or say that it is not interesting; whoever does this is simply placing himself outside of philosophy.

I would not like to lose myself in considerations that are excessively general. It is best to return to the nucleus of the philosophical problem at the present moment, and this is nothing but the meaning and destiny of metaphysics. An old question, raised periodically in philosophy, and with particular emphasis since the eighteenth century, is the problem of the possibility of metaphysics. Is metaphysics possible? This question has been asked from several different points of view—by Hume and Kant, by the positivists (and today by the neopositivists), by the phenomenologists, by irrationalists. The question is undoubtedly interesting, but I believe it is of no more than secondary importance. I mean that, strictly speaking, it would not be enough for a truly serious philosophy to reply to that question in the affirmative; it would not be enough to demonstrate that metaphysics is possible. There are many possible things that do not interest us; that something is possible is not enough to make us take an interest in it and cultivate it.

When my *Introducción a la filosofía* was translated into English,* I wrote a prologue for that edition in which I said that the best title the book could have had would have been *An Attempt to Avoid Philosophy*. If philosophy could be avoided, think of how many worries and preoccupations we would be saved. And the book in fact consists of an attempt to avoid philosophy, to adjust to a life without it.

---

* [Published under the title *Reason and Life* (Yale University Press, 1956)—Trans.]

It is, however, a frustrated attempt, since it turns out that we cannot. And this outcome might have given the book another excellent title: *Unavoidable Philosophy.*

Whether metaphysics is possible or not is a matter of secondary importance; what has to be justified is not whether it may be impossible but whether it is *necessary.* The decisive question does not refer to the possibility but to the necessity of metaphysics. Perhaps it will be said that, if metaphysics should be proven to be *impossible,* all other questions about it would be useless. It would be already disqualified, eliminated from our horizon. To believe this—and there are many who have believed it and who now do believe it—is to be outside the realm of philosophy; it is an antiphilosophical way of posing the question, alien to the kind of radical outlook that belongs to philosophy. An example of a different character—but not as different as it may appear—will serve to clarify this matter. It is not difficult to prove that human happiness is impossible. Is this enough to eliminate it from our horizon? Its necessity is evident, and with its necessity its central and inevitable position on the horizon of our lives.

If metaphysics is necessary, it will have its roots and its motives in a human *need* of such a nature that human life would be impossible without it. But, it will be said, philosophy did not always exist nor has it existed everywhere; its existence has, on the contrary, been exceptional in the history of humanity; and today it is not all men who cultivate metaphysics but, fortunately, only a few—where then is its necessity?

There is a concept that I have utilized in a thematic way for about twenty years and which serves to clarify not a few things. It is the concept of *homology* applied to the structure of human life and of history. I call two dissimilar, perhaps quite different, realities homologous that represent the same function in two distinct situations. Gills hardly at all resemble the lungs, but they have the same respiratory function; the anatomical differences between these organs do not preclude their physiological homology. But this is solely an example; when we are dealing with human life we are not required to think about "things," and for this reason homology in human life has a different nature, in the last analysis dramatic.

There is something further: the relation of homology is static. If, however, I consider two elements from two situations in a historical sense and find that one of them is derived from the other and represents in the second situation the same function that the other represents in the first, this derived element is not simply a homologue but something more: it is a *surrogate*—that is, it performs the function of the first. In other words, if situation B is derived from situation A, we may now say that the homologous elements in situation B are surrogates for the respective elements in situation A. In this way we might obtain a historical system of the relations of surrogation, which is homology in evolution, understood dynamically.

Returning to our theme, it is true that metaphysics has not always existed, but what we have to look for are its homologous functions—in other words, we have to look for something that metaphysics is the surrogate of, something that corresponded to it in other situations; we have to look for the function that metaphysics has come to perform that was performed in other, historically past situations by other, different realities.

If then we find a human need to which metaphysics is a response, or if we find those homologous functions in relation to which metaphysics is a surrogate, then we will have proven the necessity of metaphysics, we will have demonstrated that human life is not possible without metaphysics or some reality homologous to it. This would be the only way of completely justifying metaphysics: to show, not its *possibility*, but something much more profound, its *necessity*.

Understand this well: since philosophy is radical knowledge, as distinct from other kinds of knowledge, it will have to involve itself with a need that is also radical in human life—that is, something without which human life is impossible, a condition *sine qua non*, without which what we call human life cannot be lived. A man needs to have a radical certainty, to know what to be guided by with regard to what is radical in reality. Perhaps a man might possess that certainty in the sense of "being in it" (religiously through revelation, or artistically without being able to feel responsible for it or to justify it), but situations arise in which this is not possible, either because such certainty is not in fact given or is in any case insufficient for knowing what to be guided by or because there are realities regarding which one has no beliefs or because a number of certainties are in conflict among themselves. There is a situation in which a man needs radical certainty and at the same time believes that it is within his power *to seek it* and perhaps to find it; instead of waiting passively for reality to *reveal* itself, he himself actively goes to *unveil* it. This belief in the responsibility for approaching reality and unveiling it, discovering it, making it apparent, manifesting it, of questioning it and obliging it to reply—this is precisely the source of metaphysics and of its homologous functions, the human need from which it springs and which it justifies.

Naturally in saying "metaphysics" I refrain completely from identifying it with any of the particular historical versions that have been given of it. For example, it would never occur to me to identify it with *ontology*, since as soon as we do so we deprive metaphysics of its radical nature, for the simple reason that precisely what metaphysics has to do is make a radical issue out of reality—thus it cannot assume as already given that it is ontology (the doctrine of being or of entities). At most, the identifications of metaphysics with ontology might be a thesis *internal* to metaphysics, but if metaphysics is defined a priori as *metaphysica sive ontologia*, it automatically renounces its radical nature by virtue of not having made a radical issue of the problem.

What we call *being* is already an interpretation of reality, of *the way things happen*. An indication of this is found in the fact that this famous and illustrious verb "to be," which has given philosophy so much to do, does not in reality exist. Note that in all the languages of our intellectual tradition, the same in Greek as in Latin and the Romance languages, in German as in English, it is a tailor's sewing box filled with fragments of verbs taken from different roots, which very clearly indicates that it is an improvised verb, forged when man at a certain stage in his history arrived at this interpretation and had to give it a name. "Being" is an interpretation of reality, the most famous perhaps, but it is not possible (as Ortega showed, something like half a century ago) to identify it with reality itself, with the way things happen.

Thus we cannot set out from this interpretation, but neither can we forget it, for it is there and we have to take it into account (it too is a reality, although it may not be *the* reality) and justify it. I have to set out from reality just as I encounter it, and what I encounter (Ortega saw this before all others and with greater clarity than anybody else) is *my life*—that is, what I do and what happens to me, me doing things with things. Note that what I am dealing with is my life (keep in mind the possessive, *my* life), and not with my biological but with my biographical life. But when I say "biographical life" take care that what

I am not saying does not slip in surreptitiously, for I do not mean "biography" or "biographical trajectory" but biographical *life*. My life is not to be identified with its trajectory, and this is so for one elementary reason: it has several. If anybody wants to write my biography, he would relate a series of facts, utterances, happenings, actions, and passions from my birth to the day of my death—that is my biographical trajectory. But it is not my life, which includes, together with the trajectory I have lived through, that I am still living in, all the trajectories I have been able to live, and those I have not. What I have done is not to be understood without keeping in mind what I might have been able to do but did not. The actual trajectory is only one, that which in fact I lived, out of all the others that were successively possible at each moment, with their innumerable ramifications, which are what give meaning and reality to that chosen trajectory and which, for that reason, equally form a part of the reality of my life. My life is not exhausted in *me;* it is *me with things,* me with the whole of the reality that surrounds me. And one of its characteristics is to possess many possible trajectories of which one is realized.

My life is (I have already shown this in *Idea de la metafísica*) the real organization of reality, not an organization that I project upon it in an abstract and more or less capricious way, calling it world, universe, whole of reality, or *omnitudo realitatis.* I encounter reality by living. The primary meaning of reality is not "to be" nor "to exist," but "to live," and this in a personal form: *I live.* This is precisely the structure that reality has in itself; this is the real organization of reality, *its own,* not that which I project upon it nor a theory about it.

But, you will say, is this not a theory like all the rest? No. Remember what I said: *my* life is reality just as and such as I encounter it, apart from and prior to all theory. I did not say *human* life, with a characterizing adjective.* Human life, yes; that is a theory, but we shall soon see that it is not a theory like all the rest but an eminently distinctive theory. I will try to explain what I mean.

My life, my own and that of each one of us, appears as *living together.* To live is to live together, to live with others; it is to find myself with you, with a certain you, with a certain he, with a certain she. Life has a *disjunctive* character: it is this or this or this (something quite different from the individuation of a species); it is the life of each one of us. Well then, this means that I have to understand my life as *the life it is.* A certain quality or, if you prefer, a kind of "suchness" belongs to life. My life is the life it is, and I encounter other lives and understand their reality as *human* life, as life *in general.* Note, however, that this life in general would not even be comprehensible without beginning with the concrete intuition of *my* life, of the suppose that a book titled *The General Theory of Human Life* had been written and that a spirit who was intelligent singular life of each one of us. I mean that if we were to but lacking in intuition of my life were able to read it, he would not understand even one word. Human life in general does not become intelligible except by setting out from the immediate and direct intuition of my life in its singular concretion.

However, what is serious is that my life is not given to me ready-made. It is given to me, certainly—I am not its creator. But it is not given to me *ready-made.* I have to

* [The distinction Marías makes here in Spanish between *la vida humana* and *vida humana* (with and without the definite article) is not a natural one in English in this context; I have, therefore, chosen to make a different distinction, valid in English, and one that at the same time fits very neatly into Marías's line of reasoning—Trans.]

make my life with things. No sentence could possibly be simpler, more self-evident, and less compromising than this old Ortegan thesis. But let's see what follows from it: first, my life is not ready-made; second, I have to make it; third, not by myself but with things; fourth, I already have to possess this reality before living, and this is what we might call the "apriorism" of human life; fifth, life consists of projects or futurity; sixth, we have to imagine it beforehand or prelive it. All this follows inexorably from that simple and self-evident sentence: "I have to make my life with things."

In order to do this, I have to set out from a multiplicity of elements, some present and some latent—above all, the future. I mean, from reality and possibility at one and the same time. The consequence of this is that human life is not possible on the basis of perception alone. Imagine that man were only a perceiving animal: human life would then be impossible, since I am unable to perceive more than what is real. There are many real things that I am unable to perceive, but naturally none that are not real. I cannot perceive what is possible; I cannot perceive the future. And man lives in the future; life is futurity. I am *futuristic* (not that I am the future, but oriented toward the future); we are doing what we are doing precisely in consideration of the future, of something that does not yet exist. Thus, we are constantly handling possibilities, things that are nonexistent and therefore imperceptible.

Neither is description enough. It provides no more than incoherent "notes" that do not permit decision. Decision is possible only when I have reality before me in its connectedness, thus in the form of a world that permits me to choose from among its possibilities that which is going to be the reality of my life. Human life is not possible with perception alone nor with description; it needs *the apprehension of reality in all its connectedness*. But this is precisely the definition of "reason" I gave in a book that is some twenty years old.*

The phrase "to give the reason for" means exactly that: to apprehend reality in its effective coherence, and this includes what is not actual, what is only possible—the characteristic reality including what is present, what is latent, and what is to come in the future. Only because man possesses reason can he live in a human way. But that reason is the system of life itself; it is life itself that makes it possible for me to understand. I only comprehend something when I cause it to enter into the sphere of my biographical life and when I give it a function, a role to perform within it. That co-implication or complication of reason and life is what, more than forty years ago, Ortega called *vital reason*, which when it functions concretely is historical reason, since my life is not only individual life but is inserted in a society and into history. Consequently, the whole of history is the only thing that makes it possible for me to give the reason for reality.

And that is exactly what it is to live. It is not to be forgotten that the absurd, which so much interests the philosophy of our times, is a phenomenon subsidiary to the primary and radical phenomenon of meaning. Whatever does not make good sense is absurd, and we can say of something that it is absurd because the whole human reality is an attempt to make sense. To live is to move within the element of meaning; to live is to understand, to give reasons. Life is one and the same thing as vital reason.

What does this mean? That *human* life—now I am using the characterizing adjective—is not reality in a strict sense. Reality in a strict sense is my life, the life of each one of us. *Human* life is a theory, but not a theory like all the rest: it is a theory demanded by the reality of my life—by which

* [Reference is to his *Introducción a la filosofía* (Madrid, 1947), p. 175; in English in *Reason and Life*, p. 159—Trans.]

I mean that *my* life is not possible except when it is transparent to itself. I cannot live, I cannot decide what I am going to be (which is the condition for my going on living), if my life is not transparent to itself, if a certain interpretation of it as the life it is, as the human life it is, is not attributed to it. In other words, what is involved here is an *intrinsic* theory, one that pertains to the very reality of my life.

The consequence is paradoxical. It turns out that there is one reality, my life, that is not possible as a reality except by carrying a theory within itself. This intrinsic theory, *constituent* of what human life is, is the root of metaphysics, is that reality homologous to metaphysics of which metaphysics is the *surrogate* in our situation. In this situation the intrinsic theory that pertains to our life, giving it transparency and making it possible, has to be neither more nor less than metaphysics—understanding by this word the attempt I am making to reach on my own a radical certainty concerning radical reality, in order to know what to be guided by and to be able to live.

This would be the effective justification, not of the possibility, but of the necessity of metaphysics. And this is the horizon of philosophy seen when we examine the present tendencies of knowledge, of knowledge itself, and not necessarily the inclinations of those who are trying to make it real.

CHAPTER FIVE

CONTEMPORARY PHILOSOPHY AND ATHEISM

Text of a lecture delivered at the Paul VI Chair in Salamanca.

I am going to speak about the problem of atheism as it appears in the philosophy of the twentieth century, especially in the philosophy that is called existential and, more concretely, in existentialism—while trying at the same time to refer to all the ways in which this theme has been presented in the thought of recent decades.

During the nineteenth century the situation regarding the problem of God could be defined as traditional forgetfulness. I mean by this that the central current in European thought during the nineteenth century did not contain the problem of God, at least not as a living and fully present problem, but that it was treated separately or by thinkers representing one of the older traditions (for example, the Scholastic tradition in the most general sense of this word) or by a few marginal thinkers (for example, the Italian ontologists Rosmini and Gioberti or Father Gratry or even Brentano), thinkers who today appear interesting to us but who during the nineteenth century had little importance and scarcely at all attracted general notice.

To me it seems interesting to keep this in mind: that what seems to us important today in philosophy and in the history of culture in general, has not always seemed so in its time, but just the contrary. And it is incredible the lengths to which at times one has to go in order to find, from the period in which they lived, references to thinkers who now seem to us of the greatest interest. Remember the case of Kierkegaard or of Dilthey: hardly anything at all was said in their lifetimes about either of them, and that little in a few vague words that would not lead us even to suspect how interesting their intellectual labors are.

However, toward the end of the nineteeth century or the beginning of the twentieth, a return to consideration of the problem of God was initiated in a very intense way, and this took place right here in the city of Salamanca. I do not have to say that I am referring to Don Miguel de Unamuno, who had unlimited intellectual courage and dared to raise the problem of God and to make this the center of his meditation in an epoch in which this problem, and the problems of death and immortality as well, were relegated to the outskirts of philosophy or, rather, in an epoch in which to dare to present these problems was to be disqualified as a thinker.

But, in addition to this, there is something in the work of Unamuno that particularly interests us. This is: that in Unamuno God appears primarily as the sustainer of personal immortality—God is the guarantor of man's hope in an otherworldly life. This means that God does not appear as the foundation or the keystone of the universe. This God does not occupy an important place in Unamuno's ontology (assuming that Unamuno had an ontology, which is to say a great deal), but, rather, God appears as a reality assigned to the task of sustaining the personal nature of man and guaranteeing his expectations of immortality. That is, this is a strictly personal God and appears with a personal function—not with a primarily cosmic function, for example.

This is unlike anything else done in European thought

before the First World War or even between the two world wars. Appearances of the theme of God prior to the most recent decades have been very limited. For example, in the phenomenology of Husserl God has a restricted and remote place; there are some marginal references (for example, in his *Ideas*), and God appears as a "concept of limit." In Scheler, despite the Catholic phase of his thought represented by *On the Eternal in Man* (*Vom Ewigen im Menschen*) and in spite of his interest in religious themes, his philosophy is excessively oriented toward values, and the theme of God makes its appearance and is studied within a constellation defined by the idea of value. But, on the whole, the theme of God has a relatively secondary role in his thought. With regard to Jaspers, the idea of the enclosing or comprehending (*das Umgreifende*) appears forcefully and raises a problem of transcending importance, but this is not, strictly speaking, a thematic consideration of the problem of God. In Heidegger, the theme is so much evaded that it has become common (as common as it is irresponsible) to speak of Heidegger's atheism. In my judgment this is pure frivolity; but it is true, nevertheless, that there is no direct and profound consideration of the problem of God in Heidegger's work, at least in the presently existing work, although the possibility of his raising this problem in the future may be open. Gabriel Marcel has a theist position, especially since his conversion, but there has never been a formal consideration of this theme in his work either.

In any case, and in spite of these restrictions (and leaving aside the precursor, Unamuno, who is much more important but with whose work I have fully occupied myself on other occasions), the theme of God has acquired a new quality and intensity in the different philosophies defined by the appearance, in one form or another, of the word "existence" in their names. Among these philosophies we are able to distinguish three fundamental groups. In the first place is *existential philosophy*, an adequate name for the philosophy of Heidegger, whose theme is the meaning of being in general (*der Sinn des Seins überhaupt*), since this problem of being is posed in the entity we ourselves are (called by Heidegger *Dasein*—"existence," "there-being"), on account of which that problem of being requires for its elucidation a prior existential analysis of *Dasein*, which is thus the condition for the consideration of the problem of being, of that forgotten question concerning the meaning of being. For this reason, Heidegger's philosophy may be called "existential philosophy"—not because its theme is existence, but because the analysis of *Dasein* is an antecedent condition for the consideration of the question about being. In the second place, we have *the philosophy of existence*, a term that may be applied in a relatively vague sense to the thought of Jaspers, an essential part of which is *Existenzerhellung* or clarification of human existence, or to that of Gabriel Marcel in France. And, finally, we would like to reserve the term *existentialism*—which has had the most general fame and, in a certain sense, has most attracted the popular imagination during recent decades—to the thought of Jean–Paul Sartre and his followers.

As everybody knows, the definition of existentialism is extremely vague. Sartre himself once said that he understands by existentialism that philosophy according to which existence in man precedes essence. This formula would be the most concise abbreviation of what Sartre understands by existentialism, and we may provisionally adopt it as a way of distinguishing existentialism from other philosophical tendencies that are somewhat close or analogous to it.

There was a moment, especially following the Second World War, when it seemed as if these philosophical movements were philosophy itself. In spite of the intrinsically unsatisfactory character of the doctrinal content of these intellectual constructions when they are considered closely and in detail, we cannot disregard the enormous interest, the profound fascination, with which all of these forms of thought, and perhaps most especially that called existentialism, have been followed first by the Europeans and then also by the Americans and by the whole world at the end of the war and during the subsequent fifteen years, more or less.

The fact that this may now be on the decline, that the popularity of these philosophies and the interest in them may be beginning to wane, should not hide the profound attraction they have had for the man of our times. And this, in any case, has to be explained and is itself already of the greatest interest.

I would say that these systems of thought have offered solutions—perhaps false, but at least solutions—to the real problems of our times. I mean by this that a doctrine can be true or false, but in either case one has first of all to raise the question of whether it is a response to our problems or to others. It should not be forgotten that a problem is not simply something I do not know, a matter of ignorance. If somebody asks me how many hairs the many people who are listening to me have on their heads, I would not know. Is this a problem? No. And what does it lack that would make it a problem? That I should have to know this. Fortunately, not for any reason do I have to know how many hairs there are on the heads of the members of my audience; and this means that it is not a problem. But if I should have to know it—if, for example, somebody were to offer me an immense prize of several millions if the number of hairs were even and were to threaten me with a violent death if that number were odd, then this would be converted for me into a genuine problem. In order for something to be a problem it is necessary, first, that I do not know this something and, second, that I must know it.

Man has a horizon of problems that changes with time.

And the greater part of those problems cease to be problems, not because they are solved, but because they are dissolved. The history of philosophy is the history of a succession of solutions, but primarily it is the history of a succession of problems. And these problems succeed one another historically; they are successively replaced, successively dissolved, leaving room for others.

Confronted with many intellectual doctrines we may be able to say that they are true, or that they may not be true but are not solutions to our problems but to other problems, to those of the thirteenth or the seventeenth or the nineteenth century. What causes us anguish or disturbs us is not what caused anguish to the people of a century ago, or eight or twenty centuries ago, and their solutions, whatever they may be, even though they may be logically correct and objectively true by virtue of their content, are of no use to us since they are not solutions to our problems.

Existentialism, however, is in a general sense a repertory of solutions to our most serious problems, and this has made existentialism of interest to us and makes it continue to interest us. Does it satisfy us? Well, that is another question. Is it sufficient, is it an adequate response? That is a different story. Even if our problems today were exactly the same as those that in 1945 led to the success of existentialism, there would still be doubt about this. But if we take a relatively long span of time, if we talk about the man of our times, meaning by this the last two or three decades, there can be no doubt that the existentialist response, true or not, is related to what we need to know.

The point of departure for all these philosophical systems is *human life*, whether it be called *Dasein*, "existence," "subjectivity," or, more profoundly and correctly, "human life." This life has been interpreted from several different points of view, some broader in scope, others more restricted. Some of them represent a forced interpretation, others project life on a plane surface and reduce it to a two-dimensional reality instead of letting it be what actually and obviously it is. In any case, since it is our life that is the point of departure, insofar as it is personal and human, all these philosophies have revolved around the notion of *freedom*, around the condition that man has to *make* or *choose* himself in one way or another, around the *solitude* in which the life of each one of us takes place, around the themes of *responsibility, abandonment, pain, anguish, nausea* . . . which have been called the "existentialist moods." Undoubtedly they are, but it is not said anywhere that they are the only ones or the most interesting or that others have not been left unexpressed that are just as important, just as existentialist, and perhaps more fundamental.

And now we find that in this procession of doctrines (which I am not going to examine here because to do so would carry us too far afield) what we may call atheism appears as an especially important and summarily insistent tendency. There are some thinkers called existentialists and other contemporary thinkers who, for one reason or another (and it is interesting that the reasons vary greatly), take a position that, in general terms, can be called *atheism*.

The word "atheism," in its turn, is not rigorously univocal either, since it can be understood according to different interpretations; the same thing is not always involved. For the moment, my aim is to search for the justifications that atheism may be given within these systems of thought. If one wishes to understand a philosophy, one must attempt to place oneself within it in such a way that, when explaining it, it seems to us justified. It is useless (and it would be a profound error) to try to show the deficiencies or the falsity of a doctrine without trying first to understand it. One must make the attempt to justify it, to present it from within, not in order to go outside it later on and refute it (a disagreeable word if ever there was one), but, rather, in order to continue within it and, through attempting to take it seriously and think it out to the roots, to see whether it actually leads anywhere or if we encounter some difficulty that obliges us to go beyond it.

The thought of our time, and not only philosophical thought, has been preoccupied with a concept that has acquired an extraordinary development during the twentieth century, and this is the concept of *meaning.* You will recall that Heidegger in *Sein und Zeit,* precisely when posing his original and fundamental question says that this is "the question that asks about the meaning of being"—that is, what is involved is not asking about being but about the *meaning* of being. This word "meaning" also makes its appearance in British and American thought and appears with equal relevance in thinkers who are not strictly philosophical, such as Camus. Thus what is involved is questioning about the meaning of reality and especially about the meaning of human life. And the concept of meaning appears face to face with the concept of the *absurd.* The absurd appears constantly as something that lies in wait for contemporary thought, which disturbs it profoundly and against which it has to marshal all its forces. Remember once more the case of Camus himself and the importance that the theme of the absurd has in his writings. What interests him is to see to what extent human life does or does not possess meaning, is or is not absurd; and it is precisely from this perspective that he raises the problem of God and, consequently, the problem of atheism. Curiously, atheism appears at times as a proof or basis for the belief that the world has no meaning and at other times as a conclusion to which we find ourselves obligatorily led in view of the fact that reality is absurd. But there is a third possibility, intrinsically bound to the other two, which is the one that most attracts present-day man, and according to this it is precisely in order to uphold a certain meaning in life that we find ourselves obliged to put God aside and thus end up in an atheist position.

These are three different motivations and, strictly speaking, what is involved are not philosophical theses or arguments but something antecedent: three general presuppositions for the interpretations that, by different paths, lead to three different variants of atheism. In many currents of atheism in our times, and especially in existentialism, God appears literally as an impediment. How can this be? God impedes a certain conception of human life and reality. Although never formulated in the terms I am going to use, the substrate of this whole series of philosophical arguments in our time would be: "If there is a God, things cannot be like this"—understanding by "like this" a definite intellectual conception one possesses and in which one is installed. In view of it, one concludes that there is no God.

Everybody remembers the famous statement, "If God did not exist, it would be necessary to invent him." What we are dealing with here is just the contrary, the strict inversion of that point of view, which is that of deism. If there had been no God, it was thought in the eighteenth century, it would have been necessary to invent him. God is necessary in order for us to comprehend reality and, probably, in order to live rationally. Rationalism is fundamentally theistic or, at least, deist. It is interesting to note that in an epoch when Voltaire was in complete discredit among religious thinkers, especially among Catholic thinkers, Father Gratry, a century ago, very wisely proclaimed that he considered Voltaire an admirable soul, an admirable friend. Precisely on account of his rationalism, Voltaire's thought is positive, and what disturbed Gratry from the Catholic point of view was not Voltaire but Hegel. Voltaire, for all his anticlericism and his superficial anti-Christianism, was a secure ally, because his rationalism flowed into deism, which could very well have been converted into a rigorous theism.

At the present time, on the contrary, what we are dealing with would be just the opposite. Instead of saying, "If God did not exist, it would be necessary to invent him," it will be said, "If God did exist, it would be necessary to eliminate or forget him." Why? Because God does not fit into the picture, because God does not allow us to install ourselves in a certain form of thought in which we place ourselves so as to interpret reality in a way that interests us and which seems, for several reasons, correct to us. If this seems to you a risky and somewhat arbitrary construction, wait a few minutes for the texts in which Sartre literally says just this.

I am not going to try to expound Sartre's thought, which is rich and complex, penetrating and variable, and has had a long evolution. I am going to do no more than attempt to define the nucleus of the general interpretation of reality, and especially of human reality, in Sartre's thought. His fundamental thesis is that in man existence precedes essence. Man is nothing; he is what he decides, what he chooses to be; he has no essence, he has no nature. Everything in the human reality is *choix*, "choice." And when a man chooses he does so for the whole of humanity. Sartre says that if I am a worker and I join a Catholic labor union and not a Communist one, for example, I make a choice not for myself, but I choose for man. And, in joining a Catholic labor union, I am recommending resignation and saying with this act that paradise is not on earth and that man must resign himself and place his faith in another life. If I get married, even though my motives may be love, passion, or desire, I am committing humanity to a path that in a concrete way is monogamous marriage.

Of course, when Sartre considers the problem in terms

of the priority of existence over essence, when he says that first I exist and then I choose what my essence has to be, he is at the same time accepting the scheme of traditional ontology. Except that he accepts it against the grain, he inverts it, but it is clear that at no time does he make an attempt to go beyond it, to raise the issue of reality in different terms. He accepts the frame "essence-existence," just as he accepts the idea of "in itself" or "for itself," of "being" or "nothing." Thus, after all, he moves within the categories of traditional ontology, of Scholasticism first of all, then of phenomenology, although with appropriate inversions.

The fundamental reason Sartre is going to deny the existence of God is that God is *causa sui* and this notion of *causa sui* seems self-contradictory to him. Of course, he could have asked himself: If the notion of *causa sui* is self-contradictory, will I not have to seek a better notion of God? It would seem that this should be antecedent to decreeing that God does not exist. Because, furthermore, this concept of *causa sui* has never been taken seriously by anybody. It is true that it is an expression that has been employed, but in a very informal way, and nobody has ever said literally and formally that God is *causa sui*. Consequently it seems a bit strange that Sartre should take the notion of God that is of least significance within the tradition of Christian thought for the purpose of basing himself upon it in order to decree the impossibility of God on account of his self-contradictory character.

For Sartre, the whole of life fundamentally constitutes something that always fails. Man is for Sartre a passion to establish being and to constitute an "in itself." However, this is something that man cannot do. The idea of God as *causa sui* is self-contradictory, and we waste ourselves in vain. Man is a useless passion: *l'homme est une passion inutile*.

With these theses he arrives at an atheist position, but one remains a little surprised and one asks if there is not something more, whether there is not something behind this very simple argument, because the justification of atheism seems to be strangely simple and gratuitous. It would be best perhaps to take a step backward and briefly go over these theses of Sartre again in order to see to what degree they are or can be formulated in entire seriousness.

When he says that man has neither essence nor nature, and that everything in man is choice or *choix*, evidently we must make a distinction. If he is saying that man has no nature *in the sense that things do*, this seems to me enormously true, and on the other hand nothing new. Many years before Sartre, Ortega said this very thing. In 1935, in *Historia como sistema,** he said, "Man has no nature, but he does have a history." Furthermore, during the same year, he said in another place, "Man is natural and preternatural at one and the same time, a species of ontological centaur." And he added, "Man has a structure, no more or less than cosmic matter." Theses, all of them, that should be brought together in order to understand the concrete meaning of the first. When Ortega said, "Man has no nature," he meant by this that man has no nature in the sense that things do; if he has a nature, this consists in not having it exactly in that sense; or, in other words, *man is not a thing.*

Existentialist thought has renewed this certainty that man is definitely not a thing. As soon as I try to identify the reality of man with that of any thing whatsoever, I find that it is not so, that man is not a material or biological thing, that I am neither my body nor my psyche—I am not any thing. But existentialist thought tends to take a further step and, in view of the fact that I am not any thing, conclude

---

* [José Ortega y Gasset, *Historia como sistema* (Buenos Aires, 1941), translated into English as *History as a System* (New York, n.d.)—Trans.]

that I am nothing. We would say in English * that from the evidence that *I am no thing*, he jumps to the conclusion, which is of all things least evident, that *I am nothing*. While it is true that man is not a thing, it is nevertheless false to say that man is "nothing"—especially if we replace, as is necessary, the word "nothing" with its personal equivalent, "nobody."

It is to be noted that many languages know more than philosophers and scientists do. And the proof of this is that if somebody knocks at the door, none of us would ask, "What is it?"—but all of us would ask, "Who is it?"—while philosophy and science have spent twenty-five centuries asking, "What is man?" And since the question is erroneous, the reply will be erroneous too. I am not saying that man may not be a "what"; to some degree and in a secondary way he is a "what," but this is because he is a "who." Man is primarily a "who," a "somebody," and thus he is or has "something," and it is possible to ask "what" concerning that. But that "what" is based upon a "who" that is prior to it and much more fundamental.

The question should be, then, "*Who* is man?"—or, even more rigorously, "*Who* am I?"—which we could not answer naturally with anything that might be a thing, but with something that points to a "somebody" or, in other words, what we call a *person*. Yes, we do say "person," but in general we take this name in vain. Even the famous definition by Boethius (not at all to be despised for the most part) of a person as *rationalis naturae individua substantia*, "an individual substance of a rational nature," takes it calmly for granted that a person is a thing, a very special thing, a thing or substance that is of a rational nature, true.

* [This phrase belongs to Marías ("Diríamos en inglés . . ."), not to the translator; the two brief sentences in italics here are in English in the original text—Trans.]

But this definition disturbs me because it has left out what is radical and distinctive about the person, who is not a thing. And as soon as I say that a person is an individual thing of a rational nature, I have given up trying to apprehend what it is I was trying to define. And do not say that I have forced the translation and have said "thing" instead of "substance," which is what Boethius says, because substance is understood primarily from things, and the model that serves Aristotle in the elaboration of his theory of substance is the example of natural things. And there is still more: by virtue of a curious inconsistency in the Aristotelian theory of substance, affecting it at its roots, while Aristotle says that the genuine substances are those that are natural (water, iron, a tree, an animal), when he wishes to explain the ontological scheme of substance, when he really wishes to explain this substance itself, he always relies on two examples—the statue and the bed—that are not natural things at all and, according to Aristotle himself, not genuine substances. That is, Aristotelian ontology is fine for explaining those substances that are not substances. And genuine substances, such as living beings and primarily man (not to speak of God), are very badly explained within the Aristotelian theory as it is set forth in the *Metaphysics*. There is a series of problems here that I will not go into now.

The notions of traditional ontology, Scholastic or phenomenological, are not adequate. Furthermore, when Sartre says that man chooses himself, that man is nothing until he chooses, he would at least have to say that man at that moment *is man*. That is, if I find myself obliged to choose, to decide my being, and to construct my essence, it turns out that I do this with my foot in chains, like the poet to whom an imposed stanza form is given. Thus, if I decide right now to choose to be a crocodile, the consequence is that I do not become one; and if I choose to be an oak tree or a block of granite, my decision is in vain. I can choose my essence, but I have to bring it to reality within a prescribed region, a region that is precisely what we call "man."

So that the truth is that I have to decide, I have to choose *who* I am going to be: this person we call Julián Marías, who is being made little by little and in a hapless sort of way. But what I am unable to decide is *what,* what class of thing I am going to be. I have not chosen my "what," not even to the degree that human reality is a "what," because I cannot decide to be black or yellow or a woman, since I find myself with the fact that, whether I want to be or not, I am a man and white.

Thus we see that it turns out to be a bit excessive to say that human reality is choice. There are two radical ingredients in human life that are not subject to choice: the first is *circumstance,* the other is *vocation.* I have not chosen to be a man or Spanish or to be born into the twentieth century or my family or my country; I have not chosen this body and this soul I am possessed of. Nothing of all this has been chosen by me; I found myself with it and that is all. And I do not choose my vocation either. Antonio Machado says, "Nobody chooses his love." My vocation is a voice that summons me, that calls me. Where then is choosing? I have to choose whether to follow my vocation or not, whether I am to be faithful or unfaithful to it; but I do not choose it, and it is precisely for this reason that it is my vocation, my calling, my destiny. I feel myself called to be somebody, and I freely choose to be faithful or unfaithful to that calling, in the same way that I choose what I am going to do with the endowments that have been given me— my body and my soul and my world. Human choice is constitutive; man is a being who chooses while he lives, but he does not choose everything.

Beyond all this, existential philosophy, beginning with Heidegger himself, has been invaded by the presupposition of "mortality." The first example is the idea of *Sein zum*

Tode, although it would be an exaggeration to translate it
as "being for death," and I believe it is better to translate
it, "being on the verge of death." * In any case, Heidegger
insists too much on mortality. The fact that life ends and
that death is certain does not mean that one lives for death
nor that death is definitive or the last word. Human life is a
possibility open to immortality or to annihilation. Remember what Plato said: "Beautiful is this risk of being immortal." The *onus probandi* falls as much on the person who
affirms one thing as the other. And this is so for a very simple
reason, which is this: although one might believe that from
the death of my body my death as a person follows, numeri-
cally they are distinct. For, I am not my body, although I
may be bodily; and from the destruction of my somatic
organism perhaps it could be that the destruction of my personality follows, perhaps I will be unable to go on living as
a result of the destruction of my organism, but this would
have to be proven. *My* death is not the same thing as the
death of my body, and consequently the notion that personal death necessarily follows bodily death is an open
question that would have to be justified. The *onus probandi,*
I repeat, falls equally on whoever affirms immortality and
on whoever affirms annihilation.

However, existential philosophy and existentialism especially have taken mortality, the annihilation of man and
thus the reduction of man to his earthly life, as given. What
happens then? Man appears as a reality who chooses himself, who has neither nature nor essence, who is wholly an

* [The Spanish translation that Marías is rejecting is *ser para la
muerte* ("being for death," "being in the service of death," "being
skilled at dying"); the translation Marías is recommending is
estar a la muerte ("being on the verge of dying"); anyone who
remembers that Unamuno was placed under arrest shortly before
his death in Salamanca for making just such a distinction (in
response to a speech by a Falangist officer in praise of death and
ending with the cry ¡*Viva la muerte!*) will recognize that courage
takes many forms—Trans.]

object of choice, and who is annihilated at death and consequently has no life other than what is temporal and terrestrial. And this is the point at which a philosophical interpretation of atheism arises.

Sartre presents what he literally calls a technical vision of the world when he tries to think of God and says that God would have had to make man in the same way that somebody manufactures a paper cutter. And how does one manufacture a paper cutter? First, I have the idea of paper cutter, I propose making it, and, adapting myself to certain standards of what something has to be in order to be a paper cutter, I manufacture it. In this way, Sartre says, God is interpreted as a superior artificer and fulfills the same role with respect to man that the artisan fulfills with respect to the paper cutter. God makes man by beginning with the idea of man.

But this of course is not possible. Sartre says, "There is no human nature, thus there is no God to conceive it." But then, I might dare to ask, if there is no God, then why do the cauliflower, the oak tree, the crocodile have a nature? Sartre does not deny that there is a nature in things. Man is a privileged and unique being who has no nature, but if the reason that man has no nature is that there is no God to conceive it, then there is no God to conceive a nature of any kind. Sartre's argument proves too much, for it would prove not only that there is no human nature but that there is no nature in anything at all. And then I go back to repeat: what is the privilege and the differentiating characteristic of man?

In spite of all this, Sartre says (and I am going to quote him at length),

> Existentialism is nothing but the effort to derive all the consequences from a coherent atheistic position. Existen-

tialism is not so much atheism in the sense that it exhausts itself in demonstrating that God does not exist; it declares, rather, that even if God did exist, this would not change a thing. This is our point of view. Not that we believe that God does exist, but we believe that the problem is not that of the existence of God. It is necessary for man to encounter himself and that he be persuaded that nothing can save him from himself, not even a valid proof of the existence of God.*

It turns out then that there is no God because God is self-contradictory, but is self-contradictory because we have defined God as *causa sui*. Then, it will be said, let's find a better definition. Since we are not bound in indissoluble matrimony to the definition of God as *causa sui*, let us divorce ourselves from it. What is the reason that we go on identifying God with this obscure notion of *causa sui* in view of the fact that it is invalid? Might it not be that we choose it precisely because it is invalid?

On the other hand, once proven that there is no God because being *causa sui* is self-contradictory, we find that man has no nature because there is no God who might conceive it. But the immediate consequence of this (although, so it seems, not to Sartre) is that, if there is no God, he cannot conceive *any* nature, and thus there is no nature. In this way man loses his privileged ontological status of being the entity without a nature, we are left with the general abolition of nature, and man is reintegrated into the universe of "non-natural" things. Sartre calls this "coherent atheism." That it is atheism I have no doubt, but to say that it is coherent seems to me an exaggeration.

---

* [I have translated this quotation from the Spanish as it is given in Marías's text, without reference either to the French original or to the published translation in English; it seems to be from *L'Existentialisme est un humanisme* (Paris, 1946), translated into English as *Existentialism and Humanism* (New York, n.d.)— Trans.]

And there is something even more interesting. And this is that when Sartre says that existentialists are not atheists in the sense that they exhaust themselves in proving that God does not exist because if there were a God everything would be the same, that even a valid proof of the existence of God would modify nothing—then we do not understand. And I believe that the most important thing one can do when one does not understand something is to begin from there, to make a virtue of necessity. When one does not understand something and, instead of considering it adequate, one stops a moment and seriously acknowledges that one does not understand it, immediately one begins to understand. I have seen the proof of this a thousand times.

What seems to me unintelligible is the following. First, we have worn ourselves out in order to show that God is self-contradictory because he is *causa sui*—in spite of the fact that nobody says that God is *causa sui*. Second, since there is no God, there cannot be a nature in man—although the immediate consequence of this is that if there is no God there will not be a nature of any kind, and for the same reason. And finally, it turns out that even if there were a God everything would be the same, and even if there were a valid proof of God nothing would be changed. I confess that I do not understand this; it is perfectly clear that it is not clear. Thus there is nothing left to do but take a turn around us.

Remember what I have called, after an image from Ortega, "the Jericho method." Joshua took Jericho by circling around the city and sounding trumpets. Philosophy has no other method than that of circling around Jericho. Let's try to take half a turn at least. Then we find:

First, if the reason there is no God is that the notion of *causa sui* is self-contradictory, the advisable thing to do would be to look for a different, more adequate notion of God, instead of declaring God to be nonexistent for no reason other than our own failure to divest ourselves of that notion which is of no importance to us.

Secondly, might it not be that, if man has no nature, this is so for a different and more intrinsic reason than that God does not exist? Should we not seek in man himself something that would explain why he has no nature, if it is true that he has none, instead of inferring this in an extrinsic and automatic way from the fact that there is no God to conceive it? Why do we go on thinking of reality from the point of view of a technical vision of the world? Why do we go on assimilating the reality of man and his essence to the reality of a paper cutter and its essence? Is this not an excess of *thingification?* And what if it should turn out that man is not a paper cutter, that he does not resemble a paper cutter in any way?

Finally, what does Sartre mean when he says that, in the end, it would not matter at all if there were a God, that everything would be the same, and that even if it were to be demonstrated with a valid proof that God exists, nothing would be changed? But if we demonstrate with a valid proof that God exists, then God exists; then the essence of man can be conceived; then man can have an essence and a nature; then all the Sartrian evidence about the non-natural character of man, about the precedence of existence over essence, about choice or *choix*—all this is overturned.

As we have seen, if we take this "coherent" atheism at all seriously, we find in the end that we cannot remain within it. It is Sartre himself who expels us. I am not trying to show that Sartre may not be right, only that we cannot install ourselves in his point of view. I am trying to take him seriously, but he will not let me, he does not allow me, he expells me. I am unable to remain within his point of view because it is not coherent, because if one thing is true another is not.

There is another form of atheism which is not existentialist. It is that which we find in other types of philosophy, those that are founded on linguistic analysis and epistemology and that are defined by an extreme positivism practically reduced, especially in England, to the analysis of language. These philosophies are not atheistic in the sense that they say that God does not exist. They say something prior to this and perhaps more serious: that the proposition "God exists" has no meaning. That is, that to speak of God is to say nothing. One cannot say even that God does not exist, because to say that God exists or that God does not exist are two opposed theses but they are alike in that neither of the two has any meaning (and here the concept of "meaning" makes its appearance again), and because God is not an object of experience and therefore neither the thesis that God exists nor the thesis that God does not exist is scientifically verifiable—and only that which is empirically verifiable has "meaning."

This position is in a certain sense more serious, since it takes the ground away from under our feet. And this is the present-day form of atheism, for existentialism is now somewhat fallen from fortune. What is in the ascendent, the genuine "new wave" in philosophy, is this. Since the issue is serious, we would do well to examine it.

I would ask two questions. First, the thesis that only that which is empirically verifiable has meaning, is this empirically verifiable? For it does occur to me to ask of the philosopher who subscribes to that thesis: how do you know it? Well, he knows it by way of sources that, strictly speaking, are not valid for him. He takes a step or makes a leap to a different way of looking at things. The philosopher who denies meaning to every statement that is not empirically verifiable is making a statement that is not empirically verifiable.

If a philosopher were to limit himself to stating nothing but empirically verifiable theses, we would be extraordinarily pleased with him and there would be nothing to object to. But if he dares go one step further and say that only such theses have meaning, I ask myself how he knows this. And thus the result would be that we can have respect for the practice of one who eliminates from his philosophy all reference to the problem of God, but I would not feel equally respectful toward one who, in the name of empirical verifiability, prohibits this problem to me. If it were in the name of something else and supported by good reasons, that would be fine; but if it is in the name of that criterion, I do not accept it because its own origin is not within the realm of the empirically verifiable.

In the second place, what is the meaning of the limitation on problematicity derived from a certain idea of knowledge? I mean, how can one accept the view that the sphere of the *problematical* be limited by virtue of an a priori conception of what knowledge is? The genuine and a posteriori impotence of thought is something that we run up against repeatedly: I try to acquaint myself with something and do not achieve it, I fail many times over—I will conclude that it is not possible to know it, at least up to the present. What is unacceptable is the a priori decree of unknowability. To say of something that we cannot speak of it or know anything about it does not satisfy me. I must reply, "Seeing is believing; let's have a look at it." All scepticism seems fine to me as long as it is justified and a posteriori, as long as it is arrived at after having tried, and not before.

I find the root of all these forms of atheism in a desire to simplify the situation. I mean, the elimination of part of the facts of a problem in order to subdue this problem and adjust it to a mental scheme we have control over. This seems interesting to me because it corresponds to a peculiar configuration of the contemporary mind. Think of other fields where that attitude may be seen more clearly: for example, a political position. Someone desires the unification of Europe or the raising of the standard of living of the masses. There might be somebody who wants these things and nothing more, but that is not frequent. Almost always, the unity of Europe is desired as long as it will be in a certain way, for example, socialist—or fascist, like the deceased Mr. Hitler who wanted one Europe, but based on the primacy of the "Aryan" race; any other kind of unity did not interest him. Some people want the masses to have better lives, but in conformity with certain principles; if the masses have other principles, these people are not interested. That is, first a scheme is established and reality is obliged to conform to that, and if reality does not wish to conform then everything that does not fit is eliminated. This reminds me of the story of a man who left his watch to be repaired; the following week the watchmaker returned it to him, saying, "Here is your watch, and these two pieces that were left over." I am not inclined to believe that pieces of reality may be left over.

Furthermore, if philosophy decides to turn its back on a problem, the problem does not for this reason cease to be there. What happens is that philosophy loses its fundamental condition: *its radical nature.* Not that philosophy *must* be radical, but that this is what it consists in, in going to the roots—without this its philosophical character disappears. And this is the price that has to be paid for the simplification of reality.

But I promised to take one more turn around Sartre. What he is saying, does it not make some good sense? Does it not have some justification? Without doubt he is a man of great talent, and when somebody who possesses such talent says something that seems to us erroneous and false, we have to try to take another turn, for it may turn out that what he is saying does make some kind of sense.

All of us have read the novels of Camus. Camus was a

great writer and an admirable figure in many ways; personally, I like his novels much more than his essays. But in all his work Camus is full of the conviction that reality is absurd. *L'Etranger,* which is an astonishing story, reveals the conduct of a man who does a series of things that, in actuality, are absurd. But Camus has taken the precaution of performing a little operation while narrating the life of Meursault, and this is to extirpate his motives, just as he might have taken out his tonsils. Naturally, once his motives are removed, his conduct is absurd. But at the same time it is impossible. I mean that Meursault could not have done what he did if he had not actually had *more* than Camus tells us. Meursault had motives, a why and a what for, making it possible for him to do what he did. Camus, with his extremely skillful command of the storyteller's art, anesthetizes Meursault, takes out his tonsils (that is, his motives), and goes on from there. Neither Meursault nor the reader are aware; the reader too has been anesthetized by Camus' art, and we read *L'Etranger* with avid pleasure. But when I reread it, I notice that it is full of little holes, precisely those left by the motives as they were being removed.

And Sartre? Sartre is a phenomenologist. He is enormously indebted to Heidegger, as everybody has said, and at times anybody (except Sartre) would say that he is indebted to Ortega, but he is much more indebted still to Husserl. And, as he is a good phenomenologist, when he writes a story he sees that there is no human action without motivation. For this reason, the acts of his characters always have a meaning; they are not absurd. We understand quite well why they do each thing they do. What lacks meaning, what is absurd, is the whole. Each action has meaning, but life as a whole, no. Preserving the meaning of each action, he takes it away from life.

This characteristic of Sartre's fiction proceeds from the radical deficiency of his philosophy. If we take seriously what human life is, we see that an act cannot be justified except from the point of view of a project, and this, in its turn, only exists as a function of a total and more vague project that involves my whole life. And I am able to do something only while *giving the reason* for what I am doing. Thus it turns out that life itself, all by itself, brings us to reason * as *instrumentum reddendi rationem*, as *vital reason*. And this is what Sartre is ignorant of, root and branch.

And then, what does "absurd" mean? Absurd is that which has no meaning, which does not make "good sense." But this means that the absurd depends on meaning; it moves, as Hegel would say, within the "element" of meaning. Just as, when we say that something is false, we are moving within the element of truth. Meaning is prior to absurdity. Human life is already meaning; it is the element of meaning. And within it, within that radical and original meaningfulness, we say that there are things that possess meaning and others that do not because they are absurd. The absurd is derived, like a cyst or infarctation, from that great order of meaning.

And finally, what is it that Sartre wishes to justify when he writes what seems to be his greatest incoherence?—that there is no God and that every man depends on the fact that there is no God, but that, in the end, even if there were everything would stay the same. Well, probably what he is trying to say—and this does make sense—is that even though there were a God, man is free and has to create himself within certain limits. And he has to choose himself, not as a "what" but as a "who," and at each moment he has to invent his life and be responsible for it—and the fact that there may be a God does not affect this condition of man.

But this means, in the last analysis, that the atheism of existentialism is unnecessary. And that what it contains of

* [The Spanish here is *solo la vida misma da razón* (literally, "only life itself gives reason")—Trans.]

truth (and it contains a great deal) in the interpretation of human life is completely independent of whether or not God exists. Or rather, taking things seriously and seeing the whole of life from the point of view of its entire project, it would probably turn out just the contrary—that is, that in order for human life to be what phenomenologically it is, in order for it to be what it reveals of itself, it is necessary that there be a God.

I wish to end with a quotation from the old Unamuno, from the old honorary Salamancan, in which he said that the only question (Unamuno was inclined to exaggerate; we ourselves would not say "the only") is knowing whether I have to die completely or not.

> And if I do not die, what is to become of me? And if I die, nothing has any meaning now.

Unamuno said that nothing has any meaning *now*. That is, if I die completely, it is not that the whole of life has no meaning, but that this act I am performing at this moment has no importance because one day it will cease to have importance—and thus it is a question of waiting and hoping.* In order for something to have importance it is necessary that it have it *always;* under any other conditions, strictly speaking, it does not have it *now*.

* [The Spanish verb *esperar,* used here, may mean "to wait," "to hope," or, in addition, "to expect"—Trans.]

CHAPTER SIX

"MEDITATIO MORTIS" — *THEME OF OUR TIMES*

"I am convinced," Unamuno wrote in 1905, "that there is no more than one solitary aim, one and the same for all men." And he went on to explain a little more: "the human question, which is mine and yours and that of the other and that of all . . . The human question," he concluded, "is the question of what there is going to be of my consciousness, of yours, of that of the other, of that of all, after each of us has died."

There is something that always surprises me, and to a greater degree the older I get, and this is that almost seventy years after Unamuno wrote these words, after exactly a century has passed since his birth and twenty-eight years since his death, still those few lines of eager and provocative prose have not yet been taken seriously.

To take them seriously does not mean to be in agreement with them, but to listen to them, to be completely aware (that is, to *integrate oneself*, making them a part of oneself), and to take a position. A short time afterward, in 1913, in the book where he more fully developed his theme, his "only question," a book that should have been called *Tratado del amor de Dios* (*Treatise on the Love of God*) and ended up being *Del sentimiento trágico de la vida en los hombres y en los pueblos* (*The Tragic Sense of Life in Men and in Peoples*—with which, no doubt, it ended up being a book other than the one he at first projected and so had to have such a different title), he did more than express and formulate this longing, although without doing as much as perhaps he should have and not even as much as in some of his novels and in one or another of his poems he would do. In a paragraph written almost without logical or grammatical relation to those around it, written, so it seems to me, from within himself, observing and not reasoning, contemplating a reality he imagines, from which no doubt he sets out but which for the moment he considers simply in tranquillity, thereby taking possession of it, Unamuno, affecting ignorance of the "human" and of "humanity," spoke of himself as "The man of flesh and blood, he who is born, suffers, and dies—above all, dies—he who eats and drinks and plays and sleeps and thinks and desires, the man who is seen and who is heard, the brother, the true brother." And later, following certain distinctions whose intent is polemical, he added, "And this concrete man, of flesh and blood, is the subject and at the same time the supreme object of all philosophy, whether certain presumed philosophers wish it so or not. "

This man, whom Unamuno saw as he was writing his words, whom he was imagining, was not a "thing" (in spite of the definite but disorienting reference to "flesh and blood"), for Unamuno was thinking not of an "organism" but of a "who": he who is born, suffers, and dies, he who eats and drinks and plays and thinks and desires, he who is seen and heard, he who performs different actions, he who does what he does through the course of time—in short, *he who lives.* What is crucial here is that Unamuno, precisely at the moment of raising his "only question," spoke of *man,* when what he was seeing without concepts was *human life.* Unamuno was clearly conscious of that "scientific inquisition" which considered it intellectually scandalous to ask questions about death and survival. At the end of the nineteenth century and the beginning of the twentieth, the general scientific *assumption* was the annihilation of man through death. Of course, "belief" was set apart as something gratuitous and more or less sentimental, something that was viewed with condescension. The question of death and immortality—which is one question—seemed "indecent" (*quod non decet*). Unamuno many times recalled the attitude of the Athenians in the Areopagus, curious about all new things, who listened to Saint Paul, attentive and interested, as he spoke about "the unknown God," but when he spoke of the resurrection, they courteously departed, saying, "Some other time we will hear about this," * and the attitude of Festus who said, "Paul, too much reading has made you mad." At a time of insecure resignation and of insecure faith as well, to speak of death was not "serious" and carried with it one's disqualification as an intellectual. Unamuno confronted this inquisition with extraordinary courage, and this is the first thing that must be said.

The first, but not the only thing. His attitude did not please anybody: for some it signified something like a reversion to magic, the proof of an archaic mind; for those who took things as "certain" and "demonstrated" things by the power of syllogisms, it was a longing to disturb, to cast doubt upon what had been "conclusively" established in the thirteenth century. Some were not aware of how meagerly scientific their presuppositions were; the others forgot that the assumptions on which they based their "demonstrations" of immortality were more problematical than the problem itself. And above all they forgot that in order for a solution to be true it is not enough that it not be false, but it has to be a solution to the *real* problem, to what it is that disturbs us and obliges us to question. Solutions, whether true or not, to *other* problems are of no use to us, not because they may not be logically correct, but because, since they have no

* [*Acts* XVI; the quotations here are, again, translated from the Spanish in which they appear in Marías' text—Trans.]

reference to what it was provoked our question, to what it is with respect to which we *need* to know what to be guided by, they are not solutions (although they might well have been at one time).

The crucial thing here is that Unamuno did not escape the "scientific inquisition." He challenged it, certainly, but that is not what is most difficult. This is the worst of all the forms of inquisition: any inquisition subjugates almost everybody, some are in rebellion against it, very few come to be *free* of it. What is characteristic of every inquisitorial spirit (whose extreme form is "terrorism") is to *take for granted* what is not at all evident and to build upon this a whole system of affirmations and especially of negations. The rebel confronts these and denies them, but he *starts with the presupposition* and plays the game. For that reason, he remains within the sphere defined by the inquisition, he does not escape the inquisition—which thus achieves its principal goal. From this the immense capacity of all forms of inquisition (religious, political, scientific, literary, artistic) to sterilize the opposition follows, and it is by this means that they achieve their purpose of putting freedom in chains, allowing no choice but that between submission and rebellion *within their own formulation*—that is, forcing everybody to be an "ist" or an "anti-ist."

Unamuno, as I said, when he raises the question of death and immortality, always talks about "man," in the sense attached to this word by the science and in general by the thought of his time, and in spite of the fact that what he was looking at was human life. For this reason he went much further in his novels than in *The Tragic Sense of Life*, for in them he decided not to reason but to imagine and by imagining he reasoned in a more profound and real way than when, even while trying to avoid philosophy, he approached it and sought it. Of course, in one case as in the other, he was philosophizing, and in a way that only at certain moments in his life did he come to suspect. But I spoke at length about all these things more than twenty years ago in my book *Miguel de Unamuno*, and even today I do not find anything substantial to modify, or to add to, what I said there. What I would like to do now is set out from Unamuno's achievement, attempt to go further, and see where we find ourselves.

Through the whole length of *The Tragic Sense of Life* two conceptions are struggling with one another. Unamuno spoke of the "agony" of the faith that affirms and of the reason that has to deny, between the heart that will not be resigned to its own annihilation and the head that does not see how it can survive. But this book of the maturity of its author is agonizing in another sense, for it is intrinsically agonizing as a work of the mind: in it what Unamuno *thinks* wages ceaseless battle with what he *sees*. While he is proposing the question and, above all, living it, he moves within the realm of human life, of the *who* making his biography in time and longing to endure indefinitely. As soon as he goes to find, or at least to examine, the solutions offered by theology or philosophy he falls again into just any of the diverse conceptions of man, all of which ultimately agree in taking man to be a thing, regardless of the nature attributed to this thing. And from this flows his constant frustration and his discouragement about developing the problem in a fundamental and radical way.

In the closing pages of my *Ortega* I have treated in some detail what I had suggested years before: that *The Tragic Sense of Life* (which between the lines frequently enters into discussion with the youthful writings of Ortega) was the definitive polemical stimulus that caused Ortega to bring himself together in order to set forth his own philosophy for the first time. His *Meditaciones del Quijote* represents a reaction against the irrationalism that Unamuno had formulated the year before in the most energetic, passionate, and fascinating way. Unamuno established a radical opposition between reason and life, concluding that everything vital is antirational (no longer simply irrational), that everything rational is antivital, and that reason is the enemy of life, in spite of the fact that both are necessary. When Ortega said that reason cannot aspire to take the place of life and has no need to try, and added that the opposition between them is suspect and "used by those who do not wish to work," "as if reason were not a vital and spontaneous function of the same lineage as seeing and touching!"—he made clear, with that simplicity things of genius usually have, that reason, far from being alien to life, is given within life, is constituted in life, and in order to oppose it one has to begin by first, arbitrarily and violently, pulling it out by the roots, out of the life in whose body it has appeared. That is, whatever may be the idea one has about reason, whatever intellectual doctrine one may elaborate about it, its primary attribute is precisely that it is *vital.*

This is important, but it is only half of what matters to us. While clarifying what we might call the genealogy of reason and observing that it is born and has its origin precisely within life, Ortega is at the same time clarifying the meaning of life itself, going beyond what is organic toward what is biographical, leaving behind its mere "ingredients" (biological or physical) in order to arrive at an interpretation of life as *circumstantial* drama, as a dynamic dialogue of a *who* who is myself with my circumstance or world, irreducible to any "thing," since things are only that *with which* I make my life.

At this level, whatever might be said about "man" as an

organism or as a subject for psychology is secondary and irrelevant, and does not even touch the issue. Thus, all the traditional *aporías* or difficulties of philosophy remain below the threshold of the problem as it is now formulated.

Is this inconsistent with Unamuno? Not at all. In that same book he asked and replied, "Why do I wish to know where I come from and where I am going, where that which surrounds me comes from and where it is going, and what is the meaning of this? Because I do not wish to die completely, and I want to know whether I have to die or not, conclusively. And if I do not die, what is to become of me? And if I die, nothing has any meaning now." In saying this, Unamuno raised the question within the element of *meaning*—that is, from the point of view of life, which in order to be lived has to have meaning and is, paradoxically, at the same time the *who* who discovers meaning and "gives" it to all of reality, which possesses meaning in relation to life. The trouble is that instead of installing himself in the perspective he had arrived at and proposing his "only question" from it, Unamuno, when he felt the theoretical impulse, turned his back on it and began to examine Scholastic doctrines or the doctrines of the sensualists, as if from that point of view the arguments about the simplicity or complexity of the soul or about the association of images or about the presumed experiences that testified to the survival of bodily death were relevant. For this reason, what is most profound and original in Unamuno's thought has to be sought for in his novels and in his poems, where he abandoned himself to his own vision of human life, where he attempted imaginatively to anticipate the significance of *personal* death—that is, the death that brings biographical life, which secretes meaning and is nourished by it, to an end (forever?), the death of the "man of flesh and blood" who is seen and heard, of the "true brother" who can be understood because he is a "thou" as I am an "I."

Unamuno made of his philosophy a *meditatio mortis*. Was he right? Spinoza, his preferred Spinoza, had written,

> *Homo liber de nulla re minus quam de morte cogitat, et eius sapientia non mortis, sed vitae meditatio est.*
> (The free man thinks of nothing less than of death, and his wisdom is not a meditation on death but on life.)

Both are right in what they affirm, and neither of them in what he excludes; for there can be no meditation on one without the other. Death is *of life*, of somebody living, of somebody who lives, and it does not make sense to think of death without being clear with regard to that life. Even more, if death interests us, it is in relation to life, from life and for life. And furthermore (not to be forgotten, although it may appear platitudinous), it is life that questions itself about death. But, in the opposite sense, life ends in death, it *includes* death. Since to live is to form projects and, above all, to project oneself, and since man anticipates his future, death is already here, in every instant of life. That anticipatory projection of life means that no vital action can be performed without *knowing what to be guided by* (Ortega has made it evident that this is the primary and radical meaning of knowing). Well then, what good does it do me to know what to be guided by with respect to *myself?*

All certainty is penultimate, insufficient, and, if things be taken in a strict sense, equivalent to uncertainty as long as I do not know what is to become of me. The projects of life follow one another and lead to others and only acquire their meaning in relation to the *total* project that encompasses my whole life. But it is entirely imaginary to make believe that this process of projection is interrupted when it arrives at the moment of death and goes no further. The meaning of everything I do in my life depends upon whether there will or will not be a "tomorrow" (and upon how that tomorrow is anticipated) by which each one of those deeds will be supported, if the expression be allowed, in a reality that will never pass judgment. All things are defined by a "why" and a "what for," and it is impossible to avoid an *evacuatio* of all of them if one does not know which is the ultimate and definitive. If the supreme category of human things is *importance*, the perspective of annihilation would mean that nothing would really have it, since one day it would *cease to have it*. Everything would be a question of waiting and hoping. When Unamuno said, "And if I die, nothing has any meaning *now*," he clearly indicated this situation, because the meaning of each thing and of each deed, of each instant of life, depends upon there being a meaning upon which it can *always* rely. Removing from him the exaggeration to which he was addicted, we still have to recognize that Unamuno was right.

This is what, though in a frivolous way, existentialism has recognized. During the last forty years, and especially during the last two decades, the theme of death has been invading philosophy. Heidegger gave the signal in 1927 with his *Sein und Zeit* and his idea of *Sein zum Tode*, about which there has been so much loose talk. It is of little importance that the translation *ser para la muerte*, "being for death," is incorrect and disorienting and does not correspond either to what the German expression means or to Heidegger's intention (many years ago I proposed the more "literal" and at the same time less slavish translation *estar a la muerte*, "being aware of death," which would lead in an entirely different direction), the fact is that "being for death" is how that expression has been interpreted with confusing frequency. Such an interpretation has the same value as have false etymologies that, through having been believed for a long time, have injected a definite meaning into a word. The "existentialists" of the following generation (especially the French and, in imitation of them, the rest) inundated their books with references to death and to some degree organized their philosophy in relation to death, but with a "mortalistic" tendency that was never justified although annihilation is "taken for granted" within it. That is, in them the inquisitorial spirit of the old scientific inquisition from the youth of Unamuno has been united with the obsessive introduction of the "theme" of death. In this, as in so many other things, the existentialists have been at one and the same time innovators and reversionists—compare their novels with those of the "naturalists" of 1880 to 1900 and it will be seen to what extent they repeat many of the most trivial and ephemeral aspects of the works of their predecessors. (The summaries of the plots of the novels on the Gallimard list recall nothing so much as those that Valera tells about, with no little irony, in his *Apuntes sobre el nuevo arte de escribir novelas* [*Notes on the New Art of Writing Novels*], which was "new" in 1887.)

When it is said that *l'homme est une passion inutile*, it would have been appropriate to take the trouble to prove it. Why? Is it enough to decree it, either capriciously or by basing oneself on a curious survival from materialism, compatible with a strange "derealization"? Plato spoke more wisely: χαλὸς γὰρ ὁ χίνζυνος (*kalòs gàr ho kíndynos*), "Beautiful is the risk of being immortal." Philosophically it is an open question, because the phenomenon of life *just as it presents itself to us*, without subjecting it to prior interpretations received from other sources (theology or biology or a hybrid of the two), is that of a reality open to annihilation or immortality.

How could we characterize the situation to which we have come? Unamuno posed the question of death and survival in an unavoidable way. He did this (in a "literary" sense, especially) at the level of his time, from the point of view of the intuition of human life and, thus, with regard to *personal* death and the eventual immortality of the person. (The expression "immortality of the soul" has in fact functioned in an ambiguous and perturbing way, by burdening speculation with doctrines that are philosophically wholly inadequate—it will be enough to recall that Aristotle's *De Anima*, which is the basis of almost all such doctrines, is a part of the *Physics* of its author.) But when he tried to initiate a theoretical investigation he almost wholly limited himself to discussing traditional doctrines, accepting their presuppositions and never going beyond them—that is, never coming to criticize them from the level at which he had himself arrived, by which he had automatically transcended them. His "irrationalism" (or "desperate intellectualism," if you prefer) prevented Unamuno from carrying out what he had begun, which may be found in his *personal novel* and in his poetry: the adequate interpretation of human death and its horizon. (Concerning all this one may look into my *Miguel de Unamuno* and some subsequent essays.)

A year after the appearance of *Del sentimiento trágico de la vida*, the philosophical doctrine of *human life* was formulated for the first time in a rigorous and conceptual way—that is, without confusing it with biological life or psychological life or with the historical forms of life. Thus, in 1914, exactly half a century ago, the possibility of raising the question of the reality of human life as something distinct from (although perhaps not inseparable from) the problem of "man" was made evident. And, along with this possibility, the further possibility of confronting the theme of death *understood from the point of view of life,* which it affects, and no longer primarily or exclusively from the point of view of the organism or of the psyche. This understanding will of course be quite involved, but only in relation to life, and not the reverse.

However, it is a fact (at the moment a fact, although facts are always insufficient and unintelligible and require us to attempt to go further and "see how the fact becomes a fact") that Ortega, during the whole course of his life and his extensive work, never clearly dealt with the theme of death. I would say (and this is an interpretative thesis, although not unjustified) that he did not get around to raising it. And the consequence is that in this centennial year of the birth of Unamuno, in which at the same time what might have been a decisive factor in his thought is now a half century old, the question continues to be insufficiently treated; it continues to be in need of an adequate inquiry.

Note to what a degree chance intervenes in what has sometimes been believed to be subject to an implacable determinism—the dialectic of ideas. There was a certain human, all too human, friction between Unamuno and Ortega, which is quite clearly evident in all the writings of both during the second decade of this century (a decisive phase for each: of definitive consolidation of the mentality of the first, of the early maturity of the second). Had it not been for a certain mutual suspicion and distrust that deprived both of them of that capacity of mind each needed in order to penetrate the other's observations, Unamuno might have been able to gather what the youthful philosophy of his alienated friend offered him and to graft it onto his own intellectual trajectory, since it had such affinity with his own most profound intuitions and was so "genuine" for the authentic Unamuno. And Ortega might not have felt such a temptation to "elude" Unamuno, who "pained him" too much, who was so important to him and irritated him so. Ortega might not have ignored the question that Unamuno reiterated in such an exaggerated and exclusivist way, the question he called "the only," taking possession of it until it seemed that it was "his only." For a long time people had the impression, no less effective on account of its absurdity, that to speak of death was to be "Unamunized," was to invade the private and personal theme of Don Miguel.

Given this intellectual situation and the undeferable urgency of taking up the problem of death, if one desired that the certainties achieved by philosophy not be undermined and invalidated by a larval uncertainty that would make them illusory, the first thing that had to be done was to bring the work of Unamuno up to the level. Up to what level?—it will be asked. To the level of philosophy, which was the level intrinsically postulated by that work and then, within that same moment, renounced and abandoned. This is the task I performed in my book *Miguel de Unamuno*, which has been much read during the last twenty years and has decisively conditioned the present image of Unamuno and the major part of what has been written about him since then, but from which (as was to be expected) hardly any *theoretical* consequences have yet been extracted.

Is this enough? Of course not. What we might call "the second incorporation," the second bringing up to the level, is required. What is necessary is that the philosophical theory of human life reach its ultimate consequences and not evade the adequate formulation of the problem of death and immortality. Will it achieve a "solution"? It is difficult to reply to that question, because one would first have to be clear about what "solution" means in relation to a philosophical problem. But it is certain that an *adequate* formulation of the problem is the primary and decisive way of intellectual installation and will at least make it possible to take note of uncertainty—that is, to be clear about it and to know what to be guided by concerning its conditions and its limits. In any case, whether philosophical problems have solutions or not, what they do have is *biography*, and the history of the problem of death reveals strange anomalies and frustrations, in spite of the recent efforts of thinkers who have come under (and this, of course, not by chance) the double influence of Unamuno and Ortega.

Unamuno's writings, especially his novels, have been the clearest and most profound *presentation* of the imagined reality of death and of the significance of survival. It would be a grave error to deprive ourselves of that heritage at the moment of philosophically confronting the *ultimate* questions in a theory of human life. By some unexpected chance, it has been in Spain where the two doctrines have germinated, whose convergence would make it possible to attack, without being completely downhearted about it, the most provocative, irremediable, and discouraging question that is offered to the human mind. But Spain is a land of profound, refined impiety and has been dedicated for centuries to erasing and forgetting itself. What hopes are there that Spanish thought may have courage and generosity enough to devotedly gather up the inheritance of Unamuno and Ortega and not remain perpetually behind both of them? Time will tell. What is not to be doubted is that the *meditatio mortis* is a theme for our times, a condition of all thought that wishes to be truthful.

CHAPTER SEVEN

HUMAN LIFE AND
ITS EMPIRICAL STRUCTURE

Look in the dictionary for the word *pentagon;* you will
find a univocal definition: "a polygon having five angles
and five sides." The proximate genus and the specific dif-
ferentiae—there is no further problem. The mathematical
object can be captured in a bare formula. But if you look
up *screech owl*, you will find that the restrained *Diccionario
de la Real Academia Española* (in spite of its being not an
encyclopedia but a dictionary, that is, concerned not with
things but with words) says nothing less than the following:

> A predatory and nocturnal bird of some 35 centimeters in
> length from the top of the head to the end of the tail, and
> with a wingspread approximately double its length, with
> very soft feathers that are yellow, striped with white,
> gray, and black on the upper parts and snow-white on
> the breast, abdomen, legs, and face; with a round head,
> short beak curved at the point; large, brilliant, iris-yellow
> eyes; circular face; a wide, short tail; and black claws. It
> is common in Spain; it breathes heavily when at rest, and
> emits a strident and sorrowful screech when in flight. It
> feeds on insects and small vertebrate animals.

It is seen that the screech owl does not submit easily to en-
closure in the cage of a definition.

Things do not end here, however. Because, finally, if you
look up the name *Cervantes*, what you will be told is that
he was born in 1547 in Alcalá de Henares, that he went

to Italy with Cardinal Acquaviva, was in combat, was wounded at Lepanto, lived as a prisoner in Algeria, was an excise-tax collector, wrote *Don Quijote*, tried to be a poet, and died in Madrid in 1616.

Why these differences? In the first case, what is involved is a mathematical object, an "ideal" object in the terminology of Husserl, and the definition gives us simply its *consistency*. In the second case, definition in a strict sense is not possible: the "essence" of the screech owl, in spite of its being the symbol of Athena, is problematical. (Does being white pertain to the essence of the swan? Rubén Darío said, "the Olympic swan of snow"; but the Australian swan, which is black, is not the same as that of Leda.) The dictionary, in defining *screech owl*, takes refuge in the most circumstantial description; and this is not only longer and relatively vaguer, but also includes two characteristics that distinguish it from the definition of the pentagon. First of all, where does it come from? From experience, of course, from having seen screech owls. (We leave to one side the question of how many screech owls one must have seen and of the constancy of traits in those that are seen.) In the second place, it is said that the screech owl does certain things: it breathes heavily, it flies exhaling a "strident and sorrowful" screech (there can be no doubt that the *Diccionario* has a romantic vision of the classical bird that usually perched on the ample shoulder of Pallas Athena), it lives in Spain, it eats insects. But, who is it does these things? The screech owl, it will be said. But note this well: this is not the same thing as in the case of the pentagon. Here what we are concerned with is what *each* screech owl does; it is this that breathes heavily, this that screeches sorrowfully in the dusk, flashing this concrete pair of huge eyes, iris-yellow. All this, presumably, is done by all screech owls, each and every one. It is not *the* screech owl (as it is *the* pentagon) who flies in the darkness, but *all* screech owls do this.

And Cervantes? Here a very different, third thing is involved. Here what corresponds to the "definition" is a history. We are told what Cervantes did and what happened to him. That is, we are told the story of his life. ("Life is what we do and what happens to us," Ortega said many years ago, and this definition continues to be the most exact.) Even in the case of the screech owl (keep this well in mind) a mere morphological description turned out to be insufficient and it was necessary to add an outline of its behavior or conduct; it was necessary to say what the screech owl *does.* But of Cervantes, it is said what he *did,* a very different thing: not an outline of activities but certain precise, temporally localized acts, in principle nonrecurrent, irreversible—in short, historical. When the word sought in the dictionary is the name of a person, the correlative of the definition is a narration.

And the knowledge of human life, "giving reasons" for it, is only possible by way of a form of narrative reason whose philosophical formulation is to be found in the idea of vital reason.[1] But within this inoffensive affirmation others are to be found that are quite serious, and it is important that these be made clear. Since I am an ingredient of reality, to the degree in which reality is constituted as such in my life and is situated within it, all reality, and not only that of man, is affected from that point of view by the historical condition of this very point of view; that is, effective knowledge of reality, when it is not limited to mere "mental manipulation," is accessible only to narrative reason, which makes it possible to apprehend not only the abstract, but the real constitution of its objects in the area of our life. Reality always appears covered with a patina of interpretations, and the primary mission of theory is the removal of all of them in order to make manifest in all its truth (*alétheia*) the naked reality that has provoked them and has at the same time made them necessary and possible. Some years ago, in demonstrating that history alone allows us to discover the interpretative character of this social and traditional patina, I said that history in that sense is the *órganon* or instrument for the return from all interpretations to the naked reality that lies beneath them and—this should not be forgotten since it is decisive—that only in them is it indicated and revealed.[2]

However, it is not simply a question of knowledge, but of the very structure of life. There exists what we might call a material alveolus, composed of diverse elements and ingredients, within which that dynamic and dramatic reality, which is living, is lodged, but consisting, not in any thing, but in my doing things here and now with things, by means of something and for the sake of something, since my life is given to me but it is not given to me ready-made, and I have to make it from one instant to another. But precisely within that instant there is an intrinsic mixture of the present, past, and future that constitutes the structural frame of our lives. This structure might be described by saying that the past and the future are *present* in my life, in the "why" and the "what for" of each one of my doings. Within my instantaneous act, the past is present since the reason for what I am doing is only to be found in what I have done, and the future is present in the project, upon which hangs the whole meaning of my life. The vital instant is not a point without extension, but implies a temporal environment. The being of life consists in this temporal span, and for that reason the only way really to speak of it is to *recount* it. The form of statement that makes concrete life accessible is narration, the story.

The main problem raised here is how it is possible to recount or narrate. The Ortegan theory of vital and historical reason orients us in this direction. Some time ago in my book *Miguel de Unamuno* [3] I set forth a theory of the novel as a method of knowledge (what, since 1938, I have called the existential or personal novel), and in *Introducción a la filosofía* a few chapters have been constructed around the method and the theory of reason that this way of posing the problem demands, and along with that a logic of concrete thinking. Allow me to refer you here to those writings.

The consequence that follows from this is that the comprehension of what is concrete requires the understanding of certain prior, *given* structures. Because what is involved here is not that I construct certain mental schemes or models and afterward go looking through the world for something that might conform to them, but that, observing my own life, I discover conditions or requisites without which it would not be possible. And since the same thing happens in much the same way in every human life, I am thus discovering a prior and necessary structure that is studied by the abstract or analytical theory of human life. Only by means of this structure will it be possible to understand concrete human life, whether it be fictitious (novel, drama, cinema) or real (biographical and historical).

However, at this point we must redouble our caution. Human life is a reality so much unexplored that, contrary to what might have been expected, it is full of unknown territories into which few people have ventured so far, and in some places nobody at all. Between analytical theory and concrete narration an intermediate phase is interposed that nobody has paid any attention to; yet it is decisive, and about it I would like to say a few words; this is what on several occasions I have called *the empirical structure of human life*.[4]

As might be expected, the philosophy of the past has not been *completely* unaware of the question; but the more these antecedents are emphasized, the more energetically the radical difference and the insufficiency of their way of raising the issue appear. Aristotle,[5] Porphyry,[6] and, following in their footsteps, the Medieval Scholastics distinguished the "proper" along with the essential and the accidental. It is *essential* to men to be living and to be endowed with reason; it is *accidental* for him to be blond, Athenian, or aged; but to be risible, bipedal, or graying are neither essential nor accidental characteristics, but *proper* to man. It must be noted that the precise definition of the *idion* or *proprium*, even from the point of view in which the ancient logicians were situated, leaves much to be desired.[7] But the decisive thing that thoroughly distinguishes that ancient consideration of what interests me here is the assumption involved in it that what is being discussed are things, in the most adequate cases referring to man; whereas, on the contrary, what is being discussed here is human life, which, in the first place, is not a thing but a completely different kind of reality and, in the second place, cannot even be identified with man, but radically surpasses all anthropological considerations.

Thus, our subject is not the analytical theory of human life—nor the existential analytic of the *Dasein* of Heidegger —for the preceding reason and for another of a different kind that has to be kept in mind, which is that this analytical theory includes only those necessary qualities that are given in all life and which make life possible, the abstract relations that have to be filled with circumstantial and concrete contents. Only then will they be fully real; only then will they be the object of that authentic knowledge which is narrative reason. But between those two elements this *terra incognita* is interposed.

Let us recall here once again the examples from the dictionary, although only as orienting analogies, since to take these analogies literally would lead into error. The definition of the pentagon and everything that follows necessarily from it—the geometry of the five-sided polygon—would correspond to the analytical theory: it is, like that theory, a kind of knowledge that is a priori, universal, necessary, and unreal. (Concerning the radical difference that, in spite of all this, exists between these two forms of knowledge, see *Introducción a la filosofía*, pages 217 ff.)* What the dictionary says about Cervantes (that is, giving an account of his life) is concrete knowledge of a circumstantial and historical reality—in short, narration. But what are the presuppositions of that article in the dictionary? What is it that is "so well known that nobody speaks of it"? This is precisely the question that occupies us here.

The first assumption, indicated by the personal, proper name, is that Cervantes is a man, and this sends us back right at the beginning to the analytical theory. The second assumption is that by "man" we understand a series of characteristics that are more than merely the requisites necessary in order that there be human life, but that are nevertheless prior to every concrete individual biography and which we take into account. This is what I call the *empirical structure*—which is empirical, but a structure; which is a structure, but empirical. *Mutatis mutandis* (and there would of course be much to change), this would correspond to what the dictionary says about the screech owl. The reality of that empirical structure rests on something that, without being an a priori requisite of human life, belongs *de facto* and in a stable way to the concrete lives that I empirically encounter.

This something corresponds, then, to the realm of *possible* human variations in history, but is under the sway of an essential permanence and stability. For example, I find as an a priori and analytical characteristic of human life

* [*Reason and Life*, pp. 197 ff.—Trans.]

the fact of being circumstantial, of being in a world—but not necessarily in this world, nor in this epoch. Corporeality belongs to human life, but not precisely this form of corporeality; in principle, the reality called "human life" could be incarnated in an eight-footed body, but then of course it would be something quite different. Earthly life is finite; days are numbered—but what is its span? The normal longevity of man, which regulates his vital behavior, the succession and the function of the ages of man, the rhythm of generations and of historical life in general— all this is a matter of the empirical structure. This structure is what determines the appearance of our real world, not only the fact that "human life" has flourished in it, but the structure of our cities, which have doors, windows, furniture, and streets of a definite size and shape. It determines the things that refer to the diverse bodily senses—human life could have been given without sight or without hearing, although not without sensibility, and it might lose one of the senses (and, in fact, is losing the sense of smell) or acquire others that are new (and the use of technical apparatus to make radiation sensible, which is not perceptible to the ordinary senses, signifies nothing but this). It determines the repertory of what is pleasant and esteemed. All these things have changed or will change; at least they *could* change without, on that account, man's ceasing to be man. But the general scheme of his life would then be something else—that is, we would have a different empirical structure.

Thus, the boundaries between what is natural and what is historical would have to be determined. It has been usual to include within "human nature" many historical, acquired, although enduring, characteristics that are incorporated within the empirical structure of our life. Historical constants do not exist, but at most there are enduring elements, perhaps permanent elements—that is, elements that endure through the whole length of history and remain within it. In principle, we could think of them as ingredients of human life that "might last" from the creation of Adam to Judgment Day without, for that reason, ceasing to be historical.

The empirical structure is the concrete form of our circumstantiality. Man is not only in the world but in *this* world, not only is he a corporeal reality but he has this corporeal structure and not another. Let us take a minimal example in which both dimensions are articulated: sleep. The world in which man lives has a day and a night that alternate; his body has a physiological structure that imposes the need for sleep—but how much and when? Probably during many millenia man slept much more than he does now, presumably at night, and more during the winter than in the summer. Recent technological developments in illumination have changed all this and left man free with respect to the time of day and relatively free with regard to the number of hours. (A curious case is the natural situation in the polar zones.) Not only is man mortal, but he lives more or less a determined number of years and counts on that probable and uncertain horizon. And his life is articulated according to a precise scheme of individual ages and historical generations, which will be changed as soon as the increase in longevity initiated some decades ago has been generalized and consolidated.

There is another decisive dimension of human life that equally belongs to the empirical structure, a dimension that philosophy has always confronted in an inadequate way: the sexed condition of man, which until now has been wandering in search of its place in theory. Being sexed does not appear in the analytical theory as a requisite of human life. Heidegger has been reproached because the *Dasein* is asexual. And why should it not be? Human life could be nonsexual; man might be able to reproduce in some other way or not reproduce at all, since the continuity and succession of men also belongs to the empirical structure, not to the conditions of the reality "human life." But it would be ridiculous to think of the sexed condition as a mere "natural" element proceeding from the body or as a simple factitive situation of each individual; it belongs to the empirical structure, with its dual character of stability and historicity. I believe that it is only from this perspective that the sexed condition of man can be made comprehensible and that the multitude of problems, which usually appear bristling with difficulties, can be understood.

All this is, of course, not the geography of that unexplored territory (in which we exist without knowing it), nor even a map of it. It is no more than might have been brought back to their native land by mariners who did not set foot on an island they saw through the fog: its position, determined with the astrolabe, an uncertain sketch of its shape, and perhaps some floating branches or a bird (an owl, perhaps) that had perched on the mast, between two lights.

NOTES

1. Cf. Julián Marías, *Ortega y la idea de la razón vital* (Madrid, 1948), also in *La Escuela de Madrid* (Buenos Aires, 1959); and *Introducción a la filosofía* (Madrid, 1947) [*Obras*, II], in English translation as *Reason and Life* (Yale University Press, 1956).
2. *Introducción a la filosofía* [*Reason and Life*], chapters III and IV.
3. *Miguel de Unamuno* (Madrid, 1943), translated into English (Harvard University Press, 1966). Also see my article "La obra de Unamuno: un problema de filosofía" (1938), in the volume *La Escuela de Madrid* (Buenos Aires, 1959).
4. In *El método histórico de las generaciones* (Madrid, 1949), pp. 155–156. Also see my communication to the International Congress of Philosophy in Lima, Peru (1951).
5. *Topics*, I, 4–5.
6. Introduction to the *Categories* of Aristotle, 5.
7. See, for example, Signoriello's *Lexicon philosophico-theologicum* (Naples, 1906), pp. 276–277.

CHAPTER EIGHT

PSYCHIATRY FROM THE POINT OF VIEW OF PHILOSOPHY

You may blame Dr. Lafora for the lacuna that today's lesson is going to signify in the course you are pursuing. I am somewhat encouraged only by the fact that a friendly voice and the silent solitude of the Atlantic come between us, because this lecture is an unmistakable case of quackery, with all the inevitable consequences. I mean that, not only am I a stranger to the medical and psychiatric disciplines, but my ignorance of them is profound and complete. In spite of this, and in spite of his knowing this, my good friend Dr. Lafora has insisted on my addressing you one day, and his cordial persistence reached me even when I was a thousand leagues from Madrid and . . . from the theme—when I was occupied with Cervantes in the midst of the snows of New England. What reason is there then that I have given in, that I am exposing myself to the charge of having caused you to lose an hour of your lives? Perhaps my renewed contact with our divine fool Don Quijote has brought me into unexpected proximity to his labors. But, above all, I have thought that, since all of you are already in possession of all the psychiatric and medical science that one could wish, perhaps my intervention might bring you exactly that something which up to now you have been missing: ignorance. And I have always believed that ignorance, well administered, usually bears some unsuspected fruit.

I have been requested to speak from the point of view of the philosopher about the new advances in psychiatry. I must point out that having spent something more than twenty years occupying myself hardly at all with anything other than philosophy, and having written a few books in whose titles this word usually appears, does not authorize me to assume, to usurp, that point of view, which rightly belongs only to an authentic philosopher who, in addition to being such a philosopher, would also have a genuine knowledge of psychiatry—who would be a philosopher doubling as a psychiatrist. Such a strange and improbable creature, such a rare bird does exist perhaps, but certainly I am not it. Are we then confronted with the presumed capacity that is sometimes attributed to the philosopher, according to which he is able to talk about anything under the sun? Is this the way things are? That depends on what you mean by *speak*. If what you mean is to know, to inform, to define—no. If what is meant is to question—then, yes. The philosopher has to know what to be guided by with respect to reality, and this implies also, from a certain point of view, with regard to all realities. But this does not mean that he necessarily has to *know* them all. Perhaps, just the contrary, not to know them, to recognize them as problematical and doubtful, even to the point of declaring them formally unknowable—unknowable or doubtful, but accounting for them in a reasonable way: this is precisely what is meant by knowing what to be guided by.

Philosophy has to know, then, *where* to put things or, what is the same thing, in what zone of reality they are to be found. Thus, if we are talking about the point of view of the philosopher in the presence of psychiatry and I am obliged to abuse this point of view by assuming it, then the only thing that can be expected of me is a series of questions. Perhaps not even that much, perhaps nothing more than a questioning glance around me, searching . . . where to locate that discipline and, above all, the problematical and confusing object it treats of and with whom it is involved. Because psychiatry has the rare privilege that—if, like all scientific disciplines, it treats *of* an *object*—it consists *at the same time*, and inseparably, in involving itself *with* a *subject*. Do you see how, right from the start, things are beginning to get complicated?

Psychiatry, it seems, is the medical discipline of the soul. But the soul, as a scientific term, is something exceedingly perplexing, and nobody ever knows clearly what he is talking about when he talks about the soul. The profound crisis in psychology is widely recognized, for that discipline is in dire need of a radical reformulation of its problems, which can only come from some really creative theoretical mind, if by chance such a one is to be found. But the trouble (or the advantage, depending on one's outlook) is that psychiatry is not only a theoretical discipline but the practical and vital action of a doctor confronted with his patient. And he cannot hold back, he cannot suspend judgment, delay his decisions, or put things off while involving himself with the problems of fundamentals. Like life itself, he cannot wait. Whatever may be the state of psychology and its uncertainties, something has to be done now with this distressed brother of ours who needs our help.

This is psychiatry's servitude and its certainty. Because there, definitely, is its object: in that anguished man, in that estranged man, whom we do not understand or who does not understand himself. Suddenly we realize that what we call soul, psyche, cerebral and nervous structures, psychological types, psychosis, neurosis, complexes—all those are only theories, elaborations of what is properly the theme or object of psychiatry: what it is that makes this man sick, what is happening to him. And this is his life, according to the strictest technical definition. Thus it is the *life* of this man that interests us.

As I see things, all the efforts of psychiatry during the last fifty years primarily constitute the attempt to reach this point—or, in other words, to be psychiatry in a more rigorous sense. (Parenthetically, this is the direction of all contemporary sciences, whose famous "crisis of principles" means the efforts which would make logic really be logic, physics, physics, and even history, history.) Psychiatry has continually oscillated between basing itself on somatic structures and converting itself into a psychological, perhaps into a psychogogical, discipline. When, during the nineteenth century, the distinction between the sciences of nature and the sciences of the spirit (or their variants) was elaborated, it seemed that clarity had been achieved. But at the same time there was a feeling that those two points of view, whether taken in isolation or when merely added together, were not without deficiencies. Or, rather, it was seen that adding them together was precisely the problem. Strictly speaking, the knowledge of the human body, especially of the cerebrum, was too sketchy. Only during the last two decades have substantial advances been made, and neurologists know how much is still missing. And this should bring us to exercise extreme caution in questions of method. For the failure of psychiatry as mere somatic medicine demonstrates *not only* an error in method but a lack of quality in a medical sense. On the other hand, the impression of "innocuousness" produced in the clinician by many attempts to pose his problems from the point of view of the "sciences of the spirit" is also not enough to disqualify this possibility and to lead him to cling to somatic investigation and somatic therapy as the *only* path.

For the time being, we have to ask of both these tendencies that they abide by four requisites: (1) not, in any case, to go beyond the evidence in that case; (2) not to confuse empirical investigation with some embryonic theory, for example, a mechanistic hypothesis or a definite "theory of the spirit"; (3) to recognize that both these methodological orientations are based on disciplines whose assumptions they accept but which they are incapable of giving reasons for, in other words, that they are not self-governing mechanisms; (4) to remain disposed to alter or abandon their point of view whenever reality may require it.

The sciences of the spirit are not self-governing mechanisms, nor are they sufficient. As soon as one really tries to get inside them, it has been seen that they are involved with problematical concepts whose fundamentation can only be found in a metaphysical theory of human life. The philosophy of the last thirty years, under different names and with better or worse fortune, has been devoted to the development of this theory. But what turns out to be symptomatic and interesting is the fact that the most extraordinary and important creation in the field of psychiatry *sensu stricto* in the twentieth century (psychoanalysis, naturally) has had to concentrate its attention, underneath the psychological structures and their particular anomalies, on what must be its true object: life, in the biographical sense. It makes little difference that psychoanalysis has improvised problematical explanations and principles that are completely insufficient—when not wholly erroneous. The theoretical limitations of psychoanalytical doctrines (inevitable, of course, in its origins and in its initial stages), the fact that an attempt was made to produce an interpretation of human life based on the nebulous notion of the "unconscious" and supported by such fragmentary, derived, and barely relevant ideas as that of the *libido* or of the will to power—all this neither detracts from nor obscures the creative and really decisive idea that one must look within the biography for the primary root of pathological changes in personality and that the first thing to do is to narrate a history.* It is well that the violent reaction that is going to be produced—that is already being produced—against a reinvigoration of psychoanalysis, which is just as much overgrown as it is in many ways inept, does not have anything to do with what is ingenious and undeniable in Freud's conception. Certainly it is not possible to accept the solutions of the psychoanalytic schools, nor their explanatory schemes. However, something quite different occurs with the more substantive issue: the formulation of the problem. Or, if greater precision is desired, one would have to say that even that formulation is not valid. What has to be retained is the "locus" or sphere of that formulation. This, yes.

During the last few years, some theoretical attempts have been made to situate the themes of psychiatry itself in a new and better framework. Leaving aside what has been called the "logical psychoanalysis" of Wittgenstein (simply to make clear its meaning and its historical justification would turn out to be much too complicated), something has to be said about "existential psychoanalysis," as it has been formulated or, rather, postulated by Sartre in the concluding chapters of his *L'être et le néant*—that book in which, in a very curious way, originality and triteness, direct acuity and obtuse error, innovation and backwardness, literary delicacy and gibberish, ingeniousness and the climate where yawning flourishes, are all interwoven.

Sartre's point of departure is the idea that human reality is announced and defined by the ends it pursues. But as soon as he sets out he gets waylaid by two errors. According to the first of them, the empirical psychologist, when defining man by his desires, "remains a victim of the substantialist illusion" and sees desire as a "content of con-

* [The Spanish here, *contar una historia*, may also mean "to tell a story"—Trans.]

sciousness" that is *in* man; for Sartre, however, desires are not "little psychic entities that inhabit consciousness," but "consciousness itself in its original projective and transcendent structure, since it is in principle consciousness of something." The second error consists in believing that psychological investigation comes to an end when the concrete confluence of empirical desires has been arrived at—man would then be a bundle of tendencies with a certain interaction and organization. Nothing of this is sufficient. It is necessary to arrive at what is genuinely irreducible—that is, something whose irreducibility would be evident to us and would satisfy us. Neither dust nor substance, Sartre adds. What is involved is a kind of unity of which unity in substance is only a caricature: a *personal* unity. For all possible subjects of biography, being is "to unify oneself in the world." The person discovers himself in the initial project that constitutes him; in every inclination or tendency he expresses himself as a whole.

This is not the time to evaluate this conception with regard to what may be new in it, though it should be pointed out that many of its central ideas have been sounded for many years in Spanish. Nor is this the occasion to stop to examine the change that Sartre imposes on the word "project" when he writes that "what more than anything else makes the fundamental project of human reality conceivable is the fact that man is the being that *projects being God."* What interests us at the moment is to make clear the meaning of the method that Sartre calls "existential psychoanalysis" and which consists in deciphering and interpreting behaviors, tendencies, and inclinations. The source of that psychoanalysis is the idea that man is a totality, not a collection or sum, and that, consequently, everything in him is *revelatory*, since in any behavior, even the most insignificant, man expresses himself as a whole. The aim is to decipher the empirical behaviors of man and conceptually to define them. Its point of departure is experience; its point of support, the preontological and fundamental understanding that man has of the human person; its method, finally, is comparative, since each human action symbolizes a fundamental choice and at the same time masquerades behind its occasional characteristics and its historical opportunity. Comparison makes it possible to discover the unique revelation that all behaviors express in diverse ways.

Sartre points out how his existential psychoanalysis both coincides with and differs from the psychoanalysis of Freud and his disciples. The two coincide in considering the manifestations of psychic life as symbolizations of the fundamental and global structures of the person; they are in agreement in that there are no primary data—neither inclinations nor characters. There is nothing anterior to the original appearance of human freedom, anterior to history in Freudianism. The human being is a perpetual historicalization, and both methods try to discover, more than statistical and constant facts, the meaning, the orientation, and the vicissitudes of that history. What is involved for them is an underlying attitude *anterior to all logic*; what is being sought is the *complex* or the *fundamental choice*. From this follows the basic "illogism" and irrationalism of both methods, which seek a prelogical synthesis of the totality of the existent. Just as one, so the other believes that the subject does not stand in a privileged position. Freud resorts to the unconscious; Sartre appeals to consciousness, but he points out that consciousness is not knowledge and he uses the expression "mystery in the full light of day."

Up to this point the areas of coincidence and agreement cover what is essential. But then Sartre indicates the differences and, consequently, the distinguishing characteristics of the existential analysis that he postulates. This can be summarized in a few words. Sartre reproaches "empirical" psychoanalysis with "coming to a decision" on the basis of what is irreducible for it (*libido* or the will to power) instead of "letting the decision announce itself in a self-evident intuition." Choice, on the contrary, takes into account its own original contingency; thus, its contingency is the other side of its freedom. In place of a primary libido, which *later on* is differentiated into complexes and behaviors, there is a unique and absolutely concrete choice right at the beginning. For human reality, Sartre concludes, there is no difference between existing and choosing oneself, and the choice can always be revoked by the subject. The final outcome is not to gain *consciousness* (Sartre starts from consciousness) but to gain *knowledge*. Existential psychoanalysis is defined as "a method directed toward bringing to the light, in a rigorously objective form, the subjective choice by means of which each person makes of himself a person, that is, which leads him to announce to himself what he is." And it is well to remember that in another place in his book, Sartre states that an insane man is doing nothing else but fulfilling the human condition in his own way.

This formulation of the problem suffers from two deficiencies or, rather, from two types of deficiencies. On the one hand, those arising out of the absence of any indication of a *modus operandi* that would give an effective methodological character to what is called existentialist psychoanalysis. On the other hand, those proceeding from the philosophical doctrine that serves as its basis. I cannot go into detail here, but at least I want to note some of the deficiencies that are most closely related to our theme. Two of them are the major fears that condition the metaphysics of the existentialists: one, the fear of the "nature" or "essence" of man; the other, the fear of "logic." Both of them lead Sartre to place the whole emphasis on the idea of *choix* or choice, to the point of identifying it wholly with existing, and to give to that fundamental choice a *pre-logical* character. I repeat that I am not able to go into an analysis of this philosophy, but let me point out that the dimension of intellectual primitivism that is so frequently to be found in Sartre appears here, and that this consists in his taking the notions of traditional philosophy (at times from phenomenology and at other times from Scholasticism) and inverting them. On occasion I have said that what we are dealing with is an *ontologie traditionnelle à rebours,* a traditional ontology against the grain, more than with an attempt at genuine innovation and original formulation of the problems. In view of the fact that man has no nature *in the sense that things do,* it is denied that man has anything to do with nature. In view of the fact that the idea of essence, as it appears in Scholasticism or in Husserl, is inadequate, all essence in man is rejected. Since the logic that is expounded in textbooks is insufficient, the irreducible ground of human life is declared to be "prelogical" (with the same frivolity that Lévy-Bruhl shows when he talks about primitive man). Thus Sartre arrives at a notion as paradoxical as that of a "prelogical choice," as if such a thing might be possible; as if the root of human life were *choice* (when this word is given a precise conceptual meaning); as if, finally, one could actually make a *prelogical* choice, that is, prior to *giving reasons* for that very choice —something quite different, of course, from utilizing definite syllogisms or such concrete logical artifices.

I am going to try to state the problem exactly as I see it, as I believe that, were I a psychiatrist, the task would be presented to me, of having to deal with a man complaining of some mental illness, with a sick man who had come to consult me. (Although, it must be asked parenthetically, is this probable? Because the curious thing is that in Spain, as distinct from other countries, hardly anyone ever *goes* to the psychiatrist; they are *brought* there. And this, it might be said in passing, creates for the Spanish psychiatrist an extremely strange situation that carries with it the consequence that his relation with the sick person begins with presuppositions quite different from the relation the somatic clinician has with his patient.) Let us imagine that I now have before me a man, presumably diseased. To begin with, he is here before me in the present moment, and that is all. The psychiatrist cannot, however, let himself be guided by the pure present instant, because in that way man would be unintelligible. In order to understand a man we have to invent him, by which I mean that we have to imagine or reconstruct the novel of his life; only through being inserted into that is this gesture, this word, this silence that I now have in front of me comprehensible. Life is, according to Ortega's old definition, "what we do and what happens to us." Life is given to me, but it is not given to me ready-made, but I have to make it myself, instant by instant. I have to do something now, by means of something and for the sake of something, in order to live. For this reason, the instant is not an intemporal point, but within it there is an essential conjunction of present, past, and future, which constitutes the frame and structure of our life. That structure might be formulated by saying that the past and the future are *present* in my life, in the "by means of" and the "for the sake of" that are within each one of my acts. In my act at this moment the past is present because the reason for what I am doing is only to be found in what I have done before, and the future is present in the project that constitutes me, from which all the meaning and the very possibility of my life hang. The vital instant is not a point without extension, but implies a temporal environment, which, in its turn, is systematically related to the totality of the life that is spread over a temporal span. Thus the only way of understanding a man is to imagine, to relive, or to prelive the novel of his life; thus the only real way of talking about his life is to *recount* it.

The form of statement in which concrete life becomes accessible is narration, the story. For this reason, and only for this reason, all human behavior is significant and revelatory. A word, a gesture, a mistake, an error, a decision, a silence, a forgetting—in each of them the whole temporal frame of life is implicated, the entire biography, including the future in the form of intention, acting there in order to cause that gesture to occur. Our dealings with our fellow man, even with a stranger, presuppose that constant interpretation and divination by which we construct and invent the biographies of our contemporaries, in this way giving meaning to the human horizon that surrounds us, in this way making community life possible.

But the psychiatrist, in addition to that reconstruction which the expressive character of gesture makes possible, has a need for the imagined biography to possess a foundation *in re*. For that reason he takes up a pen and paper and is ready to write. What? This is precisely the problem.

More or less, a "clinical history." As you see, theory is usually less valuable than practice, and actual practice in the medical profession has anticipated by many centuries the theoretical understanding of the reasons for what it has been doing all along. A Freudian psychoanalyst of whatever persuasion propels himself toward the past of the sick person and begins a retrospective exploration of his biography. The presumed existential psychiatrist directs himself rather toward the future. For the first, the most important thing would be to discover some special moment in the past of the sick person, a moment that at a certain time had been cast off into the unconscious and from there began to exercise a disturbing influence. The second would try to discover the fundamental and constitutive choice of the sick person, symbolized in his accessible and empirical behaviors. There can be no doubt that both methods are, in principle, right and even that *both* are necessary. But what turns out to be difficult is precisely the task of integrating them. But there is something even more important.

Supposing that the uniting of both these modes of exploration—one directed toward the future, the other directed toward the past—had, by some stroke of good fortune, been brought about (leaving aside—what is not insignificant—the theoretical difficulties raised by the differing presuppositions of the two attitudes, by which I mean the idea of the *unconscious* and the idea that the fundamental project is a matter of *choice*), we must still ask whether one can really begin here, because the individual biography is accessible only by beginning with a general structure. Certainly our dealings with our fellow man carry us to a definite level of comprehension right from the beginning. Sartre speaks, in an expression that is excessively reminiscent of Heidegger and not very enlightening, of the "preontological and fundamental understanding that man has of the human person." However, I think that what is involved is something simple enough that it could be explained if we were to take a deep breath at this point. But the psychiatrist, if he wishes to create a science, cannot content himself with the irresponsible understanding that just anybody has of some anybody else. Our intelligence of our fellow man in the most trivial dealings, and even of ourselves, presupposes a definite foreshadowing of the knowledge whose fully developed form is what may be called the abstract or analytical theory of human life. Only on the basis of this theory will the comprehension of concrete human life, real or fictitious, become possible.

But this is, at one and the same time, too much and too little. This abstract theory, for the same reason that it allows for the comprehension of *all* possible human life—

of whatever age, sex, or condition, of whatever epoch or country, including imaginary life—since it includes all the requisites or conditions under which what is called "human life" may be given, is not sufficient for coming to terms with the particular characteristics of this sick man I have in front of me. Thus, we would have to go to his individual and very concrete life. But this, which is in summary the more or less clear aim of all psychoanalysis, is this possible? I believe that between the analytical theory and the concrete narration of an individual life a decisive intermediate stage is interposed, to which nobody has paid any attention, which obstinately thrusts itself into view. I alluded to this in a fugitive way several years ago in a passage in my book on *El método histórico de las generaciones* (Madrid, 1949), pages 155–156; and returned to this theme in a communication read at the International Congress of Philosophy in Lima, Peru. I would like to repeat some paragraphs from that communication:

> It must not be forgotten that the analytical theory of human life is not anthropology; it comprises only those requisites that are given in all life and that make it possible, the abstract relations or *blank spaces* (*leere Stellen*) that have to be filled with circumstantial and concrete contents in order to be actual knowledge of realities. Between these two elements the *empirical structure* intervenes—which is empirical, but a structure; which is a structure, but empirical. Its reality corresponds to the field of possible human variation in history, a variation that is conditioned by an essential stability. Man has to live in a world, but not necessarily in this one nor at this time. Corporeality is essential to human life, but not exactly this form of corporeality. Terrestrial life is finite, man is mortal, subject to the rhythm of different ages and to aging; but the normal longevity of man belongs only to the empirical structure, and through this to the rhythm of historical life and of generations. All these things have

changed or will change; at least, they could change without man's ceasing to be man, although the general scheme of his life would be different.

Thus, it is necessary to determine the boundaries between what is natural and what is historical. It has been usual to attribute to "human nature" many historical, acquired, but enduring, things that are incorporated into the empirical structure of our life. Historical constants do not exist, but at most enduring elements, permanent elements if you wish—that is, elements that endure through the whole length of history and remain within it. In principle, it would be possible for certain ingredients of human life "to last" from Adam to Judgment Day without, on that account, ceasing to be historical.

The empirical structure is the concrete form of our circumstantiality. Man is not only in the world, but in *this* world; not only is he a corporeal and incarnated reality, but he possesses this corporeal structure and not another. Not only is he mortal, but he lives a definite number of years—at least he counts on a horizon of a certain duration—and his life is articulated according to a precise scheme of individual ages and historical generations. A decisive dimension of human life whose philosophical formulation has always been inadequate also belongs to the empirical structure: the sexed condition of man, which is a decisive component in his life that until now has wandered in search of its place in theory. Being sexed does not appear in the analytical theory as a requisite of human life; but it would be ridiculous to think of the sexed condition as a mere "natural" element proceeding from the body or as a simple *de facto* situation of each individual. It belongs to the empirical structure, with its dual character of stability and historicity. And I believe that it is only from this perspective that it can be made comprehensible.

In my judgment, all this would have to be taken as the concrete point of departure. Only from the point of view of a precise image of the empirical structure of human life can the psychiatrist, in a rigorous sense, consider the individual life that he has in front of him. Note that the word that comes up from time to time, in spite of all attempts to avoid it, is the word "normality" (or "abnormality"). In view of the fact that it is not easy to accept an invariant "human nature" of the sort that could be believed in during the eighteenth century, one falls into a kind of nominalism in which there can be nothing but individual cases, all of them with the same claims to legitimacy; and within such a scheme the notions of normal and abnormal are dissolved. The most that one can rely on is a vague idea of statistical frequency that has very little utility. Only in relation to a precise idea of the empirical structure of life in each circumstance can a rigorous and productive meaning be given to the notion of normality. Only on this basis can the trajectory of individual lives be sketched and the precise characteristics of each biography be made intelligible.

It is an error with incalculable consequences to believe that an isolated fact—for example, a childhood or adolescent experience—can have any significance apart from a structure, since it is only within this structure that it is constituted as such and ceases being a mere physical fact, to be converted into a biographical incident. It is no less erroneous nor less serious to believe that the vital project is an absolute development—that is, independent and without reason—which would lead one to believe that any vital project is possible in any circumstance, which is very far from being the truth. On occasion I have tried to explain the relations between what is personal and what is historical in one's vocation in a way that demonstrates how it is not possible to choose knight errantry as a vocation unless one is crazy, as happened with Don Quijote. But this vague and precipitous diagnosis, "being crazy," is the popular and direct expression for what I just got through saying in a more technical way, that the vocation of knight errant is impossible today, and so it was also in the sixteenth century. For this reason, the first thing Don Quijote had to do was to escape from his world, act with violence against it, and convert it into another—where flocks of sheep were armies, inns were castles, and a cavern in La Mancha was the cave of Montesinos.

Consider then, since this is almost always what is most important, the idea of himself that a man has and which is usually the root of his possible psychic disturbance. Understand me well. When I say "root," I do not mean *cause;* I am not trying to determine the etiology of mental diseases and say that they proceed from the idea that the subject has of himself and not from a cerebral or medullary lesion, for example. I mean that the disease *as disease*—that is, as something that happens to the man and constitutes his "being sick," not the mere organic state of his body—*takes root* in a fundamental way in that idea that the man has of himself. The fact that a man feels himself to be old or of weak intelligence or sexually inadequate or a coward or a failure in society or dominated by his wife; the fact that a woman thinks of herself as lacking in refinement or ugly or without femininity or "wasted" or without freedom or oppressed—all this depends on a certain structure, in relation to which those ways of being are constituted, as well as the consciousness of them. I am certain that in periods of tranquillity, such as the nineteenth century was, especially during the second half, many men lived in contentment with their level of personal courage who in other periods would have felt abnormal and secretly distressed. It is evident that the significance of thirty years to a single woman is not the same thing in 1830 as in 1930—nor is it the same in 1952.

All this leads to the idea that the individual aspiration of each person—which is realized to some degree or other and

thus allows for a certain combination of happiness and unhappiness, which is more or less authentic, more or less in
accord with the social or personal situation in which one
finds oneself—is always cut out according to a more ample
general pattern that is one of the broad ways in which the
empirical structure of human life is made real, one of the
broad historical forms in which this structure makes itself
actual. Only within this frame can the psychiatrist situate
the present sick man's biography, which he labors to reconstruct. Within that sphere the disease as such is constituted
and, consequently, the relation of the doctor with the
patient. And, as I noted at the beginning, there is a rigorous
theoretical significance in that relation, since the intellectual treatment of the theme or object of psychiatry is inseparable from the human relation or the medical treatment
of the subject who is that same man, and, to begin with, is
inseparable from the idea of disease itself, I mean the situation of being diseased. Are these all the same: disease in a
situation involving magic, or being mysteriously condemned, or an immoral condition, or a microbic invasion?
I alluded before to the fact, which seemed to be of only
anecdotal interest, that the clients of Spanish psychiatrists
rarely come of their own accord to be examined (such as
happens in stomach ailments, in earache, or in circulatory
troubles), but are most frequently brought by their fami-
lies, and thus at a definite phase in the course of the disease.
Does this not reveal a peculiar relation of the Spaniard to
mental disease, which is not the same as that he has to mere
somatic ailments, which is also quite different from that
which the American patient has to mental affliction? I was
going to say "to the *same* mental affliction," but at the point
of doing so it occurred to me that it is not the same, since
precisely that fact, that difference between going on Fri-
days to see the psychoanalyst and being carried there one
dramatic day following a painful family conference, means

that we have two completely different human realities that, strictly speaking, are two incomparable ailments of the same "nosological type" as are described and characterized in a treatise on psychiatry.

This is the location or sphere where that fabulous theme called psychiatry is presented to my ignorance—that is, the localization of that reality which is the "soul" or psyche from a definite point of view or, in other words, the localization of this aspect or facet of human life. But it is exactly at this point that the problems begin. I am not referring, of course, to professional problems of psychiatry proper (that is, to "intrapsychiatric" problems), of which I have to keep myself prudently and respectfully apart; I am referring to certain *theoretical* problems that I believe to be prior to the practice of any possible therapeutic technique and which might be looked upon as a structure anterior to psychiatry itself. A clear vision of these problems would have an undoubted methodological value; it would be equivalent to a new set of instruments of a different kind. And this is not a superfluous thing, for psychiatry, like all other medical disciplines, is a technique—that is, a skill in doing something, a knowledge whose purpose is the handling of certain realities. However, it is usually forgotten that handling *sensu stricto*—literally, handling things with the hand—is not the only, but is *always* preceded by another more subtle way of handling, which is the *mental* handling of those same realities. As I see things, it would be advisable for psychiatry to provide itself with a repertory of mental instruments—that is, *concepts*—with which it would be able to approach the sick person as he really is in order to perform upon him its effective curative action.

To say the same thing in a few words, it would try to come to understand the real situation of the sick person. It would have to relate his life to the general framework of an empirical structure, in the sense that I have already explained; but with this, which has to be the beginning, nothing more has been done than to begin. It is necessary now to take one more step and determine his *concrete* situation. But here the greatest difficulty arises. Because it would be chimerical to try to determine a man's situation "objectively," apart from his aim in life. All the facts that might be enumerated—sex, age, physical and intellectual endowments, social and economic condition, nationality, epoch—acquire effective value as *elements in a situation* only when onto them one projects . . . a project, an aspiration, a vital program. Only from the point of view of aspiring to be a dancer does articular rheumatism acquire its precise significance; only snobbery makes a person look upon the happiness and contentment of a family of wealthy shopkeepers in an unfavorable light; the hope of being a Don Juan causes a man to view his own wife from a particularly uncomfortable perspective; and the faith or lack of faith in the prospect of an enduring life is what truly determines the reality of cancer in one who has it. Thus, the situation receives its own being from the influence upon its components that emanate from a form of individual human life. As a consequence of the interaction between the two, the authentic concrete aspiration, the effective vital program, is constituted, and with it the actual outline of a biography.

But this too is not sufficient. Every human act is determined by a constellation of all the available possibilities. What a man *does* has meaning only in relation to what he *can* do. A reconstruction of a man's sphere of possibilities (or a woman's, of course; and I expressly emphasize this because there are usually enormous qualitative and quantitative differences) is indispensable in order to understand his life. But even with this, it is still not enough. Among the things that are possible, a man chooses; from all his possibilities, some and only some are called into existence. It seems (and this is the impression that is usually extracted from existential philosophers) that the person remains ascribed to his choice, separated from everything else. However, this is in a strict sense untrue. To choose is to *prefer*, and to prefer means nothing but placing or bringing forward, to cause one thing to come forward and precede the rest. Thus, it is an essentially relative action that cannot be understood if one pays attention only to what is preferred, but only by taking into consideration, *at the same time*, the two terms of preference—by which I mean the *preferred* and (if I may be allowed the expression) the *postferred*, the postponed. This means that each ingredient on the horizon of possibilities functions within a context. And the fact of preference does not prove that the preferred is *desired*, but only that it is pre-ferred to the other possibilities. And for this reason it might very well not *directly* express the vocation or aim of the one who chooses, as when somebody condemned to death prefers hanging to being shot or as, in a fire, one prefers leaping out of the window to perishing in the flames. And, on the other hand, the possibilities that are excluded and disregarded might very well be desired, at times in the most violent and painful way. I have said on occasion that for man being is *to be this and not something else*. And this is but one of many possible ways of expressing the inevitability of human unhappiness.

This intrinsic limitation is what determines the actual course that a biography follows. Such a mental labor alone would place the psychiatrist in a position from which to establish efficacious contact with the sick person. And within the scheme thus achieved the disease would appear in its own true light.

Upon arriving at this point I would have liked to bring your weariness to an end. But it seems to me impossible to leave on a note of equivocation. Maybe, then, you will pardon a few more words. It may perhaps have been

thought that, when assuming the point of view of philosophy, I forgot about the body and tried to attribute a
biographical nature to the disease, as if it might have originated solely from the way in which the man senses himself
within his life, from the vicissitudes of his life, from the
drama that it constitutes. Nothing could be further from my
intentions than such forgetfulness. The disease may very
well come out of organic change, including a trauma of
external origin. Nothing could be less "biographical." But
when we talk about psychiatry and about psychic or mental
disease, we are saying, without saying it, that what is involved is the *biographical* significance of the disease. It has
also been discovered—you know this much better than I
do—that an ulcer of the stomach may have an etiology and
consequently a significance that is biographical. But we call
psychic or mental not so much those diseases that have a
definite "psychic cause" as those whose reality *as diseases* is
primarily biographical. Thus, the amputation of a leg—
when it turns out not to be biographically assimilable, when
psychologically the incised tissue does not heal over properly (if you will allow me the metaphor)—is converted into
a psychic disease. It is the amputation itself that *is* the psychic disease. Because an amputation is not the cutting away
of certain fleshy and bony masses at some point on the
planet, but the removal of a member that belongs, not to a
body, but to a man—naturally by way of his body.

And that is all. Please excuse this intervention in which
I have wandered so far from my spatial localization and so
far from the theme on account of my ignorance of it. I have
only been able to contribute to the course what I have:
difficulties and problems. I have acted out in front of you a
glance at the horizon, looking for a place in which to situate
psychiatry, looking especially for a place in which to
locate the man who is its theme—and, in passing, the other

man who practices it. If I have caused you to look too, this will be the only possibility that my intervention in this course, in addition to being impertinent, may not be wholly in vain.

CHAPTER NINE

THE CORPOREAL STRUCTURE OF HUMAN LIFE

Human life has many aspects. It is essential to it that we cannot say how many, since they are not "given." What is interesting is the plurality, the fact that it has "sides." Greek, a language (as it turned out) especially apt for philosophy, constantly used particles that are almost always omitted in translation, for if we change μὲν and δέ into "from one side," "from the other side," and "through one part," "through another part," these awkward formulas become insufferable. Those brief syllables *mèn* and *dé*, without overburdening the diction, gently remind us that there are "sides," "directions," or "orientations" to life, that life is multilateral, *mehr-seitig* (as Dilthey said), *many-sided*.

But it would be a mistake to take these aspects in isolation; at least, to do so would signify that they are not being taken in a philosophical way—as aspects *of life*. If one talks about the world, the body, time, or about happiness, *and nothing more*, one is not philosophizing. It is something else again if one treats of being in the world,* corporeality, temporality, or happiness as aspects *of* life and thus in relation to its *structure*, as dimensions of this structure. Only

*[I use "being in the world" or "being of the world" as equivalents for *mundanidad*, since the more obvious one-word equivalents have connotations alien to Marías's thought, while the only disadvantage of the phrase I have chosen is the undue emphasis that may come to be placed on "being" if this word is mistakenly abstracted out of the phrase in which it is used—Trans.]

from the point of view of life can those aspects be seen as they concretely are in reality and with a radical vision of them—that is, seen from the root.

Thus, I am not going to talk here about the body, but about the corporeal structure of life. This distinction is highly pertinent, since it is precisely in consideration of the body that thoughts concerning what life itself is are usually led astray. In fact, if one begins with an idea of "life" as something in which diverse "forms of life" are to be lodged —the modes of being of different living beings, corporeal (plants, animals, man) or incorporeal (angels, God)—one will not understand a thing, since one is taking a certain abstract characteristic and making the meaning of the word "life" out of it, thereby putting in place of life a theory or interpretation, which might be true but which would forever remain a theory. One usually thinks of biology, especially when the body is mentioned, but this is not what we are dealing with here, since biology is a theory made by biologists, and its reality is, naturally, a consequence of their *life*. As Ortega always said, the primary meaning of life is that of *biographical life*. But when talking about biographical life, we must take care to avoid a sophistry that has become quite frequent: forgetting all about life and surreptitiously replacing it with a "trajectory," which is only one factor in that life. What we are concerned with is not "biographical trajectory" nor "biography," but biographical *life*—that is, a reality that includes among its characteristics the fact of being biographical. To such a degree is it impossible to identify life with its trajectory, because pertaining to it in an essential way are *several* trajectories, not only the actual trajectory, but all those that have been successively possible at each moment and whose extraordinarily complex interweavement constitutes the true reality of a life. To confuse life with its trajectory is to assume that life is identical with one of its dimensions or, rather, not only that, but with a mere fragment of this dimension, a fragment that does not have any significance at all apart from the rest, apart from all the other trajectories that have not been made real, that have not actually come to pass.

All thought that begins with theories (not to say scientific theories) is lacking in radical nature and disregards the *reality*, "life." This becomes especially serious when the somatic factor is being considered. Through the whole course of the history of philosophy we have seen how serenely the functions of personal life have been explained down to the last detail in ways based on biological or physiological theories that science has a short time later corrected or modified so substantially that, by that time, no one would any longer think of trying to base any kind of adequate explanation on them. These explanations, when such theories have not been discarded outright, have been found to be erroneous and useless on account of later discoveries that invalidated them.

This does not mean that much of what is biologically true has nothing to say to philosophy. It has a great deal to say, although not directly—that is, not as "knowledge," not as a portion or presupposition of the philosophical knowledge of the body, but as a heuristic principle that induces philosophy to think in a certain direction and, especially, as an ingredient within the effective interpretation that one possesses of the body, which conditions the way of "living" it and using it and, consequently, conditions its reality. Recall, for example, the profound change that the theory of microbes introduced into the manner in which corporeal realities were experienced; the vision of microbes as "little animals," which was the predominant one, caused everybody to almost feel them running about on the surface and on the inside of their organisms, carrying with them a tinge of danger and threat. The recent irruption of the idea of viruses in pathology, in going beyond the previous image, has in a certain sense pushed to one side the idea of "contamination" that dominated a century and, paradoxically, has "cleaned up" our image of the body at the same time that antibiotics, on the one hand, and the image of microbial flora, on the other, have almost completely destroyed the experience (in itself so recent) in which the organism was believed to be populated by strange animalcules to which it was difficult not to attribute a minimum of quasi personality, as we do with all macroscopic animals. All this has an undoubted significance for a philosophy that would confront reality and not merely schemes abstracted from it. However, the attitude of the *parvenu* of science has to be avoided. This is the attitude which believes that the man of a few years ago, or (in any case) of a few centuries ago, "did not know" what the body is, or what water is, or what fire is, or in general what the world is. Of course, there is a certain sense in which it is true that he did not know, but then neither do we, and that is why we go on questioning. But there is another sense in which he knew these things as immediately and as efficaciously as we and all other men of our time, or of any other time, are able to know them: to the degree that they actually are vital *realities*.

It should not be necessary to point out that when I refer to the corporeal structure of human life, I am not speaking of this as the radical reality (which is *my* life), nor even of metaphysics insofar as it is the theory of human life, the necessary and thus universal structure of all human life. I am moving on the plane of what I call "the empirical structure" of human life as the combination of all those factors that, without being a priori requisites, belong *de facto* and in a permanent way to the human lives that I encounter, that I empirically discover, and which, consequently, constitutes the field of possible human variation in history. We might say that *man* is the combination of the empirical structures in which human life is presented to us; and thus anthropology, in the radical philosophical sense of this word, would be the study of this empirical structure, while the theory of human life as radical reality is metaphysics.

This empirical structure is what might be called "nature" (if it were necessary to use this word). It would then be seen that, if it can be said at all that man *has* a nature, it cannot be said that he *is* a nature, nor that he is simply natural. Neither in an upward direction toward the analytical theory, which all by itself is unreal, nor downward toward singular concretion, which is an absolutely personal position and freedom, can human life in any sense be reduced to "nature." One more clarification must be added: in order to grasp this empirical structure either in a real or in a fictitious sense, in order to grasp it as a *rooted* reality, one has to concern oneself with its system of roots, and this means to see it at its roots in the *radical* reality. Any study that moves within this dimension has a presupposition, which is the metaphysical theory of human life.* Having treated this presupposition in other writings of mine, I begin from it to examine here one decisive aspect of this structure which is life: the concrete form of its corporeality.

The problem of the corporeality of human life, *on the plane of the empirical structure*, is inseparable from that of its being in the world. I say on that plane because things would be different at the level of the analytical theory: "being in

* A full development of these ideas will be found in my book, *Metaphysical Anthropology: The Empirical Structure of Human Life*, published by The Pennsylvania State University Press (University Park, 1971).

the world" or "circumstantiality" would in principle not be bound to the condition of corporeality, by which I mean that there could be "human" life, presumably circumstantial, without corporeal structures. Naturally, the meaning of the circumstance or world would be different, but not any less real. *In fact*, however, the circumstantiality of life takes place in the form of corporeality. If human life were not corporeal (or if it is not in some ways, or ceases to be corporeal), it would not cease being of the world—the "other world" is a world also, though of course another. Corporeality imposes the exact forms that being in the world takes, and these forms are local and particular. Angelic life, for example, would be "circumstantial" but not local, and thus would have a different world structure. To the "transfigured body" of a saint (a body in a different sense) a different manner of being in the world would have to correspond, and this is what is expressed in speaking about the "other" world. Being corporeal, I am "localized," assigned to a place; but it is also the body that allows me local liberation from place (there can be other forms of liberation), and that is precisely what movement is.

The world is not a thing nor a collection of things; it is the ambit where things are, myself among them. The being of circumstance consists in *circumstanding*—more exactly, in my circumstanding.* The world is intrinsically *my* world, although not *only* mine. The body is also circumstance, a portion with a special function, but within circumstance, that is, *outside of me*. And the same thing can be said of the psyche, so that the distinction between *exterior* world and *interior* world (or psyche), however important it may be, is secondary with respect to the char-

* [The word Marías uses here, *circunstar*, is an etymologically appropriate coinage, composed of the prefix *circum-* and the verb *estar*, "to be"; thus, the obvious translation would be "circumbeing," but to translate it thus would mean losing its relation to "circumstance"—Trans.]

acteristic they have in common, the characteristic of *world*. What is decisive is that reality surrounding us invades our life with a corporeal character because of our own body.

The characteristics of being in the world are united with those of my reality, and consequently with those of my corporeal structure. For that reason, sensibility is a correlative of the structure of the world. Philosophers have ordinarily talked about *mundus sensibilis atque intelligibilis*, by which it is to be understood that the *same* world that is sensible is also intelligible, since human perception is interpretative and interpretation perceptive. "Over and above passive seeing there is an active seeing, which interprets while seeing and sees while interpreting, a seeing that is a looking," Ortega said in his *Meditaciones del Quijote*. The *kósmos noetós* and the *kósmos horatós* are one single world, and the intelligibility of this world contains within itself the possibility of increasing, and increasing as much with regard to what is involved in the intellectual analysis of it as with regard to what depends on sensibility proper, on the perceptive capacity of man, which is not naturally "given" once and for all, but which experiences essential amplifications that are specifically human, due to technics. By means of technics, new realities come into my world— that is, this world grows by virtue of possibilities appropriate to man, bound to his corporeality, but which go beyond what this corporeality is "by nature."

Somatic structures give order to those of the world. The perceptual and mobile condition of man brings it about that there is a "forward and backward," "up and down," "right and left." If the human body were radial, like that of the starfish, or like the medusa or the ameba, the structure of the world would be different. As it is, it supposes a center, myself, who is, however, slightly "off-center"— what is behind me is not real in the same way that what is in front of me is. There are directions, and among them are some of a privileged character. In relation to corporality, the world has a vectorial organization. In my essay "La interpretación visual del mundo" (*Obras*, VI),* I studied the way in which visuality conditions the concrete form of being in the world, for vision is not merely a sense of *things*, but it is in addition a sense of the world insofar as it is a world.

It is within this context that the question of the "size" of man should be studied. It does not make any sense to predicate the size of *me*, of the "I" that I am, of the who that is each one of us; but insofar as I am "incarnated" and my life is corporeal, some size or magnitude does pertain to me. It might be thought that what is involved is simply the size of the body, a physical reality of such and such dimensions; however, vital size is not simply geometrical (or, if you wish, "metrical"), but operative. Human life has size because it can operate within a certain order of magnitude; this is the precise and experiential meaning of what is called "the human scale." However, man differs radically in this regard from all animals and from all entities that are merely "natural"; his operative size is not *given* but varies with social conditions and through history and is at least in principle indefinite. The image of a man who by means of a complicated scaffolding "handles" (and constructs) a huge building, thousands of times larger than he himself is, is the elementary example of this condition. Man operates in orders of magnitude that are not immediately human: the ocean, celestial spaces, the interior of the cell and of the atom. Technology is the intermediary that adapts reality to the human scale; between man and those extreme magnitudes mechanisms are interposed that perform that adaptation. But those mechanisms are also corporeal structures that have to be adjusted to the somatic structure of

* [Translated in this volume as "The Visual Interpretation of the World," beginning on page 189—Trans.]

man. That is, technology makes physical liberation from the servitude imposed by the body possible, but in its turn it has to be subjected to that initial corporeal structure, which places certain limits in each instance, although these may not be permanent and could be transported (if this is the word) to a different frontier. Thus, the "vital size" (that is, the biographical size) of man is not given once and for all, but from moment to moment within each situation. And this factor, along with the somatic organization, which is also in principle modifiable, forms an essential part of the empirical structure. This situation might be symbolized by the fact that the instruments with which the ingredients of the atomic nucleus are explored, or with which the trajectory of a projectile nearing Venus is corrected from a distance millions of miles away, have to be adjusted to the precise dimensions of man's hands and eyes.

The encounter with my body is not primary. The first thing I must involve myself with, the first thing I find in my surroundings, are things. But it must be said at the same time that the encounter with each thing is simultaneous with the encounter with my self as that which is *with* those things. And secondarily I encounter myself as a corporeal reality that is with corporeal things. Reality is that which I encounter, just as I encounter it. For this reason, each thing presents itself to me as reality, although naturally this characteristic is inseparable from my encountering it, a factor that cannot be surreptitiously eliminated later on, leaving an assumed characteristic of "reality" that without any encounter would simply not have any meaning. In my encounter with reality I find myself *with* it; for that reason, it may be said that everything known is "com-prehended" (giving to this word an unaccustomed meaning), since I am *with* what it is that I know.* Almost twenty years ago I observed that the traditional symbol of knowledge, the arrow that hits the target, is incorrect. More exact would be the archer and the target, for here the archer is present twice—first, where he is; and, secondly, in the target, to the degree that it is a target for him.

It is not quite the same thing to be *in* as to be *with* things. I discover things before becoming aware of my body and I discover it *with* things. We might say that I live *from* my body. By virtue of sensibility, my body is "transparent"; for that reason, I can pass through it to reach out for things. The body is transitive; it sends me to what is other than myself. It is on this basis that I have been able to interpret death as an "opacity" descending upon the body by virtue of which the body loses its "transparency" and no longer allows me to take myself beyond it. Instead of letting me pass to the other, it is interposed as a barrier; it isolates me and leaves me without a circumstance—at least, without this circumstance or, if you wish, without "this world." The body in death suddenly ceases to fulfill its function; it segregates me from the world, isolates me, and leaves me in absolute solitude. Of course, with these observations one has not yet begun to consider the problem of death; only a first step has been taken in order to make clear what one might wish to say. But this does seem not to be superfluous, since the most serious thing about the problem of death is that when this word is pronounced one hardly knows what is being talked about.

The body raises a decisive question, which has probably not often found an adequate formulation: Do I *have* a body

* [Marías writes *con-sabido*, breaking the word into its components, meaning "with" and "known"; since it is not possible to treat any of the English equivalents of *consabido* ("aforementioned," "understood," etc.) in this way with a similar result, I have chosen to use a more general word that is at least within the same category of meaning—Trans.]

or *am* I a body? Throughout the history of thought the predominant belief has been to consider man as a corporeal reality, although of a special kind. In contrast to this thing-ifying tendency in the interpretation of man, the opposite view has arisen, culminating in Joseph de Maistre's formula that man is an intelligence served by its organs—that is, that he "has" a body which he makes use of. I believe that this is an incorrect way of considering the issue. First of all, man is not an intelligence; he is intelligent, but that is a very different thing. Those who object to saying "I have a body" usually do not object to saying "I have a world," and they would never say "I am a world." But we have seen that corporeality is the concrete form of our being of the world and that the world pertains to me no less than the body, by which I mean no less essentially (perhaps more). Strictly speaking, *I am corporeal* in the same way that I am of the world or circumstantial. If we return to Ortega's old thesis, *yo soy yo y mi circunstancia* ("I am myself and my cir-cumstance"), we see that *yo* appears twice and with a two-fold meaning. It can be said of the first *yo* ("I"), which in-dicates and designates my entire reality, that it is corporeal and of the world, and even that it "is a body." But of the second *yo* ("myself"), which is the moment of "I-ness," the *who* that is opposed in a relation of polarity to cir-cumstance (which includes the body and the psyche or, if you prefer, the animated body), it would not make sense at all to say that it is corporeal. Once more we have to reject any interpretation of the body as a reality *per se,* so that we may return to the original perspective, that which seems to me most fecund and which is, in any case, what interests me here: the corporeal condition *of* human life.

This corporeality takes on many necessary and definite forms; a complete exposition of them would constitute a decisive part of the theory of the empirical structure. It will be enough here to note some especially significant aspects that may serve to illustrate that perspective which seems to me most fertile.

As a corporeal reality, man does not seem to be very "well endowed." His life appears (and this is how it has been felt for millenia) as a series of limitations: not being able to fly, or to submerge, or to swim in a natural way, etc. Man's natural weapons are exceedingly modest: he is not well protected, he is not very strong, he is not very agile or very swift, he is badly defended. The most interesting thing is that, along with all this, man feels his natural characteristics as "limitations," when not actually as deficiencies or strict deprivations. That is, the "natural" vision that man has of himself is not based as much on what he *is* or *has* as it is on what he is *lacking*. But this means that this vision in itself is *not* natural, that it is not composed with regard to what reality is but, rather, from the point of view of unreality, out of imagination and not out of perception, out of the possibilities that he feels deprived of. Man has always looked at animals, at some animals, with an extraordinary biological envy, as if he were himself dispossessed of the characteristics of those animals, and this means (looking at things from the opposite direction) as if in some way they really did belong to him.

But this, seen from the perspective of human life and not from that of biological life, means that those limitations are understood as something positive: they are reality's challenge to man's aspirations, aspirations that are at first unreal and imaginary. Those limitations are not mere "lacks," but deficiencies or deprivations—as if man in his natural reality were an essentially mutilated being. Here, of course, we come upon the locus for the insertion of *technics* in human life. Man flies today more efficiently than any bird; he submerges to depths which no fish has ever reached; he has more strength than the largest of whales, more effective weapons than any animal. Not only does man surpass each animal, but any of them—that is, all. And all this amounts to saying that man's "nature" has expanded in all directions, that man is (if you prefer) a nature in expansion.

Technics were at the beginning a surrogate for *existing* possibilities, for possibilities that did exist, but existed outside of man, in other animals, and of which man was corporeally deprived. Later on, they were converted into means for the projection of man's own imagination. Finally, they have been becoming independent even of the concrete desires of man to such a degree that they now drag him along. Today there exists the inescapable impression that man does not know where he is going, that he is being carried by his technics toward ends he has not proposed but which are being imposed upon him. And this situation gives its most rigorous meaning to the expression I used a while ago, "nature in expansion."

Another decisive aspect is the surprising and protracted debility of the human infant—in other words, the existence of the child as distinct from the "cub." Looked at negatively, the child is an invalid for a long time, can do nothing for himself, and depends on others for his nutrition, protection, warmth, etc. He has to be taken care of by adults for many years. During an important part of the vital human trajectory, his corporeal structures, especially those of the mind, are quite different from those of adults; what this means is that human life has a phase during which it must be defined by means of characteristics other than those that are considered appropriate to it. Strictly speaking, things are even more complicated, since one cannot speak of childhood as a unitary and homogeneous reality. Just as the adult man cannot be equated with one who is not an adult, so the nursing baby cannot be equated with the adolescent. One would have to say that several empirical structures are given in human life or, if you prefer, that a constitutive variation pertains to the empirical structure to a degree qualitatively different from that which would be valid for an animal which, following a brief period as a cub, achieves its relatively definite adult state in a very short time.

However, the radical characteristic among those that constitute the corporeal structure of human life, and the most difficult to grasp in a theoretical way, is sex. Sex has, of course, an obvious somatic, corporeal dimension, but it goes far beyond that dimension. I believe that the most fruitful thing we can do in order to orient ourselves is take advantage of the distinction that is offered us by two adjectives in our language: "sexual" and "sexed." This last designates the sexed condition of human life in general, on which human life depends and on which sexual activity, which is a limited and restricted aspect of life, is founded.

Human life is not made real in "men" alone, but in men and women, quite distinct somatic and physiological realities. This structure does not really belong to the notion "human life" insofar as that notion is the theme of the analytical theory; this structure is not a *conditio sine qua non* of all possible human life. For this reason, the factor of sex does not appear at the level of the analytical theory. Heidegger has sometimes been reproached because his *Dasein* is "unsexed," but such an objection does not make any sense, since, although what Heidegger understands by *Dasein* is not the same thing as what I call "human life," it moves on the level of the *existentiale Analytik des Daseins*, where the dimension of sex does not occur. And this is not, of course, merely accidental or factitive, but structural. As a matter *of fact*, human life does take place in a stable and permanent way as a sexed reality, which is thus strictly a characteristic of the empirical structure.

But if now we try to look more closely at what it consists of, difficulties arise. It appears that there are two "classes" of human beings or persons: man and woman. But what do these classes consist of? What is the principle of the distinction between them? It could be thought that sex is a *specific* difference, and then we would have two species of the genus *Homo: Homo vir* and *Homo mulier*. But since biology traditionally defines "species" from the point of view of reproduction, the consequence would be a monstrosity: human reproduction would take place between two species, and man would be a hybrid like the mule.* Is it possible, then, to believe that difference in sex is a mere *accidental* difference that affects individuals? Might there be men and women in the same way that there are short and tall, fair and dark? All this is, of course, inadmissible. If we wish to remain within the categories offered by traditional philosophy, let us try one last resort: that the difference or distinction of sex is neither specific nor accidental, but *proper*— in the sense of the *ídion* or *proprium* of Aristotle, Porphyry, and the Scholastics. But this attempt only serves to reveal to us the insufficiency of the notion of "proper" when it is applied to human life, for we would have to ask: What is it that is proper to human beings, to be man or to be woman? With a characteristic like *risibilitas*, the favorite example of the Scholastics, things are clear: it is proper to man because *each* man (and in principle man only) can laugh. With graying, the same thing occurs: each man can get gray. But what happens when we come to sex? We have to ask *which* is proper. And then we see that we cannot consider human life as a "thing" in any sense of the word.

---

* [No equivalent for the phrase "like the mule" occurs in the Spanish text, but it seems necessary to add this phrase (in spite of its making some easy puns available), since the word "hybrid" is most commonly used to refer to the offspring of crossed varieties *within a single* species and not to crossbred offspring of *different* species, such as Marías is postulating here and such as the mule is—Trans.]

What is involved is the form of *installation* in circumstance, and one of its radical ways is the sexed condition.

Here we have to fall back on the idea of *disjunction*, which I stumbled on in 1946 when trying to comprehend (in my *Introducción a la filosofía*) the relation between "human" life and "my" life. On the level of the analytical theory we have seen that human life exists in the concrete form of being this *or* this *or* this, and that what is involved is not a division of the species into individuals, since the species as such is indifferent to that individualization, but that human life cannot even be thought of except concretely and individually in disjunction, since it is this *or* this other, that is, *each one*. Thus, human life exists, not merely in individuation, but disjunctively—in a circumstantial disjunction that pertains intrinsically to what we might call the "consistency" of this life. Well then, we now find that, on the level of the empirical structure too, human life is realized disjunctively: man *or* woman. This means that what is involved is not a division of human beings into men and women, as one might divide black cubes and white cubes into two different groups in such a way that the groups are separate and independent: among the whites there is no blackness, and vice versa. Disjunction does not separate or divide, but *unites*. In fact, the disjunction itself is present in the *terms* of the disjunction, or it may be that the disjunction constitutes the disjunctive terms.

That is, the disjunction into man and woman affects the man and the woman, establishing between them a relation of polarity. For this reason, we can say that each sex co-implies the other or, in a more direct and effective way, complicates the other. The sexed condition does not consist of the terms of the disjunction; it *is* the disjunction itself seen alternately from the point of view of each of its terms. We observe it from the point of view of each one of us insofar as we are related to the opposite sex. The reality "woman" cannot be understood without co-implying the reality "man," and vice versa. This interpretation, it seems unnecessary to say, is miles away from some of the more recent theories about sex.

But there is a risk that is constantly lying in wait for thought *at all levels*, and this danger, which is that of thingification, must be evaded. I mean that the inertia of traditional thought is so great that, just when it has hardly bypassed one danger of taking reality to be a thing, it starts to go forward and falls again into the same temptation. Human life is not any thing, although it includes innumerable things as its ingredients or resources. It is possible for us to talk as much as we might wish about things of all kinds as long as we do not lose sight of the fact that what we are dealing with are "things of life" but that life itself is not in any sense a thing. And let us not forget that it has an essentially *projective* character, which has to be made to intervene in every concrete characteristic.

Thus, human life is projected *from* one's own sex *toward* the other. The sexed condition, far from being a separation into two halves, by which one half of the community is divided from the other half, causes life to consist in each fraction of humanity *involving itself* with the other. In this way, the sexed condition introduces a kind of "magnetic field" into community life; human life is thus not inert coexistence but dynamic living together. This is why community life has a dynamic configuration and structure, why it is intrinsically a project, an enterprise. Man and woman, installed in their respective sex, experience reality entirely from within it. This radical installation is *prior to all sexual behavior*. It is the sphere in which sexual and asexual behaviors originate—but never *unsexed* behavior, for such does not exist. I mean that the sexed condition penetrates everything in life, which is, without exception, experienced from the point of view of the disjunction into man and woman. Any reality whatsoever, even the most remote areas of sexuality and not excluding mathematical theorems, is experienced by virtue of its installation in one sex or the other, thus within a context and from a perspective that is in each case irreducible to the other. The experiences that accompany the explanation of the Pythagorean theorem in a classroom are different for boys and for girls, and consequently differ sexually for them, in spite of the fact that what is being considered is something perfectly asexual.

From this point of view we should see how undoubtedly correct Freud was in placing sex at the center of his consideration of man and how erroneous not to distinguish adequately between what is "sexual" and what is "sexed," so that all his interpretations deviate unduly toward the first, which is, in spite of its enormous importance, relatively secondary—by which I mean that it is less radical than that other constitutive and all-absorbing condition. During recent decades the hypertrophy of what is sexual has served to conceal and obscure the genuine reality of what is sexed in human life. Because even the concrete characteristics of what is sexual in man (for example, its constancy, in contrast with the fugitive character of animal sexuality) are intelligible only from the point of view of that anterior, all-enveloping condition. Always, when Freudians talk about childhood sexuality, we feel an impulse toward repugnance, and if they are talking really seriously, a decided inclination to believe that they are joking. But nothing of this would occur if one were to talk about the *sexed* condition of childhood, since this is obvious and childhood life is determined by it, and more than is believed, from the very first moments.

It is sometimes noted that nobody is wholly man or wholly woman, and intermediate states are pointed out. But this confirms that sex is a way of installation in reality and not something separable from its roots. It is a way of biological installation, but only in part; it is in addition psychic and social. "Man" and "woman" are reciprocal structures; the structure that we call "man" in a masculine sense is not wholly comprised in being positively and exclusively man, but consists in being man in the presence of femininity. They are mutual structures, each one of which is present in the other in the concrete form of projection. Being man means to be related to woman; and being woman, related to man. What somatic characteristics illustrate is projected onto the whole of life and is converted into the corporeal structure *of life*.

One more characteristic still has to be emphasized. All human reality is *interpretative*. The body is, of course, interpreted; it is a rooted reality that I encounter in my life and that, at first, is covered by a patina of interpretations. That is, the body is not merely a biological reality, but from the beginning social and historical. For that reason, when an attempt is made to reduce life to the functioning of an organism among bare physical things, far from being a step in the direction of a radical insight, what is real is being supplanted by a questionable theory.

On account of its being a reality of this nature, the body signifies and *is* many things, according to the way it is viewed, and there can be different uses of the body, all with a historical character, so that a spirituality of the body is possible and one might even write a history of the body. The structures originating in the sexed condition are equally interpreted, and the interpretative coefficient that affects them is inseparable from their biological substrate, which does not wholly comprise them in any way. The child at a very early age begins to perceive and distinguish men and women, recognizes them, and responds to their presence in two different ways—just as, on the other hand, he reacts in a third way to the presence of another child. An interesting and subtle problem is that of determining the age at which the transition from a child's to an adult's interpretation begins and whether it is the same age for both sexes. This recognition on the part of the child is founded more on external interpretative differences, in the last analysis on social differences, than it is on strictly biological differences. In relation to biological differences, insofar as they express sexuality, man behaves in different ways: he displays them, or conceals them, or accentuates them by stylizing them—for example, by means of the kind of visual emphasis that is in fashion. It is usual to add conventional structures that are the external signs of sexuality—for example, skirts and trousers. This is the alphabet that the child manipulates in order to orient himself. At some periods in history, these differences are accentuated—beards, hair styles, clothing that is distinctive to a maximum degree. At other times they are made tenuous and almost erased. But when this happens, there is a very subtle system of compensation that rectifies the situation: when the man's beard disappears woman "responds" with make-up, or the same articles of clothing that are worn by all are stylized to the degree that they are converted into attributes of distinction—for instance, woman's trousers. In the same way, customs that, instead of being differential, become common (like horseback riding, sports, driving a car, smoking) are activities that, as soon as they are performed by women, are done in a way that is stylistically distinctive and are converted into accentuating powers of femininity.

This brings us to a final question: the biographical use of the body and its personal significance. Man's relations with his body, his diverse ways of sensing himself "in it," vary to such a degree that this alone would be enough to demonstrate that I am not reducible to my corporeality. More than that, each of us has to "come to a decision" with regard to the question of what significance his corporeal condition is going to have for him. This decision is not, of course, primarily individual, but social and historical. It is a collective decision, a great prevailing decision dominant in each society and in each period of history, and each individual man and woman has to contend with it, sometimes in an unpleasant way. But, in the second place and on top of this consideration, there is a personal decision by virtue of which each person "makes" his own body, starting from the biological, social, and economic resources that have been given him, and he uses it in an untransferrable way.

There are profound differences, conditioned by age and sex, in the sense of corporeality and, consequently, in the sense of corporeal relations between persons. The appropriate way of dealing with a small child is to take him up in your arms and caress him physically (his size is, of course, a decisive factor that abstract thought tends to disregard). The caress, more than the word, is the proper way of addressing oneself to a child. Biology and pediatrics have recently come to recognize the scientific justification for something that has always been known at more profound levels. (Well, perhaps not always, because everything in man is historical, and it is quite possible that the reality we call "child" may be, in its way, conditioned by the frequency and character of the caresses bestowed upon it; exaggerating of course, one might think of the child in itself as a product of the caress and a recent "invention.") The relationship with woman, although different, has decisive elements in common with the relation with the child. It is evident that additional factors alter the situation, but not on this account is the natural aptitude of the feminine body for caressing any less obvious, and along with it the dependence that woman *sensu stricto* (as distinct from the female) has on being caressed. For this reason, caressing between women or between man and woman is "decent," in the literal and etymological meaning of that which *decet,* while one experiences an immediate repugnance to corporeal contact between men that appears to have the character of a caress. This causes us to believe that the body of the child, of the woman, and of the man are "bodies" in three quite different senses—that is, that they represent three distinct forms of corporeality, three distinct ways of involving oneself with other such forms of human life.

This human life is expressed in the body, and thus the body is intrinsically expressive. I said before that it is a "transparent" reality, by virtue of sensibility. But everything real is opaque. A block of stone has an inside and an outside, but its interiority is merely factitive and not essential—that is, I might externalize any point, though of course not all. Its exterior or interior condition is purely accidental. In contrast, a living being, especially an animal, has an inside and an outside, exterior portions and others that are internal (its vital organs); they can be externalized by violence, but only through such injury to its reality as might lead to the death of the living being. In a certain sense, the human body is a real thing and as such opaque. Its transparency comes to it from what it possesses of life and, in the last analysis, from its personal character. But at the same time *human* reality as such is intrinsically occult, arcane, without possibility of exteriorization, since it is absolutely interior. Literally, it is not interior, but *intimate;* it consists of intimacy. This is the torture, the frustration, and the delight of all man's attempts at communication within all forms of community life, from thinking together and education to friendship and love.

This essential "monastic confinement" of life within its corporeality explains the *expressive* character of the body: just as water oozes through the pores of an unglazed clay pot, so traces of intimacy ooze forth in the expressions of the body. It is this that makes physiognomic knowledge of the person possible, and at the same time necessary. Rationalism has looked down on this knowledge because it seems so difficult to validate and seems to have no clear means of identification, but when the body is seen, and especially when the face is seen in motion, one observes the "within" that conceals and at the same time reveals itself. The face, it is usually said, is the mirror of the soul; but it would be better to say that the face is the soul made visible, as Descartes said that *l'idée est la chose même conçue*. Intimacy oozes out of the body and, like all reality, it needs to be interpreted. Expression itself is the result of the interpretation that each person makes of himself. It is for this reason, and not on account of biological factors, that expression is so revelatory. These factors are also revelatory, no doubt, but that is because they too are, in great measure, interpretative, although not personal. In them the repertory of interpretations deriving from one's parents and one's ancestors is observable. *Inheritance* is not only a biological but also a social inheritance, and even the biological nucleus is also interpretative.

My life is possible only by virtue of an intrinsic theory of it, in which I interpret myself to myself and project my life as *such* a life. At first, of course, as such a "human" life, but in addition and necessarily as *my* personal and untransferrable life. Each man interprets himself to himself, and that personal interpretation shines through his body in the expression on his face.

And now human time, age, makes its appearance again. The face of an old man or of a mature man is not the same as that of a young man. The face of the former tells what he has done with his life, what he has understood it to be. In the young man, who has not yet lived, his face is still unwritten, not yet engraved. But if human life is futurity, one has to take privileges from the past and give to the future what is due. What the mature man and woman have done is written on their faces; the face of the young man or woman projectively anticipates what they intend to be or to do. The only difference is that the young face, lacking furrows, is more difficult to read, and requires more imagination.

CHAPTER TEN

THE VISUAL INTERPRETATION OF THE WORLD

For Benjamín Palencia

Visual images and metaphors have always been an accompaniment of knowledge. At least in the Western world, man has usually thought and believed that to know something is, in effect, to see it. The Greek *noûs*, which is so problematical in translation when one wishes to express its rigorously cognitive meaning, is first of all "vision." Whatever may be the profounder meaning of *noeîn*, its obvious meaning, on which all the others are based by means of various transpositions, is "to see." The same thing occurs with the famous word *theoría;* and the Romans utilized the same visual metaphor (although with an essential difference in shading) in order to talk about *contemplatio* and to translate the Hellenic *bíos theoretikós* as *vita contemplativa. Idéa* and *eîdos,* two terms taken from the sphere of visuality, "aspect" and "that which is seen," have had an extraordinary proliferation in the vocabulary of knowledge: idea as reality, idea as a mental instrument, *idea* in English, where it is almost identical with "image"; in the Latin version, *species,* with its corresponding visual root and all its derivatives— "speculation," "inspection," "aspect," "respect," and, in another direction, "skeptic" (a person who looks distrustfully from one side to the other), and, somewhat further away, "consider." What follows from this?

All this naturally culminates in the identification of knowing with the metaphor of light. *Phôs* and its derivatives, *phaínesthai* and *phainómenon*, the duality of light and shadow in the Platonic myth of the cave, the doctrine of *lumen naturale*, the luminous images that accumulate whenever man has the impression that he really knows, as in the eighteenth century—Illumination, *Aufklärung*, Enlightenment. And the contrary in opposed ages: obscurantism, the "Dark Ages."

However, it has frequently been felt that the visual is insufficient and that the exclusive use, or the absolute predominance at least, of visual metaphors as the explanatory principle of knowledge is unjustified. The need to integrate what the eyes give us with what the other senses offer is so obvious that there is no need to insist on this point. And then one realizes that the unilateral metaphorical interpretation of knowledge as the optimum reality omits decisive dimensions that would have to be included in a thorough experience of knowledge. The relation of faith to hearing (*fides ex auditu*), Aristotle's insistence on the phenomenon of touch, the connection of knowledge with taste * and of one who is *sapiens* with discernment of tastes, images related to taste, smell, and hearing in references to mystical knowledge, from the "unsayable sayings" (*árrheta rhémata*) of Saint Paul or the "sonorous solitude" of Saint John of the Cross to the "pomegranate juice" of Saint John of the Cross or the sexual interpretation of *knowing*—all these are other such moments in which we touch on (to use a significant tactile metaphor) the insufficiency of visuality. But

---

* [The words used here in Spanish are *saber* ("to know," "to taste of," "knowing") and *sabor* ("taste," "flavor"), both of which are derived from Latin *sapere* ("to have a pleasant taste); related English words that make this connection clear are "sapience" and "savor," also derived from the same Latin root—Trans.]

it should not be forgotten that Saint Paul, who, it is true, speaks of seeking God "gropingly," nevertheless, when he comes to refer to his encounter with God, to his actual knowledge of God, resorts once again to visual images, whether "as an enigma in a mirror" during this life or "face to face" in the other. And, speaking of the *invisible* perfections of God, he says expressly that *intellecta conspiciuntur* through created things.

This predominance of the visual or visional conception of knowledge—is it not excessive? Is it not evident that there is a dimension of arbitrariness, perhaps of caprice, in it? It seems beyond doubt that other aspects, related to senses other than that of seeing, have to be brought into the notion, and even into the experience of knowing. However, the things that are (in an Aristotelian sense, I mean, not those that are simply for a day or so, but those that last and endure), are usually justified. Is there some reason explaining the surprising predominance of the visual interpretation of knowing and thus of the reality that is known?

Aristotle, in the beginning lines of his *Metaphysics*, comes across the preference for visual perception over other kinds and gives an explanation for this: *pollàs deloî diaphoràs*, "it brings to light many differences," he says. If the primordial function of knowing is to distinguish, to discern, to discriminate, it does seem that seeing is the sense that comes closest to fulfilling this function and, within its sphere of sensitivity, most faithfully realizes that task of discernment, of sifting, of which, in their turn, judgment and judging consist (*krísis, krínein*).* But this does not seem to be sufficient; nor is it decisive either. As I see things, there is another, much more radical dimension, and this brings it

---

* [This sentence is based on some etymological relations that are no more clearly exhibited in the Spanish text than they are here in English: the relation of *discernir*, *discriminar*, and *criba* ("sieve," "act of sifting") to Greek *krísis* ("act of sifting") and *krínein* ("to sift")—Trans.]

about that the sense of sight may actually be privileged, that the visual interpretation of knowing with regard to reality may consequently be justified, if not in an exclusive at least in a preponderant sense.

Sight is, in effect, specifically the sense of the world—or, if you prefer, of being in the world. The other senses offer us things or features of things arising from them: their corporeality or bulk, their temperature, their smoothness or roughness, their state of consistency, the voice that issues from them, the odor they give off or exhale, or a diffuse odor surrounding us, their taste, etc. And these modes of being present are woven together and combined in ways that everybody is aware of. Sight *also* functions in that same way; unquestionably there are many times when it acts as one sense among the rest. And in general the phenomenon of vision is usually studied in such a way that it can be assimilated to that function of presenting things or their features—concretely, their *aspects*. But that function is not the only one, nor the primary one; above all, it is not the particular or irreducible function of sight. What is characteristic of all the other senses is that, in each case, they give us an individual thing or something pertaining to it: the apple I touch, the odor of roses, the voice of a friend or the sound of the automobile that passes, the taste of the wine I am drinking. When the senses present a multiplicity of things to us, it has to be in the form of a succession or at least in some manner of separation; I can separately touch the apples in a basket, successively listen to the voices of several people in a conversation, etc. I can also simultaneously touch the fingers of my left hand with those of my right hand, or those of somebody else's hand, paying attention to each one of them. When it does not occur in this way, *confusion* results, as when the vague sound of waves or of a crowd reach me, or when I listen to an orchestra without distinguishing the different instruments or go into a house permeated with a diffuse odor—smoke, for example.

Sight too behaves in this way, but to a subsidiary degree —that is, when it is functioning abstractly and artificially. For, under normal circumstances it presents a multiplicity of features simultaneously, and not only as an aggregate or sum of them, nor a mere combination, but as a *context*. The ingredients of *what is seen* appear bound together by a system of mutual relations. In other words, they constitute a visual *field;* and each thing, when it is focused on individually and exclusively, appears with a halo or border of visual (and to some extent seen) realities that are not taken into consideration. We can say that sight always goes beyond its object, that it transcends things as such in order to pass on to their visual context or field. But what is most interesting about this is not the simple plurality of the elements that compose the field, but its characteristic of appearing *antecedently* to them. In other words, the structure that pertains to the visual field is not that of a combination, but that of a "within," and thus that of a "with"—that is, that of an *area*. Sight discovers multiple things *within* this visual field, and for this reason they are one *with* another, within a context. This is the fundamental structure of the world as a reality distinct from things and antecedent to them all.

And this is not all. The mere *area* does not exhaust the characteristics of visuality, which at the same time gives *organization* to its ingredients. The perspective is the very structure of vision in reality. While the simultaneous hearing of a variety of sounds tends toward confusion, and only a practiced ear and sufficient concentration can introduce order into this multiplicity, the visual field is organized in relation to a definite perspective and is constituted by it. This is another of the conditions of *being in the world* insofar as one is actually in the world. It is true that visual perception may have a *spectral* character; but when this is emphasized, along with its unreality in comparison with the reality that accompanies touching or tasting, when it is observed that what is seen reduces itself in principle to a mere *object*, there is a tendency to forget two things. First, the reality with which things are present in tactile perception, for example, is to a considerable extent the result of their association with visual perception. I mean by this that the visual discernment of things in a field or world, at a distance and in an organized perspective, confers a reality upon them that touch, later on, comes to confirm or take over (if this expression is proper). It is insertion in an area or context, manifested primarily in vision, that gives reality to things that are heard or touched or tasted, for the primary encounter with these things does not usually occur in these ways. The second thing that is often forgotten or disregarded is that vision is not exclusively a visual phenomenon, by which I mean that actual vision—as a human activity, not as a phenomenon of the psychological laboratory—has a muscular component: accommodation, movements of the eyes and even of the head in order to orient oneself and to scan the visual field, adjustments of the light, the attempt to concentrate, etc. When a man talks about an idea, intuition, or evidence, when he mentions clarity of understanding or utilizes visual images of any kind in making reference to knowledge, he is including within them everything that in fact occurs in actual vision, where the merely spectral presence of objects is only a special case.

It is precisely the anatomical organization of the human visual apparatus that reinforces the reference of vision to the world and to reality as they are. Disregarding the fact that man has binocular vision, with all its notable consequences, the situation in which man has two eyes on a level and light is propagated rectilinearly automatically introduces an orientation and a structure into the visual field and, as a consequence, into the world. Ahead and behind, to the right and to the left, up and down, near and far, appear with full immediacy and exactness in visuality, but only in a residual or incipient (in either case, a vague) way in the other *isolated* senses. But, above all, the fundamental structures *here* and *there* are manifested primarily in vision. Touch, taste, and smell are senses of immediacy; hearing presupposes the intervention of distance, but let us not forget that hearing *by itself* is the sense most given to unreality. It is not by chance that the acoustic art, music, is not only an art without an object but consists precisely in liberation from objectivity. Sight alone brings things that for the other senses are absent (that is, distant) into presence. And this presence does not consist in suppressing the distance or eliminating it, but just the contrary: sight places before us what is *not here, but there*—that is, the visual presence of distance itself. Only in exceptional cases when, on account of the lack of terms of reference, the vital reality of distance is not given (as when one is looking at the stars), does then the simple and absolute *there* make its appearance, forever qualified by that same absence of immediate references or of a path from *here* to it.

And this qualitative structure of visuality has a quantitative consequence that, in its turn, is converted into a quality in a new sense: this consequence is the fabulous expansion of the repertory of things perceived. While the other, more immediate senses reduce us to our body and its most immediate neighborhood, vision extends the horizon and incomparably multiplies our possibilities. It is due to visuality that the characteristic of *repertory* pertaining to the world appears in a form adequate to the projective activity of man.

There is still another aspect in which, with even greater clarity, sight is revealed as the sense of being in the world. I refer to the appearance of modes of negation as something positive. The other senses offer us positive realities or, in effect, they simply do not function. I hear, touch, smell, or taste *something*, or I do not exercise these sensory activities.

To the degree that the tactile sensibility does not possess the characteristic of concrete reference to a definite object, it is in constant change and always positive: I feel, and I feel in one way or another. Sight does not behave only in this way. What is visible is always associated with what is invisible, and the invisible is not only whatever *is not* seen but (at least *hic et nunc*) that which *cannot be* seen. The organization of the visual field, determined by the perspective or point of view and by the structure of things (this last should not be forgotten), establishes an articulation that is highly complex, coherent, and variable (all these traits are equally important) among its elements, in accordance with their visibility or invisibility. Some things *hide* others; the determination of what is hidden or concealed possesses a primary visual significance. There is, finally, the radical form of invisibility which is the lack of light. Expressed in vital terms, this is gloom or darkness, which is not, as some Scholastic thinkers believe, *ens rationis* (as it might be from the point of view of physics), but a positive and vital reality with which I find myself and which I have to take into consideration like any other. I encounter darkness as an irreducible reality within my life, and as a reality that is even an object of visual perception. And darkness is, neither more nor less, the image of *nothing* and probably was the mental and historical source of the concept of nothing. Nothing as a positive reality, as the negation of reality, is sustained by itself and depends upon it; it is the reality (positive, consequently) that has the total negation of itself. Analogously, darkness is the form of the visible (or visual) presence of invisibility itself as it is. Upon opening our eyes in the darkness, *we see that we do not see*. The only reality that is in any way analogous to this in other sensory spheres is silence, but in a much more tenuous way and with decisive differences that would take a long time to analyze and demonstrate in detail.

Finally, there is a dimension of the world that, on account of its being the radical condition of human life, transcends each of the senses and permeates them all, but which acquires a special concretion in the sense of sight. This is *time*. Temporality is experienced through the entire sensory system and never by its means alone. Vision, however, contributes a decisive element: its articulation. Day and night, which are manifested primarily in a visual form and only secondarily and in an extremely vague way through the other senses, give the first indication of the temporal rhythm, of duration in a strict sense, and of the quantification of time. That decisive feature of human life which we refer to when we talk about *days being numbered* is most forcibly manifested through visuality. Think of the complex of consequences that this has for the organization of memory, and even more for the mechanism of anticipating and projecting and, consequently, for the very reality of life.

Among what I call characteristics of the *empirical structure* of human life, visuality is of primary significance because, if being in the world in an absolute sense is not radically bound to it, then the concrete empirical structure of the human way of being in the world is.

But an immediate objection will be raised. What about the blind? Can it be said that the blind man is not in the world or that he is at least in a world *other than* that of those who are able to see? Is the structure of being in the world different for the blind man? Is it not enough to say that he perceives the world, the same world, in a different way, impoverished perhaps, precarious, but still the same? I would respond to this objection by accepting its import, although denying that it is an objection to what I have just finished saying. The blind man lives in the same world as those who are able to see; he has the same structure of being in the world. How is this possible, if it is true that the sense of the world as such (of our world, it is understood) is sight? Simply because *in vital terms* (not in sensory, physiological, or psychological terms) *the blind man possesses a visual world*. The blind man lives in a seeing society. The world is not only or primarily a repertory of physical things perceived sensorially, but of human realities interpreted by society; it is a historical and social reality. The interpretations that are injected into the blind man by his surroundings from the beginning of his life (even if he is blind from birth) are visual; the structure, including the physical structures, of his world is built up in relation to (in *view* of, we would say) visuality. Language, images, metaphors, even many logical relations, contain references to visuality. The blind man, of course, lacks a sensory intuition of all this; he does not see it, but nevertheless he functions with all those visual structures. The blind man lives literally in a visual world, which he sees with the eyes of other people— that is, with what his life possesses of collective life. Society is the blind man's guide.

Imagine the difference between a blind man (an individual who is blind) and what a blind species would be. That is, what man would be if man were unable to see, if the empirical structure did not include visuality. It is obvious that an individual of the blind species would be very much different from the blind individual of our species, which is that of normal men endowed with sight. And this may help us to understand the articulation of somatic elements (for example, perceived features) with social elements (ideas, beliefs, customs, language, values, logical relations, etc.) in the constitution of the empirical structure.

The traditional ways of justifying the primacy of vision over the other senses were inadequate, but this primacy itself is fully justified. The reason this is so is that thought has always obstinately clung to operating with *things,* and from the point of view of things the primacy of sight over touching or hearing or tasting is secondary and a matter of emphasis or degree. However, what is involved is not things but the *world* and being in the world, and since sight is the specific sense of the world, this validates and justifies the historical prevalence of the visual interpretation of the world.

CHAPTER ELEVEN

HUMAN HAPPINESS: THE WORLD AND PARADISE

One of the few things that men are in agreement about (and men are in agreement about very few things) is that happiness does not exist; and yet there is no doubt that man is the being who needs to be happy.

This is quite an anomalous situation, and it reveals to us that this theme of happiness, in spite of its promising name and its air of innocence, is going to turn out to be very thorny; for the most problematical thing is determining what it is that we call, perhaps all too simply, *happiness*. I refer to two groups of difficulties—two types, if you prefer. The first difficulty, the least of them all (let us begin with what is lesser and secondary), is that there are enormous differences among men in what they need in order to be happy. That is, enormous differences are encountered when one tries to determine what each man or each type of man (race, people, class, epoch) needs in order to be happy. But there is a greater difficulty, and this is that these differences are based on the fact that "being happy" has itself many different meanings. Leaving aside what one needs in order to be happy and what the resources would be for attaining this, the very expression "being happy" may mean profoundly different things. On occasion I have said that "being happy" does not mean the same thing when it is referring to an Eskimo that it does when referring to Lord Byron. What is involved, I repeat, is not that one or the other needs such different things in order to be happy, but what one or the other perceives as happiness, what they understand by being happy. The Eskimo would quite probably consider Lord Byron extremely wretched in his happiest moments, and no doubt the reverse would also be true.

This brings us to an important problem, one that we run into immediately—we always come across this problem at every turn, no matter where we may happen to be going. And this is the problem of so-called (since it has to be called something) "human nature."

I will not go into this metaphysical question here; I have on other occasions explained my position somewhat with regard to it. It will be enough to recall here that throughout history it has frequently been said that the life man leads is not natural, that man (to make a long story short) lives a life that is not at all natural, but is, on the contrary, absurd. And then we are advised to lead a natural life.

Occasionally man is afflicted with a disease of naturalism. The most sensational and famous was Rousseau's, but there were many others before him and a few more afterward. Rousseau proposed *going back to nature*, just as the Stoics, two thousand years before, had called for a life in conformity with nature. But the troublesome thing is that we definitely do not know where that nature is. When we want to go back to it, we look around us, we search for it, trying to locate it, but we do not find it. What I am saying is that we do not know what the natural life would be for man that we are invited to follow.

Evidently, what we are doing—living in cities, on streets full of people, exhausting ourselves in the pursuit of things, going to shows, writing books and reading them, listening to speeches—is not natural. Rather, it is taken for granted that it is antinatural. But, is it that the natural thing would be to live in the top of a coconut tree? That is not at all certain. Wouldn't it be more natural to live in caves? Or in dwellings built on stilts? Is it natural for man to work? It seems not. And not to work? Likewise, no. Is it natural to be nomadic or sedentary? This does not seem to be clear. Is it natural to become rich or to remain poor?

It turns out, in short, that this natural life, which is so frequently recommended to us, is proposed to us in a vacuum, in the abstract: "Be natural," "Lead a natural life." But when we try to determine exactly what a "natural life" would consist of, we find out that we do not know, and for quite a significant reason—that there is no natural life, that it does not exist. Man is essentially artificial or (if you prefer) historical, and, consequently, that expression "natural life," when it is applied to man, is purely a meaningless notion.

And this, of course, has direct repercussions on the idea we have about happiness. By happiness we understand a certain form of life, of which we can say only the best things we are able to say. To say that a life is happy is to say the best thing that can be said of it. But note that this formula "the best thing" is also enormously vague, has only a formal character, and is, therefore, very difficult to define and to fill with contents.

No, it is not a simple thing to give rigorous and concrete contents to this expression. Happiness is in a certain sense the enjoyment and possession of reality. Does anybody doubt this? By happiness we understand primarily a certain possession of reality. But here is exactly where the problem begins. When at last we have reached a point that seems to be secure, when it seems to us that we have finally grasped something concrete, then our difficulties begin—and they come in through a double door.

Because, indeed, what is *reality?* What is this about "possessing reality"? In reality, *reality* does not appear anywhere. There are realities, a great diversity of realities: there are stars, fields, trees, animals, men, and, of course, women; there are books, memories, sensations, perceptions, history, societies, spirits, God. All these are realities. They are (using the word in the vaguest way) things. But reality? Reality seems to escape us. To possess things, to possess each thing, is not to possess reality.

But what is even worse is that if we take the other term of the expression, *to possess,* we do not find ourselves in any better shape. For the word "possess" is also quite ambiguous. What does "possessing" mean? In how many ways is it possible to possess? To possess is in a certain sense *to perceive;* in some way I possess the things and the persons I see, and those who see me and hear me equally possess me. There is another possession that is tactile, which is touching, palpating, grasping. There is another that seems to be even more vigorous, and this is tasting, especially eating. When we eat something, we make it our own, we assimilate it (that is, we make it similar to ourselves); and in a certain sense that is the most active type of possession. There is another form, which is sexual union. And another quite different, which is knowledge of reality—and here it must be noted that knowledge may be expressed in many ways. Finally, there is another way of possession to which man aspires, and this is the identification of the things that are possessed.

In summary, then, involvement with reality consists in a series of efforts, in the last analysis always frustrated, attempting to take possession. Especially in the forms of human involvement, very concretely in friendship, and in a much more active way in love. What is involved in love is a titanic effort to possess a person, a disproportionate effort to be possessed by her, to let oneself be possessed and to possess. And the possessive intent always pours out to some extent into dissatisfaction, because that possession is inevitably deficient and problematical.

But what am I saying? The possession of the reality of

the other? And our own? Is it that we possess our own reality? Can it properly be said that we are the possessors of ourselves? We shall see that this too is more than problematical and more than deficient, and that this is so whether we look at it from the *reality* side or from the side of *possession*.

This means that the normal and inevitable form of human life is discontent, which is a constituent of man in this world. It may be noted, incidentally, that discontent is, furthermore, in some ways supremely consoling. I have pointed out, while living in the United States, where things usually function well, at least in comparison with other countries, that this has its counterpart. When things do not work, when almost all are out of order, when we go to turn on a light and it does not go on, when the train we are waiting for does not arrive on time, when we buy a product and it turns out to be of inferior quality, when the employment of our taxes does not seem to be having any effect— when all these things happen, we put the blame on somebody and say that society is corrupt, that it does not function, that public services are in a sorry state, that the government does not do its duty or does it badly. And this consoles us, since it makes it possible for us to consider those evils as temporary and to believe that if things were to be improved, we would no longer have such troubles.

But when things function well, at least in most cases, when there is nobody on whom we can, strictly speaking, place the blame, then we see that, no matter how well things function, life is in the last analysis something very limited, narrow, and at times pitiable. And then this impoverished and deficitory character of life appears as something intrinsic, since we no longer have incidental causes on which to lay the blame.

This means (and let us extract the inevitable consequences) that man is a contradiction. Man seems to be formally defined by discontent, which is absolutely inexorable, and at the same time man is the being who needs to be happy, who absolutely needs to be happy and will not resign himself to being other than happy. Thus we arrive at a notion of man as impossible. And we have to hold onto it, since man actually is an impossible being. Thematically, to be a man consists of trying to be something that cannot be. This task, truly improbable and almost incredible, of which I am speaking, is what all of us do all the days of our life and is called *living*.

Human life has a strange and paradoxical structure. It has a temporal and successive character. It is the contrary of eternity. Recalling once more the old definition of Boethius: *aeternitas igitur est interminibilis vitae tota simul et perfecta possessio*, "eternity is the simultaneous and perfect possession of unending life." Human life is just the opposite of this in every way. It is not unending, but terminates, and quite soon (I am speaking at the moment of earthly life), almost as soon as it has begun. In the second place, this life is not possessed all at once, simultaneously, but in a successive way; we go along possessing it in fragments, little by little. And, finally, this possession is imperfect; we possess no more than an instant of our life, the present. We possess the past in a very deficient way, by memory, and the future in a way that is even more precarious, to the extent that we are able to anticipate it, and nothing more.

Man is, then, just the contrary of eternity and, in this sense, of the being of God. The formula for human life is this: "our days are numbered." For this reason, as Ortega well observed, man can do nothing but approve: he has to choose well. For, if man had an unlimited life, what would it matter if he made a mistake! If an hour of our lives, in which we are expecting something, gives us nothing, or at most a boring time, this would have no significance if we could count on an indefinite time ahead of us—what more could that lost hour have given us? An indefinite number of others would always remain intact. But the trouble is that this is not the way things are. The trouble is that we have a certain number of hours, perhaps more, perhaps less, but always finite, and thus each one of them is irreplaceable. If an hour is lost, it can never be regained.

This is something like what happens when one has very little money. One has to decide, for if one buys a piece of furniture, a suit, an appliance, and it doesn't fit the need, one cannot now buy something else, for the error is irreparable. If we look closely at this situation, we find, however, that with life things are even worse than this. For, when all is said and done, money does have a homogeneous structure—that is, if the suit we bought is not what we need, it does happen that we can get another, though not without loss, perhaps at the cost of giving up a dessert or going to a show or inviting a friend to dinner. But the possibility does always exist, at least in principle, that the error can be rectified with *other money*, at the cost, that is, of a sacrifice. But it turns out that human life is not so much like money as like that prosaic reality called "ration tickets," which were in use until a short time ago in almost all countries and are still in use in some. That is, we are not concerned now with having enough money (ten, twenty, or a hundred dollars to spend however we wish), but with having 300 points for food, 120 for clothing, 40 for diversion, 20 for transportation. And, of course, these points are not interchangeable, so that if you take the wrong train and go to Seville instead of going to Barcelona, using up all the points available to you for transportation, you could not now give up a pair of shoes or going to a bullfight, but you simply could not get to Barcelona.

Well, this is what happens in human life, since its time is not only "days that are numbered," but it also has structure and quality. We might say "days that are ordered." This is what is called *age*. Human life has ages. Each year of our life is different from the preceding and from that which follows. If we lose our childhood, we have lost it irrecoverably. If a child does not play with a hoop or top at the age of six or eight, it is ridiculous to think that he may do so when he is an established professor or senator, since at that age one does not play with hoops and tops. Each age has its own occupation; thus, as soon as the moment passes in which something has to be done, it can no longer be done—or if, sometimes, it is nevertheless still done, that is even worse.

Man can do nothing but guess right and choose well, for he stakes his life in each decision, on every choice. This is why his life is a drama, as Ortega repeated from time to time. What obscures this reality is that man risks his life in bits and pieces, he goes along risking fragments of his life; but since each of these is irreplaceable, the loss of life in them is no less real. And this has to be added: given the systematic structure of human life and its irreversibility, each act involves the whole of life; so that in risking our life in pieces, we are placing our life at stake in its entirety. And the only thing that gives zest to life is the possibility and at the same time the necessity—the ambiguous privilege, in short—of risking everything from time to time on one throw of the dice.

There is a tendency of our times that preoccupies me a lot, and this is the tendency that consists in evading the irrevocable, in trying to conceal the radical character of human life—which is that and nothing else. It is from this that my antipathy (even from the purely human and earthly point of view) toward divorce arises, not so much in consideration of the unsuccessful marriage as for the sake of successful marriage. I mean that marriage accompanied by the possibility of divorce, where one may count on "putting things right," lacks that characteristic of decisive risk, of "wagering everything," which is essential to it. For I believe that marriage can only be successful when everything is risked on its outcome, when the man and the woman stake everything on this one throw of the dice and hurl themselves without reservation into that enterprise, burning their ships, just as that old countryman of ours, Hernán Cortés, did—if it is true that he did.

Thus we find that irrevocability is the very condition of human life. Since life is irrevocable, it is quite chimerical for man to be determined to divest it of that characteristic. What happens is that in this way, little by little and without noticing it, he goes along losing life, at the same time that he loses its purest and most delightful possibility, which is precisely to risk it. In other words, he expires day by day at his own hands, he goes along being left without life, without even having dared to risk it.

Man has to guess right, then; he cannot be mistaken, he has to choose well. In each instant, he has to prefer, that is, choose among the possibilities. And no possibility is sufficient or satisfactory, since each thing (as we have already seen) is not reality. It is real, it has something of reality, but it is not reality. As we take hold of each thing, we have the real thing in our hand, but reality escapes us. It is from this that the constitutive discontent of human life flows.

And this discontent is, furthermore, double. If on the one hand no thing satisfies us and every choice is defective, on the other hand omission is painful. That is, in choosing we take our selection from among several possibilities that are excluded, and our heart frequently goes after the excluded ones, which we would also like to know, to enjoy, and to possess. Life is constant preference and choice, and this process of choosing is a mutilation. We go along constructing a life that, we may suppose, is *the best of all possible lives* (it will not be said of me that I am not an optimist). Let us suppose, then, that at each instant we choose the best, with a marvelous perspicacity. In spite of all this, our life has been outflanked, to the right and to the left, by other possible lives that we might have wanted to live but that have been left abandoned, like imaginary dead bodies, on both sides of the trail behind us.

Consider what has become of my childhood vocation of pirate, which, given the real conditions of this world, I have not been able to realize, and which has had to be replaced by this other, much less glamorous, career which is philosophy. And this has happened to many of us, perhaps to all of us. The same thing has happened to you, has it not? We live surrounded by the ghosts, bearing our names, of all the possible lives which we might have wanted to live and which we have gone along casting aside, slitting their throats mercilessly, to the right and left of the trail.

Happiness thus consists (now that we are beginning to see what happiness rests on, we can try to define it formally) in the realization of a certain aspiration or vital project that is constructed within a repertory of definite circumstances. That is, what is involved is a certain pressure that I exert upon circumstances, circumstances which make it possible or impossible for me to realize that aspiration, project, program, or (more rigorously) vocation. If I achieve it, we say that I am happy; if I do not achieve it, we say that I am unhappy, unsuccessful, miserable, unfortunate—it would be worth our while to pause a few minutes over this series of words.

It is obvious that one's vital project is never fully realized. Nor is it, generally, frustrated completely. This is why human life is usually a compromise between happiness and unhappiness. But Ortega recorded many years ago (and he was completely right) that man's life, in its general course and at all periods in history, is happy, that if we take the entire course of the life of each man, then the life of all men in each period of history is more or less happy. And this is the way things are because the vocation, the aspiration of each man is closely bound to the repertory of his historical possibilities. Thus, vocations, types of vocation, aspiration, have a certain uniformity within each epoch and approximately correspond to the conditions in which one lives and, consequently, to the conditions that make it possible at least in some measure to realize those vocations or, what is the same thing, to be happy. What happens is that man is extremely insincere, and it is always painful for him to confess his happiness. Furthermore, misfortune has a very good press—to acknowledge that one is passably happy is to appear to admit that one has a strong streak of frivolity or hardness of heart, and nevertheless . . . Take, not a whole epoch that is especially difficult, as ours is; take a portion of it, a portion that may be really atrocious, without alleviation: war, a beseiged and starving city, bombarded and insecure, or perhaps a prison or a concentration camp. So many men, and even women, of our times have known and know these realities that it is not irrelevant to appeal to personal memories. Well, if we are sincere, there is nothing we can do but admit that, within a situation that was in general atrocious, we were sometimes happy. Once the effort is made to change the "threshold" of what is disagreeable and the higher threshold of what is intolerable, happiness flourishes in the muddy trenches, in streets swept by mortar fire, in prison, under danger from enemy guns. For this reason alone, of course, man is able to survive many experiences, since man cannot live without a little happiness, and it should be clearly observed that he is quite capable of finding it in the midst of unimaginable distresses. In the face of the unreflecting cult of anguish, of gloom, of nausea, I observe what is more properly human (something that brings one to feel a certain pride in being a man) in that marvelous capacity for extracting a few drops of happiness

212 PHILOSOPHY AS DRAMATIC THEORY

out of sorrow, out of suffering, out of misery, and out of
fear, for knowing how to find in misfortune a spark of good
fortune.

At all moments man invents and shapes his own novel.
These novels have, depending on their historical period,
quite different characteristics. The romantics were great
novelists, not so much on account of the novels they wrote
(most of them mediocre), but because of those they lived—
above all, for those they tried to live. If the lives of the
romantic age are studied, it will be seen that almost all of
them are singularly brilliant and attractive. From the intellectual point of view they are at times deplorable, almost
always preposterous; but as possible lives, as invention, project, aspiration, and vocation, they are full of nobility,
beautiful, and even marvelous. And as the nineteenth century advanced all that grew more gray, more monotonous,
those novels began to repeat themselves, plagiarism arose,
and little by little a literary genre came into being that was
much more lamentable. And today something quite similar
is happening: the range of individuation in human life has
become even more restricted.

We live in a world where each man is indexed and filed
away, practically stuck down with a pin to a piece of card-
board or a block of cork, the way entomologists usually do
with insects. Today it is known (that is, nobody definite
knows it, but it is known by society, even more by the
state, and of course its police) who each one of us is, where
we are, what we are doing, how much we earn, what we
know, what immunizations we have received; and one cannot get out of this situation, one cannot flee to some other
place, because there is no longer any *other* place. We are
subjected to a system of enormous social pressures that in
great measure block the spontaneous development of personality. Ortega referred at times to a curious fact. In every
city of Europe there used to be at one time a certain number

of eccentric people, picturesque, amusing, with a degree of insanity but with more than a degree of charm, who stood for the possibilities of invention at the margins of normal life. Well, the number of those ingenious eccentrics has diminished considerably. I have still observed them in their decline. Today, in Madrid, in Paris, in London, there are hardly any survivors. This picturesque and preposterous fauna, half Bohemian and half crazy, is to be found in the same situation as those employments that are marked by the now already familiar expression, "to be phased out."

If life, taken in its entirety and statistically, is to some degree happy, happiness itself when considered seriously and *sensu stricto* is utopian, formally impossible, and contradictory, because of the inexorable nature of choice and preference and the consequent deferral of what is also pleasing, desirable, and interesting to us.

As we arrive at this point there is nothing we can do but pause for a moment and then begin to consider something different. For it is too frequently forgotten that man lives in the world, and what this signifies is not often enough remembered. People keep repeating that the world is the enemy of the soul, and this has a profound meaning about which (it may be noted in passing) almost nobody has ever thought for five minutes. It is said that there are three enemies of the soul—the world, the flesh, and the devil. And my good friend Eduardo Mallea has even written a novel on the subject. But how many people have stopped to think what it means, in reality, to say that the world is the enemy of the soul? About the devil, that seems quite clear, especially in these times; about the flesh, a little less clear, because it is usually misunderstood; about the world . . . it will be worth while to think about it, and this is not easy.

But what I would like to emphasize here is that, in the face of most of the objections that are made to the world, if the world had a voice, probably it would rise in irritation and refute them. It would, no doubt, say: "But who do you people take me for? Is it that you think I am Paradise? Because I have never said that I am Paradise. I am the World."

In this imaginary dialogue with the world, I believe that the world is right—for, normally, man has the idea that the world should be paradise. Of course this is the deeply meaningful idea of the lost paradise. We come from paradise and we are still not consoled. And this seems appropriate to me. I too am not consoled—nor need it be said! But it is one thing for me not to be consoled and something else to go on believing that I am in paradise. This, no. I am completely convinced that paradise is lost, that it was lost, for themselves and for us, by Adam and Eve, and that, for this reason, we are today only in the world. And so it seems necessary to me to take the world as world and not to raise objections against it from the point of view of paradise. That is, that our discontent with the world should be on account of what is obnoxious about it as a world, and not because of what it does not possess of paradise.

And this suggests to me a theme that I wish to touch on, even if only incidentally and cursorily, and this is man's frequent nonacceptance of reality—nonacceptance by man and, at least in a certain aspect, even more by woman. It frequently happens, in fact, that women ruin and partially destroy their lives for no reason other than that they were once twenty years old; and for the sake of that age, which belonged to them just once, they deny all the rest. And, of course, in denying all other ages, they contradict them, they fail to experience them, they live them dishonestly. I have no special preference for the age of twenty. No doubt it is a marvelous age, but it is like all ages, since all the ages of human life are marvelous on condition that they be what they have to be. A woman twenty years old is usually enchanting, no doubt about it. But she can also be enchanting at twenty-five, at forty, at seventy, and quite probably at eighty—and if she reaches a hundred, certainly!

Of course, those charms have to be different and do not coincide with that of twenty. Each woman has her moment of perfection, what the Greeks called her *akmé,* her flowering, at a definite age. And it is an error to believe that this moment is given, above all in our times, in early youth. Some women, very few, have their optimum age at eighteen or twenty, and from then on their life is in a certain sense a falling away. But much more frequent are the cases in which the *akmé* occurs much later. And, in any case, each one of the ages has its own possibility of perfection, in all orders, including that which rightly matters most to the woman. Consequently, that nonacceptance of reality involves the destruction and emptying out of life.

This is no more than a special case of that human attitude which consists in not accepting the structure of the world— that is, the inexorable conditions of the world, inexorable by virtue of its being a world. It is generally believed that the good is the absence of difficulty and of limitation. But this is, of course, the very formula for paradise; paradise is nonlimitation and nondifficulty.

It should be noted, in passing, that this is a negative formula. An that is why, as soon as man begins to think for more than ten minutes about paradise, he grows bored. The reader races through the first two chapters of *Genesis.* He comes quickly to the part about the serpent, temptation, sin, and the expulsion of Adam and Eve from Paradise. Then he begins to enjoy himself. And since only two chapters are involved he passes cursorily through them. Furthermore, he already knows what is going to happen and from one moment to the next he is expecting the serpent to appear. In other words, the paradise of the reader is already a paradise with a serpent—something that was not true for

Eve and for Adam, who did not figure on the serpent at all.

For all these reasons, the usual formula for paradise is negative, and it is on this account that as soon as we begin to think about it we are attacked by boredom. This seems terribly serious to me, and I will have to come back to it. The fact is that we are habitually involved with negative formulas for things that are only negatively desirable, like aspirin, which takes away our headache and is undoubtedly marvelous. But as soon as it has taken our headache away, we have to seek something finer since we no longer have a headache. And that is almost always what is understood by paradise: a world without a headache—without limitation and without difficulty. It is necessary to look for a more adequate idea of paradise and, incidentally, of the world.

First of all, I believe that the world has to be understood as an enterprise. The world presents itself to man as a repertory of possibilities and of incitements. It is not simply a place where one is. *To be at* * is, for man, to be experiencing something, doing something, inventing something; and things are in each instant new possibilities. Recall what the world is to the child—the most fabulous repertory of possibilities. Furthermore, the child is the one who has the most accurate idea of what reality is, since for him things are not something fixed and immutable. The grand piano is a mountain; his father's library is a trench; his grandfather's huge easy chair is the Comanche chief's tepee. And this only for a while. A little later, the easy chair becomes the navigating bridge of a brigantine, for now the child is playing pirates. That is, each reality assumes different functions and presents diverse aspects; thus it continues to be the possibility and promise of different lives.

For the child, the world is an enterprise: "Are we going

* [Marías uses the verb *estar* here, not *ser;* the distinction, remember, is that between "being in a situation" (*estar*) and "being by nature" (*ser*)—Trans.]

to play such and such?" At times I have observed that when the child makes the initial proposal for the game, when he "establishes" the presuppositions of the playful fiction and thus begins to live in a definite world, he uses the past tense. He never says "I *am* a pirate," but "I *was* a pirate," or "I *was* a thief and you *were* a policeman." (I wonder, shall it always be in that order, where the one who proposes the game always takes for himself the role of the thief?) That past tense, that *was*, is the time of fiction. French newspapers do the same thing when they use the conditional to say that what they are saying is not the truth: *Le Ministre des Finances aurait présenté sa démission* —that is, he has not presented it, but the newspaper wants him to.

If the world is a repertory of possibilities, if life is a project or aspiration, something that advances upon the world, this means that pressure has to be exerted upon the world. And when one really begins to exert pressure upon the environment, instead of sliding over it as usual, it turns out that the environment, even the most trivial and ordinary, begins to ooze like a squeezed lemon.

Conduct the experiment of going one afternoon, some gray afternoon in a drizzle if possible, through the ugliest and most desolate section of the city you live in. Go through the grayest, most disagreeable section of town, the one with the least style, the least poetry. Look for the worst. Walk through those streets and try to exert pressure with your eyes upon each thing. Take reality as the reality it is and press against it. You will see how, inside of ten minutes, you will begin to find everything marvelous, absolutely marvelous. You will begin to feel that enormous contentment in reality that man usually feels, as Ortega has observed, to the degree that he is advanced in years. And from this it follows, that the adult is generally happier than the adolescent, in spite of everything that is said to the contrary, for he accepts more of reality and feels more contentment in what is real, without requiring that it be extraordinary.

I believe that what is usually called "contentment in limitation" is something decisive. When something is good, when a thing is fine, although it be limited and modest and come to an end right here and now, it is necessary to admire it, to feel contentment in it and even enthusiasm for it. It has to be accepted, although it is not an unlimited and marvelous thing, although we know that it has very precise and perhaps immediate limits.

Well, so the world is a bittersweet reality. That is why I said it was like a lemon. It is a bittersweet reality because it is constantly mixed with what is negative and unpleasant, with resistance and failure. But this does not require us to become oblivious to the splendid truth of the inexhaustible novelty of the world. *Omnia nova sub sole.* Everything is new because the point of view from which it is seen is constantly in motion.

> *Todo se mueve, fluye, discurre, corre o gira; cambian la mar y el monte y el ojo que los mira.* ("Everything moves, flows, passes, runs, or turns; the sea and the mountain and the eye that looks at them—all change.")

Thus sang Antonio Machado. Yes, everything changes, everything passes, and thus all reality is always different, always new, and to live is to discover reality at every moment. This is why man always has something in him of Adam, and, of course, woman something of Eve. That is, man, who has lost Paradise, preserves of it one thing: the power to go on discovering it, the power to go on giving names (or, it may be, interpretations) to things. To say all this in one word, the world has an *argument* just as novels do, just as plays do. It is not a mere inert storehouse of things, but it has a plot, it has unknown depths and perspectives, and is thus a promise of adventures in which we submerge ourselves as we are living.

Life has a certain horizon. There is no more appropriate expression than this. When one is a child or very young, it seems that one is on the way toward a tranquil and steady state, which is that which is called "being grown up." But when the child becomes grown up, he discovers instability anew; he finds that he cannot install himself, but that he has to go on advancing and inventing what to do. No matter how far he goes the horizon is always in the distance, for it is absolutely inaccessible. This is the character of life, defined by the constitutive instability of every situation. But there is a privileged moment in which, at the depths of the horizon, something appears that is going to transform everything and thus transform the very meaning of life: a black hole. It is not even necessary to name it, is it? Everybody knows that it is called *death*.

The discovery of the black hole comes at a certain age, different in each individual, rarely in early youth. Of course, the adolescent thinks a lot about death and frequently talks even about taking his own life, and sometimes does so—at least, some one hundred and twenty or hundred and thirty years ago, he did so. But it is one thing for the young to talk about death, think about it, and even, if excessively grief-stricken, to seek it; and something else *to take it into account*. For death appears to him as something distant, which does not exist on the effective horizon in view of which he is in fact operating—that is, within the normal distance to which he projects himself. There is a quite youthful sentence from Don Juan Tenorio that must be repeated: "Too far in advance you expect me to believe in it." * Don Juan, the spirit of youth, always has the im-

* [A terse idiom, *Largo me lo fiáis;* it has to be completely unfolded in order for it to make sense in English—Trans.]

pression, whenever anybody speaks to him about death, that they are talking about something outside of time—and this, mind you, even though he knew that he was gesturing at the point of a sword.

There is a decisive moment in which human life becomes a crisis. This is the moment at which death ceases being an idea and becomes an operative certainty—that is, a reality that is taken into account as an element on our effective horizon. If I am asked what I am going to be doing on such and such a definite day some twenty years from now, this would make no sense at all; it is not possible for me to project anything concrete—that is, I am not able imaginatively to reach that point. This is what happens with a young person. He knows he is going to die, of course; it could be that he thinks a lot about it, but he does not know where to put death, he cannot *situate* it. It seems to him very remote—that is, he does not take it into account, it does not function as a real ingredient of his actual horizon. And if death by some chance approaches him, it seems to him to be an accident, something anomalous occurring to him or, rather, something that is going to occur. We could say that, for a very young man, death is always *structurally remote*. In contrast, things are different for the adult: death is *here*, always and at every instant, not present (that would be excessive), but he has to take it into account in each act of his life, because it is *latent*—and because what is latent will not let us forget that it effectively "is."

But life, on account of its characteristic of absolute certainty, since living consists in a certain absolute position, claims and demands an infinity. Life cannot renounce itself except from within itself—that is, while at the same time surreptitiously affirming itself. For this reason, human life intrinsically requires its own perpetuation. In other words, the demand for its own immortality pertains to life, united at the same time with the affirmation that it is mortal, with the view that "its days are numbered," and with the imaginative anticipation of death. All the disparate terms of the question have to be grasped at one and the same time, if it is not to be falsified. Whatever may be the solution that is given to the problem, these are its data. The neglect of this complexity, whether from one side or the other, is a radical form of inauthenticity, displaying two opposed manifestations: one that takes annihilation for granted, another that equally takes survival for granted and considers it obvious —that is, without a living faith in it.

In fact, there are many people—believers, Christians, Catholics—who consider enduring and eternal life real, who believe that each person will go to heaven or to hell, but who have never thought for even a minute about eternal life as such. I mean that they abide by the verdict or the outcome of judgment, without thinking even for a moment about the very substance of that verdict, without being able to say truly: *expecto resurrectionem mortuorum et vitam venturi saeculi.*

Man passes his life inventing things. I have said on another occasion that more than half of the things man has invented, he has invented in order to console himself for having to die, and the other not quite half of those things he has invented in order to defend himself against desolation while he lives. And desolation is, first of all, solitude among people, solitude in a place where companionship should be. If you wish an extreme formula, it must be said that desolation is the contrary of the communion of the saints.

That is why it is highly precautionary and precipitous— thus not at all Cartesian—to say that "hell is the others." This is not certain, not certain at all. It all depends on what others and, especially, on what is done with them; it all depends (does it not?) on what our own vital project is with regard to them. The others are heaven and hell, according to cases. And this brings us back again to paradise.

Notice by what path we return to paradise, which we believed conclusively lost.

Now we are dealing with Paradise with a capital *P*, with the heavenly Paradise, of the heaven we expect, that we are trying to gain, not with that supposed and chimerical paradise with which we usually confuse the world. People talk about *eternal life;* they even talk about *vita beata.* But these expressions, are they not "round squares"? At first sight, it would seem so. We have seen that life is temporal and successive, precisely that. What does it mean then to talk about *eternal life?* Is this not the very formula for impossibility? We have seen that life is defined by discontent, by disenchantment, by dissatisfaction, by limitation, by exclusion—in sum, by intrinsic unhappiness. Is it possible then that *vita beata* too may not be another formula for contradiction?

First of all, let us remove a danger from our path: the image of beatitude as something inert. Note that the Spanish word *beato* has two meanings: *beato* is one who has achieved *beatitud,* "blessedness." But in another sense it represents one of the most deplorable realities on earth: *beato* is one who has fallen into *beatería,* "hypocritical piety." Consider the accidental semantic proximity of *beatitud* and *beatería.* It is frightening. It is frightening and it gives us much to think about. It reveals to us that what is involved is a hinge, a hinge where two quite different realities are joined.

On the other hand, when we talk about *eternal life,* the expression should not be trivialized, by which I mean not "naturalizing" it. Because eternal life exists as such only in a supernatural way and by virtue of participation in divine life. Because, in a strict sense, God alone is eternal. I stand absolutely opposed to the kind of inflation of eternity that prevails these days. We are in an era of inflation, and the adjective *"eternal"* is no exception. People talk about "eternal art," "eternal truths," "eternal Spain" (and *la France éternelle*), and in this same way about many other things. And *eternal*, well, strictly and absolutely God is eternal and nothing else. Other realities are, at most, sempiternal and everlasting, when they are not temporal plain and simple.

This eternal and supernatural life, therefore, cannot be planned. It is possible to plan toward it, which is something quite different. It is possible to try to gain heaven, as René Descartes said. This, yes: it is perfectly human and feasible to try to gain heaven, to plan toward an enduring life, but not to plan *it*. It is unplannable because it is unimaginable. And to plan something is precisely to imagine it, to prelive it in imagination. It is to shape the novel of our life. It is to invent the next adventure. And the heavenly adventure is unimaginable, and thus we are unable to plan it.

Of course, as soon as one has finished saying this, one has to give a tug on the rudder and come around in a different direction. That is, after denying that enduring life can be imagined, I have to invite the imagination of it. What does this contradiction mean? Simply this: it has to be rigorously emphasized that eternal life is inaccessible from this life, that it transcends our earthly possibilities, in the sense that we cannot in any way try to *reduce* it to something already known. But at the same time the effort to imagine it in some way is inescapable—analogously, with great caution, knowing that our imagination makes mistakes when it is forced and, above all, that it is defective.

The idea of happiness would have to be utilized methodically, not as a more or less insipid idea, not as a conventional idea of what is good and what is proper, not as a certain impassiveness and absence of pain, nor as a certain stability that inside of ten minutes would bore us, in the way that the usual manner of representing the other paradise bores us. Nor would a simple magnification and inertial amplification of what we here consider good be enough.

Paradise is another world; it is *the other world.* Emphasize "other" as much as you wish, but only on condition that you do not forget "world." What is involved is the New Jerusalem, the heavenly Jerusalem: *Et vidi caelum novum et terram novam,* it is said in *Revelations.* And world is already enterprise. The primary source of beatitude, the vision of God, the contemplation of God, absolutely infinite —this is the unending and inexhaustible enterprise.

The idea of enduring life is almost always thought about in a very schematic and abstract way; and the tremendous, prodigious belief in the resurrection of the flesh, in the bodily resurrection of the dead, is usually forgotten. For example, theologians have sometimes asked about the age at which resurrection will take place, at what age people will be resuscitated, whether at the age at which they died or at some other age, whether one who died in childhood will be resuscitated as a child and one who died old and diseased will be resuscitated at least old, although without his diseases. And the opinion is common among theologians (fortunately, nothing is known of this, since the Church teaches nothing on this subject and leaves it to the disputes of men) that everybody will be resuscitated as an adult, neither old nor young, but of adult age and mature. But this solution seems to me to represent a mental attitude that is inadequate and uncongenial to questions of this order, since it seems to be the projection of narrow human intellectual habits upon enduring life. It seems to me, in short, to betoken an unspeakable lack of confidence in God.

Human life appears to us as something that is irreplaceable *as a whole.* Consider, for example, the life course of a beloved person. Recall the painful, heartrending feeling with which the father watches his children grow; he is in some ways pleased that they are growing older, but at the same time he feels the pain of losing the child of three months, the child of two years, of four, of seven, to find himself little by little confronted with a young man as tall as he is, with a man he may prefer to all those children, but who will never console him for the loss of them. Of course, parents generally have recourse to an expedient, which is to have another child, and later on another, and in this way, although the children keep on growing, there is always a child in the house. But in the end this cannot go on forever, nor is it in itself sufficient to dull the pain of losing the child—the children, rather—who was at one time within each one of the grown-up children.

Thus, to resign oneself to the notion that in the other life we will be resuscitated only at one age seems to me a kind of pettiness and cowardice unworthy of the Christian idea of God. It seems to me to reveal very little belief, very little confidence in divine omnipotence to think that such a painful earthly limitation will have to endure. I believe that God will know how to manage things very well (even though we do not know how) in order that the successive spacing out of human ages on earth will not persist in heaven. That is, I believe that God will arrange it so that those many ages do not disappear in eternal life and be reduced to only one, and so that the totality of the ages of each one of our lives will be rescued and will be supernaturally preserved.

I do not understand how it is possible for there to be Christians (but there are, almost all of them) who would admit the possibility that the Child Jesus may not really exist—and nothing less than this is what is involved here. Because the Child Jesus, object of a moving and profound cult throughout the whole of Christianity, does not exist, according to a very widespread theological opinion. He existed, yes, in Bethlehem in Judea more than nineteen hundred years ago, but he *no longer* exists, because Christ, corporeally resuscitated, would exist in heaven at his adult age of thirty-three years, exactly that which those theologians believe to be the most probable age of resurrection. That is, Christ would exist in heaven just as he was when he walked on water and was crucified. More exactly, as he appeared to Mary Magdalene and at Emmaus. But the Child Jesus would not exist, neither he who lay in the straw at Bethlehem nor the boy who disputed with the scholars.

I am not able to renounce all this, and I believe that God has some way of doing things that will not disappoint us—that is, our hopes and expectations cannot be condemned to frustration, that the good we imagine and desire will not suffer such a fate, because it will turn out to be greater, never more paltry or narrow. God will know how to bring it about that all ages are able to coexist in heaven and that nothing at all be lost from any of them. As I also expect that he will know how to accomplish things in such a way that nothing of all our possible and desired lives will be lost either, those lives that, as I said before, we have gone along leaving abandoned to the right and left of the trail.

Here it is that I see a way, a possibility of imagining, vaguely and by analogy, what Paradise will be, what enduring life will be—very vaguely, just precise enough to make it possible to desire it truly.

Because, let us not deceive ourselves, the great diabolical temptation is a kind of emptying out of reality that leaves everything pallid and bloodless. In contrast to the testimony that God saw the newly created world as something that was "very good," the devil whispers in our ear that nothing is worth the trouble. It is not to be forgotten, for example, that there is a type of reasoning that defends the faith in such a way that it undermines it, giving ridiculous reasons, reasons that are not reasons, that cause, as Saint Thomas said, *in irrisionem infidelium*, that makes the unfaithful laugh. Nor is it to be forgotten that there is a hostile kind of faith, a faith that believes *against*, in which to affirm is always to affirm against, and which in this way destroys charity. One has to fear, finally, that security, that simple security, that simple, inert, inoperant, never provocative certainty, which never provokes nor awakens the appetite, the appetite for the other life, the inextinguishable appetite for Paradise—in other words, that dead faith, that simple security and certainty in the inevitable which does not know how to kindle expectation and hope.

CHAPTER TWELVE

ATARAXIA AND HALCYONISM

All Greek thought is crisscrossed by a continuous grumble: In order for man to be happy, he has to be master of himself. Does this then mean that he is not? And if he is not, why is he not and in what way? What is it that, in one way or another, leads man astray, uproots him from himself, enslaves him, deprives him of himself? This theme has passed from the Greeks to the whole of Western thought. (And, probably, if one looks through Oriental eyes, the entire Occident appears as a culture that *forgets* this situation and that, for this reason, does not apply the remedies, a culture in which man, occupied in exercising his dominion over things, is never or seldom master of himself.)

Self-sufficiency, independence, freedom, serenity, imperturbability—such seem to be the Hellenic ideals, especially to the degree that, with the passage of time and the accumulation of experiences, failures, and disappointments, Greek thought begins to feel uneasy and suspicious, from its acquaintance with so many things, and to retreat within itself. One after another of the philosophers, from very different schools of philosophy, and even those that are opposed to one another, all seem to agree that happiness always presents itself with the same countenance, that of a man who has not let himself be carried away or wrenched out of himself by anything, who has achieved imperturbability, *ataraxía*. This is nothing but one of the forms of that radical sense of independence, of self-sufficiency, that defines Greek man—I mean, who is defined by his sense of the need for it. For a Greek, something is truly real only when it is sufficient unto itself, self-sufficient, autarchical— when, therefore, it is able to isolate itself from everything else (thus substance, *ousía*, which is a detachable reality that does not require any other within which to exist or upon which to adhere, as upon a subject, foundation, or sub- strate), when it is a law unto itself and *autonomous*. Even freedom is thought of in this way. Aristotle's *eleútheros ánthropos*, the "free man," is a man who has an estate (*ousía*) and thus has no need for anybody else. It is true, of course, that he does at least have a need for that estate. This difficulty did not escape the keenness of the Greeks, and thus during the Hellenistic period the *wise man* gradually divests himself of more and more things, and his ideal, in the hands of the Cynics, comes more and more to resemble, in a disquieting way, that of the beggar. Until, finally, a decisive question arises that is, of course, no less disquieting: Will this not turn out to be an easy simplification? Will the Cynic beggar really be independent and master of himself, so that he needs nothing and is a person who is indifferent to everything and to whom nothing matters? Will he not have reduced his own reality so much, will he not have impoverished it in such a way, that he may no longer have *anything to be master of?*

Our own time, on the contrary, has arrived at the exalta- tion of *anguish*. From the time of the Romantic Age (as was to be expected), from the days of Kierkegaard (1813– 1855), with its luxuriant revival in all the *existentialisms*, anguish has enjoyed an excellent press. It is believed to be an extreme and privileged situation of man, in which alone, perhaps, he is properly a man. In other places [1] I have oc- cupied myself with this contemporary predilection for anguish. And yet there are many and, no doubt, real similar- ities between our own times and the crisis of the ancient world, that time of historical maturity in which man faced the critical situation with a "morality for hard times" composed of imperturbability or *ataraxía*, with an ideal of humanity that is precisely the serene and perhaps detached wise man. Would it not be appropriate to look back with some carefulness at that ancient ideal of *ataraxía?*

What has been decisive is that the classical doctrine of *ataraxía* is to be found in the schools of Skepticism, above all in Pyrrho (c. 360–270 B.C.) and in written form in the *Outline Sketches of Pyrrhonism* of Sextus Empiricus, who lived in the second century of our era. It will be appropriate for us to note in detail what Sextus Empiricus understood by *ataraxía.*

> Skepticism [Sextus Empiricus wrote] is a faculty that in every way opposes phenomena and noumena, and departing from them we pass, by way of the equilibrium of things and of opposed reasons, first to abstention (*epokhé*) and then to imperturbability (*ataraxía*). We call it a faculty, not in a superfluous way, but purely and simply in the sense of a "power." By "phenomena" we now understand things perceptible to the senses, and for that reason we oppose to them the intelligible . . . By "opposed reasons" we understand, not at all affirmation and negation, but simply those that are in conflict. We call "equilibrium" the equivalence of credence and distrust, in such a way that none of the reasons in conflict surpasses any of the others in credibility. "Abstention" (*epokhé*) is a fixed position in the mind (*stásis dianoías*) by virtue of which we neither affirm nor deny anything. "Imperturbability" (*ataraxía*) is serenity and calmness of soul (phykhês aokhlesía kaì galenótes).[2]

A little further on, Sextus Empiricus defines the aim of *sképsis.*

> Consecutive with this would also be to explain the aim of Skepticism. The end is that for which all things are done and considered and is itself on account of nothing else, or

the highest of all desired things. We have said up to now that the aim of Skepticism is imperturbability *(ataraxía)* in what concerns opinion and moderation of the passions *(metriopátheia)* to the necessary degree. In fact, you began to philosophize by attempting to judge and decide which fantasies are true and which false, with the aim of achieving imperturbability, but you came across the disagreement *(diaphonía)* of which we have spoken and, not being able to come to a decision about it, you abstain. But then, as if by chance, tranquility *(ataraxía)* in matters of opinion follows immediately upon this abstention of yours. In fact, he who believes that something is good or evil by nature is in a continuous state of unrest, and when he does not have what he considers good, he believes himself to be pursued by what is naturally evil and goes after the good, according to his understanding of it. But once this is obtained, he falls into an even greater unrest, because he is unreasonably and excessively agitated and, fearing change, he does everything he can so as not to lose what he considers good. On the other hand, *he who makes no decision about what is naturally good and evil neither refuses nor pursues anything with any intensity and is, therefore, free of disturbance (atarakteî).* What happens to the Skeptic is thus what is told of the painter Apeles. It is said of him that while painting a horse and trying to imitate the lather of the horse's sweat, he failed so thoroughly that in exasperation he hurled the sponge on which he cleaned his brushes at the surface he was painting, and the sponge, upon striking the picture, made a perfect likeness of the horse's sweat. It is in this way too that the Skeptics expected to achieve imperturbability, attempting to come to a decision about the differences between phenomena and noumena and, not being able to do so, they abstained; but, immediately upon abstaining, as if by chance, imperturbability came over them like a shadow following a body.[3]

What is involved, then, is a negative imperturbability or *ataraxía*, emerging out of a certain desperation, composed out of the renunciation of what is considered impossible. Ortega once recalled [4] that expression of Cicero's, referring precisely to those "Academics" who were *quasi desperata cognitione certi* (*De finibus*, II, 14). Ortega said, "The expression is extremely paradoxical and perhaps might well be translated in this way: We are possessed by the desperation of not being able to know."

What is decisive is, evidently, the connection between *ataraxía* and abstraction or *epokhé;* the latter is the means by which tranquillity is achieved. In one way or another, as we shall shortly see, this general presupposition permeates almost all the interpretations of *ataraxía*, both before and after that time. We need to know whether it is justified, whether it pertains to the most profound and radical meaning of *ataraxía*.

In a less extreme form, as was to be expected, an analogous interpretation flutters beneath the diverse forms in which *ataraxía* is presented in the Epicurean and Stoic schools. It could be said that *ataraxía*, tranquillity, is the very substance of the doctrine of Epicurus. According to the testimony of Sextus Empiricus,[5] "Epicurus said that philosophy is an activity that by means of discussions and reasonings strives for a happy life." How does it attain this? By *tranquilizing* man with regard to his religious fears, especially concerning the anger of the gods and above all concerning death. When Epicurus occupied himself with physics, and in particular with meteors, he always gave *several* explanations, since, strictly speaking, it was not the explanation that interested him, but only the possibility of finding a natural explanation. What is involved is always "knowing what to be guided by," but in this case in a purely negative sense. He was not interested in what it is that produces earthquakes or hailstorms, but simply in the fact that they are *in no way* supernatural, that *there is nothing to worry about.*[6] Epicurean *ataraxía* is liberation from fear. When Lucretius expounds this doctrine, he locates the supreme good in overcoming fear of the gods. He pictures human life as oppressed by the gravity of religion. Epicurus dared to confront this fact and triumph over it.[7] And for this reason genuine *pietas* does not reside in acts that are considered religious, but in being able to contemplate everything with a serene mind, *pacata posse omnia mente tueri.*[8]

In Stoicism, for its part, virtue (*areté*) rests on rational conformity with the order of things. The goal of man is *homologouménos têi physei zên*,[9] *convenienter naturae vivire*, to live in harmony with nature. From Zeno and Chrysippus to Cicero, Seneca, and Marcus Aurelius, the same theme resounds through half a millenium in the Stoic schools of Greece and Rome. Nature coincides with what is rational; what matters is that men behave *in accordance with reason*, come what may. Almost all things are indifferent (*adiáphora*), although in the end the pressure of reality obliges us to recognize that some are *preferable;* in a rigorous sense, things are neither good nor bad. Nothing affects the Stoic, who is self-sufficient, dependent on himself alone; he endures and renounces (*sustine et abstine*). *Ataraxía* is the properly human state. Seneca comes to say that *not being moved* is a sovereign state that is vast and very close to the condition of a God; it is what Democritus called *thymía* but which he, Seneca, preferred to call, in Latin, *tranquillitas.*

> *Quod desideras autem, magnum est Deoque vicinum, non concuti. Hanc stabilem animi sedem Graeci θυμίαν vocant, da qua Democriti volumen egregium est; ego tranquillitatem voco.*[10]

The tranquil man, he who contemplates things with a serene gaze—at what cost does he purchase his tranquillity?

Perhaps that of losing interest in things. The freedom of the Epicurean and the Stoic is a liberation *from* things, from interests, from fears—perhaps also from hopes. It is, without doubt, an impoverishment of the world, an invitation to inactivity, to the *suspension* of the Skeptic. It is not to be forgotten that *apàtheia*, so frequently identified with *ataraxía*, has come to acquire underneath its literal meaning (absence of passions) that of *apathy*. The Epicureans usually equated *ataraxía* with *aponía*, which reveals its negative character: absence of disturbance, absence of pain, neither restlessness nor pain. *From* all this the wise man is free. But is that enough? Beneath freedom *from*, is it not freedom *for* that is decisive? Is a positive, active, affirmative interpretation of *ataraxía*—tranquillity, calmness—possible?

The oldest and most fundamental meanings of *ataraxía* refer to other concepts and operate in what Ortega would call other "pragmatic fields." Probably the oldest philosophical text in which the word appears is a doxography of Democritus (around 460–370 B.C.), preserved in Joannes Stobaeus. Plato and Democritus, says Stobaeus, locate happiness in the soul, and Democritus

> also calls happiness (*eudaimonía*) *euthymía* ("good humor," "spirit," "self-confidence") and *euestó* ("well-being," "prosperity") and *harmonía* ("good constitution") and *symmetría* ("proportion," "equilibrium") and *ataraxía;* it consists in the distinction and discrimination of pleasures, and this is what is loveliest and most appropriate for man.[11]

Here we have an entirely positive and active context for ataraxia. Good humor, joy and contentment, merriment, harmonious equilibrium. There is no concern here for abstention, for suspension of judgment or of activity, but rather for distinction (*diorismos*) and discrimination (*diákrisis*) among pleasures. There is no effort here to *endure* passively or to give up interests with indifference, but to consider the situation in which one finds oneself and the things in it with an alert eye, in order to discern, distinguish, and discover prosperity and well-being. In his interpretation of ataraxia Democritus is, in effect, the joyous philosopher of the tradition.

If we leave aside a Pythagorean testimony, in which ataraxia is equated with purity (*atáraktoí te kaì katharoí*),[12] and an Aristotelian passage in *The History of Animals*[13] that is of secondary interest, we find a confirmation of the positive point of view in the *Nicomachean Ethics* of Aristotle. In Book IV, with reference to evenness of temper or *praiótes*, ataraxia appears in a context of equilibrium and moderation. The even-tempered man wishes to be *atárakhos*, that is, to live free of contention and disturbance and not to let himself be carried away by passions any more than in the measure and during the time that reason directs.[14] That is, ataraxia consists of a middle way (*mesótes*), and not, by any means, of a lack of response, impassiveness, or absence of indignation and courage—all of which are expressly condemned. Thus it is not the nonexistence of emotion but the moderation of emotion. The *atárakhos* feels indignation, annoyance, and anger; but he is the master of them, he restrains them, and dominates them, he is not *rattled*.

This is not, however, the most interesting of the texts in which Aristotle occupies himself with ataraxia. In Book III, it appears with express reference to courage and fortitude (*andreía*). The brave man (*andreîos*) is one who in the face of danger (*phoberá*) maintains himself *atárakhos* and behaves as he should (*hos dei*). Here, then, ataraxia is not *apathy*, it is not properly imperturbability in the negative sense of the word, but rather fearlessness.[15] One tries to keep cool in the face of danger, to confront it without being rattled. This is so to such a degree that a little while before Aristotle equates the adjectives *áphobon kaì atárakhon* (without fear and without disturbance, courageous and serene), and for this reason insists that the man who maintains himself in this way, fearless and imperturbable, in sudden and unforeseen dangers (*en toîs aiphnidíois phóbois*) is more courageous than the one who behaves in the same way in dangers that are already known and manifest (*en toîs prodélois*), since the former kind of bravery proceeds more from character than from preparation.[16]

In other words, ataraxia consists in a state of *alertness*, which is serenity and foresight *directed toward action*. Courage in the midst of dangers, and above all in the midst of sudden, unexpected, and unforeseeable dangers, is an attitude composed of serenity, of acutely perceptive calmness, that allows one to act promptly and with certainty, even without prior preparation. The word *alert*, so expressive, translates this disposition in a way that cannot be improved upon. With the interjection *all'erta* (from *erta*, "the act of rising") * soldiers were called "to rise and take up their positions in the event of an attack." [17] Notice the enormous semantic gap between the abstention or suspension of the Skeptics, the apathy, the absence of disturbance and pain of the Epicureans, and this serene and tense state of alert in the face of every unexpected danger.

In spite of this, the fortunes (the bad fortune, we would say) of the idea of ataraxia have almost always emphasized its negative side. Montaigne, always quite perceptive, was clearly aware of this.

* [The interjection *all'erta*, as well as the word *erta*, is not Spanish, but Italian, from which both Spanish *alerta* and English *alert* are derived—Trans.]

Les pyrrhoniens [he writes], *quand ils disent que le souverain bien c'est l'ataraxie, qui est l'immobilité de jugement, ils ne l'entendent pas dire d'une façon affirmative; mais le même bransle de leur ame, qui leur faict fuyr les precipices, et se mettre à couvert du serein, celuy là mesme leur present cette fantaisie, et leur en faict refuser une aultre.*[18]

The affirmative form of ataraxia would appear rather in its classical Spanish version: *el sosiego,* "restfulness," "tranquility." Some years ago, in an article entitled "Los nombres de la angustia" ("The Names of Anguish"),[19] I occupied myself briefly with the different ways in which "anguish" is understood and interpreted, as these are reflected in the different names it has received: anguish, agony, affliction, anxiety, turmoil, discontent, restlessness (and, of course, other contrary words, where they exist). I grouped these words around three distinct cores of meaning. The first is dominated by the experience of being in a *tight squeeze:* anguish as narrowness,* and from this oppression or lack of air, suffocation; agony as compression; affliction as the pressure actively exerted by something or somebody and suffered by the one who is afflicted; anxiety as permanent and enduring anguish. In turmoil there is no narrowness, but *instability,* fluctuation, oscillation up and down and back and forth, insecurity, uncertainty, discord, the danger of foundering. The last names, finally, are negative, privative words: *dis*content, rest*less*ness—the lack of contentment, inappropriateness, untimeliness, disappointment. And restlessness? I said:

Desasosiego ("restlessness") is privation or lack of rest; the noun *sosiego* ("restfulness," "tranquillity") comes from the verb *sosegar* ("to take a rest"). It seems then

---

* [The Spanish for "narrowness" is *angostura*—Trans.]

that in order to have tranquility one must oneself take a rest, since tranquility does not already exist, since it is not given as a gift. And the Spanish word *sosegar*, from the same root as *sentarse* ("to sit down"), means "to take a rest," "to calm down," "to settle," "to make firm, secure, serene." Restlessness is the loss of restfulness, of settlement, of the calmness that man had achieved, that he had attained as a result of taking a rest.

Among all the names for anguish this is the one I prefer: *desasosiego*, so completely Spanish that it is not to be found in any other language unless it has been imported from ours, so entirely appropriate to the best that we have been, so exact—because it shows us that anguish is only a deprivation, that what is proper to man is not anguish but *sosiego*, "tranquillity," but that this, in its turn, is not given without effort, but that man has to conquer it and earn it, that in order to have restfulness, he must first take a rest.

Man, even in the most oppressive situations, is capable of retiring within himself and taking a rest, perhaps by means of a vigorous effort. It is always something that a man does, which he has to achieve; but when he has attained it, he does not come to another thing, but to himself. Tranquillity is the authenticity conquered from agitation and alienation.

Saint John of the Cross admirably grasps this nuance in "The Ascent of Mount Carmel."

En una noche oscura
con ansias en amores inflamada,
¡oh dichosa ventura!,
salí sin ser notada,
estando ya mi casa sosegada.

A oscuras y segura,
por la secreta escala, disfrazada,
¡oh dichosa ventura!,

a oscuras, en celada,
*estando ya mi casa sosegada.**

What is decisive is *ya* ("now," "already"), which confers upon *sosegada* ("rested") its character of participle. The end of an act of resting is the state to which the soul comes; at the conclusion of arduous effort the house is *now* rested. Although Saint John's commentaries frequently detract somewhat from the immediate effectiveness of his poems, his own commentary in this case is quite revealing.

And this "since my house is rested now," namely, the sensitive part which is the house of all the appetites, *rested now by the vanquishment* and the slumber of all of them. Because until the appetites slumber *through mortification* in sensuality, and sensuality itself is already rested in them in such a way that no war is waged against the spirit, *the soul does not go out into its true freedom* in order to enjoy union with its Beloved.[20]

And further on he talks about "the main difficulty that there is in bringing this house to rest on the spiritual side and being able to enter into this interior darkness which is the spiritual nakedness of all things." [21] And he still insists on the "supernatural restfulness" in which "one must always try to exist with tranquility of understanding." [22]

But the classical passage that illustrates *el sosiego* as a Spanish form of existence in the seventeenth century is

---

* [Here is a more or less literal version in English:
   On a dark night
   with longings by loves enflamed—
   Oh, fortunate hazard!—
   I went out without being observed,
   since my house was rested now.

   In darkness and secure
   by a secret ladder, disguised—
   Oh, fortunate hazard!—
   in darkness, into an ambush,
   since my house was rested now.
                                       —Trans.]

that from the account of the life of Don Francisco Manuel de Melo, the Portuguese-Spanish author of *Historia de los movimientos, separación y guerra de Cataluña en tiempos de Felipe IV*, which Ortega so much liked to recall. Melo, hardly into his youth, embarked on the flagship *San Antonio*, under the command of General Don Manuel de Meneses, on the 23rd of September, 1626, to go to Flanders with two regiments recruited in Portugal.

The ship was hardly out of sight of the coast when a storm began to rise in such a fury that, according to the pilots, such a battle of winds and seas had never been seen before. And thus everything announced to the grieving and departed voyagers an approaching and inevitable shipwreck, as was finally confirmed *after nineteen days of the storm in the waters off Saint-Jean-de-Luz* in a small cove of this port on the coast of France. In this disastrous situation night fell, which was passed in confusion, vows, and the making of wills; but the General, however, although not ignorant of the great peril he was in, had the strange resolve to put on the best clothes he possessed. Everybody else then followed his example and did the same thing, so that, when dying as they fully expected to, their bright winding sheets would be recommendation for a decent burial.

In the middle of all this, the General took out some papers he was carrying with him and turned to Don Francisco Manuel, who had accompanied him most of the night, and calmly said to him, "This is one of Lope de Vega's sonnets, which he himself gave to me when I went just now to the palace; in it he praises Cardinal Barbarino, *legatus a latere* to his eminence Pope Urban VIII." He read it and began to pronounce his judgment upon it, as if he were examining it in a serene academy. But upon arriving at a line that seemed useless to him, he spoke at length, revealing to our author all the defects he found in it, no doubt for the purpose of distracting him from the immense danger he saw him to be in.[23]

This is the passage. Bad weather, a raging storm, certainty of shipwreck, and death probable. You will recall that the night "was passed in confusion, vows, and the making of wills." But in the midst of the danger—without, however, being ignorant of it—the commander of the fleet, Don Miguel de Meneses, puts on his best clothing, all the others imitating him, and *sosegadamente* ("calmly") —that is, after having taken a rest within himself—turned to Melo, with Lope's sonnet in his hand, and began to deliver a literary criticism of it in the middle of the storm. This is Spanish tranquillity, which Velázquez should have painted.

The condition of uncertainty and disorientation, "not knowing what to be guided by," when man abandons himself to it, frequently leads to *anguish*. When he tries to evade this condition without overcoming it, when he pretends that he can go on acting as if he knew, though he does not know and, above all, does not exert himself for the purpose of knowing, that is *fanaticism*. The fanatic throws dirt in his own eyes and tries to nullify his intellectual confusion with an emotional confusion. He is a squid that, in order not to see that the water is muddy, discharges a cloud of ink into it. Anguish and fanaticism are two of the main complaints of our times, as they were, in different forms, at the end of the ancient world. The attempt to go beyond them was ataraxia—that is, as we have seen, the negative version of ataraxia, which is suspension and abstention, disinterestedness and indifference. But we have already seen that this is nothing but a degeneration of the more radical and older meaning of ataraxia, whose positive forms are the state of alertness and an active and tense tranquillity.

When some years ago the activity of the *Instituto de Humanidades* was initiated, Ortega wrote these foresightful words:

When in recent times the question "What is man?" was asked for the first time with vigor and urgency, it was very quickly discovered that he *was nothing of* what up until now had been presumed. The consequences of this discovery must be the admission that we do not know what man is and a courageous determination to go about finding out. But the type of man who predominates these days is possessed of the basic belief that he already knows everything—he is, by definition, not "the man in the street," but the man who "knows all the ropes," * the man who does not know that he does not know—the fanatic. This is why, in his mind, the discovery that *man was nothing of what has been believed until now* is transubstantiated, without further consideration, into the firm doctrine that *man is nothing,* and he winds up, with unseemly haste, with unjustified high-handedness, in a nihilism that is as radical as it is arbitrary. In the face of all this, the *Instituto de Humanidades* takes pride in its own ignorance, which is the unquestionable privilege of man and the maximum stimulus that moves us to undertake a series of efforts in common for the purpose of trying to go on responding to that desperate question. And all that with jovial tranquillity—a temperament as *existential* as wrath, bitterness, and anguish can be—over having the advantage (a humanist would say) of placing ourselves under the direct protection of Jove, since from him joviality proceeds. This human tranquillity bears a sign that is just the opposite of the contentedness usually attributed to the bovine species, which, if we are to take the risk of affirming that the animal feels it, would be a gift of restfulness, composed of insensibility toward

* [Ortega contrasts *el hombre de la calle,* "the man in the street," with *el hombre al cabo de la calle,* literally "the man at the end of the street," but meaning "the man who is well informed"—Trans.]

danger. But man's tranquillity is what man himself elegantly creates in the midst of agony and harassment, when upon feeling himself lost he cries to others or to himself, Keep cool! The privileged quality that some thinkers today concede to *extreme* situations, rehabilitating a bit of Kierkegaard's romantic frenzy, does not seem to be established upon an adequate foundation. It is not in *anguish* but in *tranquillity* that such situations are to be surmounted and order brought into them, where man can truly take possession of his life and effectively *exist*. In that tranquillity he genuinely humanizes himself. The only thing that must be said against tranquillity is the same thing that must be said against anguish and against every other pure emotion on which man tries to found his existence: that each one of them carries within itself the seed of a particular corruption. Every human temperament can *exist in its true form* or in a defective way. Thus, tranquillity may degenerate into routine, mere adaptation, or conformity, just as anguish, degenerated into mania or fear, makes a man frantic and vile.[24]

And this active tranquillity, this positive ataraxia, jovial and alert, possesses its myth—the myth of Halcyon. The halcyon, or kingfisher, is one of the most beautiful of aquatic birds, with a strong, sharp beak, short tail, and brilliant colors: greenish blue, with a white and brown breast. The halcyon, *martín pescador*, kingfisher, *Eisvogel*, venerated in the islands of the Pacific, theme of medieval legends, a mythic and mythological bird. During the Middle Ages it was believed to have acquired its brilliant plumage (it was originally a common gray bird) upon flying toward the sun when it left Noah's ark. On its upper feathers it took on the tints of the sky, and was singed on its underside by the heat of the setting sun. Perched on a rooftop, it is like a weathervane, with its beak pointed toward the direction from which the wind is coming.

But the most significant myth is the classical myth, told

by Apollonius Rhodius, Hyginus, Ovid,[25] and which had already appeared in Simonides, noted by Aristotle. Halcyone, daughter of Aeolus, and her husband Ceyx, on account of having called themselves Zeus and Hera, were converted into halcyons. According to a different version, Ceyx was drowned, and Halcyone found his body, thrown up onto the beach by the sea; the gods, moved to compassion, converted them both into halcyons. And (this now is the nucleus, the most significant part of the myth) by command of Zeus or of Aeolus, the winds ceased to blow during the seven days before and after the winter solstice, so that the halcyons might make their nests without danger of the winds carrying off their eggs. Those were the days called "the halcyon days," *alkyonides hemérai.*[26]

In the middle of the winter, season of storms and tempests, during the most bitter weather, the winds stop blowing and *tranquillity is created.* In the stillness, over the quiet, restful waves, which will again be agitated, the halcyon flies, working eagerly, skillfully building its nest, laying its eggs, so that life may continue in spite of all the storms. In this myth of the halcyon, which might be the totem animal of our world, it seems to me I see the culmination of the active, lucid, and human interpretation of tranquillity.

NOTES

1. "Ese que se llama angustia," and "El pensamiento y la inseguridad," in *Ensayos de convivencia* (Buenos Aires, 1955).
2. Sextus Empiricus, *Outline Sketches of Pyrrhonism*, I, 4.
3. *Ibid.*, I, 12. See *Sexti Empirici Opera*, vol. I, Πυρρωνείων 'γποτυπώσεων ΑΒΓ, recensuit Hermannus Mutschmann (Leipzig, 1912). The translation into Spanish [from which this translation into English is made—Trans.] is by M. Araujo in my anthology, *La filosofía en sus textos* (Barcelona, 1950), I, 214–217.

4. Prologue to Emile Bréhier, *Historia de la filosofía* (Madrid, 1942); also in *Obras completas*, VI, 407 fn.

5. *Adversus mathematicas*, XI, 169: Ἐπίχουρος—ἔλεγε τὴν φιλοσοφίαν ἐνέργειαν εἶναι λόγοις καὶ διαλογισμοῖς τὸν εὐδαίμονα βίον περιποιοῦσαν (quoted in Ritter-Preller, *Historia Philosophiae Graecae*, 457). Concerning all this, see Julián Marías, *Biografía de la filosofía*, 2nd edition (Buenos Aires, 1956).

6. See Diogenes Laërtus, Book X. Cf. also William Chase Greene, *Moira: Fate, Good and Evil in Greek Thought* (Harvard University Press, 1948), pp. 333–335.

7. Lucretius, *De rerum natura*, I, 62–101.

8. *Ibid.*, V, 1198–1203:

    nec pietas ullast velatum saepe videri
    vertier ad lapidem atque omnis accedere ad aras
    nec procumbere humi postratum et pandere palmas
    ante deum delubra nec aras sanguine multo
    spargere quadrupedum nec votis nectere vota,
    sed mage pacata posse omnia menti tueri.

9. As early as Heraclitus, the expression ποιεῖν κατα φύσιν ἐπαΐοντας is encountered, presaging the Stoic ὁμολογουμένως τῇ φύσει ζῆν. See *Biografía de la filosofía, III, ii.*

10. Seneca, *De tranquillitate animi*, II.

11. H. Diels, *Die Fragmente der Vorsokratiker*, 6. Aufl., II, 129. Democritus, A, 167: τὴν δ᾽ (εὐθαιμονίαν καὶ) εὐθυμίαν καὶ εὐεστὼ καὶ ἁρμονίαν, συμμετρίαν τε καὶ ἀταρξίαν καλεῖ, συνίσταοθαι δ᾽αὐτὴν ἐκ τοῦ διορισμοῦ καὶ τῆς διακρίσεως τῶν ἡδονῶν, καὶ τοῦτ᾽ εἶναι τὸ κάλλιστόν τε καὶ συμφορώτατον ἀνθρώποις.

12. *Ibid.*, I, 475 (*Pythagoreische Schule*, D. Ἐκ τῶν Ἀριστοξένου Πυθαγοικῶν ἀποφάσεων, 8. Iambl. V. P. 206).

13. Aristotle, *The History of Animals*, IX, 45, 630ᵇ 12.

14. Aristotle, *Nicomachean Ethics*, IV, 5, 125ᵇ 33 ss.

15. *Ibid.*, III, 9, 1117ᵃ 29 ss.

16. *Ibid.*, III, 8, 1117ᵃ 17 ss.

17. See Joan Corominas, *Diccionario crítico etimológico de la lengua castellana* (Madrid, 1954), vol. I.

18. Montaigne, *Essais, livre* II, *chapitre* XII.

19. In *Ensayos de convivencia* (Buenos Aires, 1955).

20. *Obras del Místico Doctor San Juan de la Cruz*, ed. del padre Gerardo de San Juan de la Cruz (Toledo, 1912), I, 94–95. (The emphasis is mine—J. M.)

21. *Ibid.*, p. 97.

22. *Ibid.*, pp. 206–207. The authenticity of this passage is disputed.

23. "Noticias de la vida de don Francisco Manuel de Melo," in *Tesoro de los historiadores españoles* (Paris, 1840), pp. 277–278.

24. *Instituto de Humanidades, organizado por* José Ortega y Gasset y Julián Marías (Madrid, 1948), pp. 16–17.

25. *Metamorphosis*, XI, 410 ss.

26. See Aristotle, *The History of Animals*, V, 8, 542ᵇ, where he talks about the ἀλκυονίδες ἡμέραι and quotes the lines from Simonides where the halcyon is called multicolored: ποικίλας ἀλκύονος.

CHAPTER THIRTEEN

ENERGY AND THE REALITY OF THE WORLD

Thought usually operates with old ideas. To a certain extent this is inevitable, even when one tries in an original and creative way to comprehend a new situation. That is, when one is coming to an idea that is also new, the concepts one is wielding are inherited; they are already here, prior to the situation that has to be understood, and they slip into the new doctrine a coefficient of anachronism. Only by being aware of this can its consequences be attenuated. Thought that takes this inadequacy into account in some measure corrects it and injects into the old concepts (or at least into their functioning) a different meaning that is better adapted to the actual situation.

At times that process of correction, the lack of which can lead to very serious errors, turns out to be especially difficult. Two causes, although not the only ones, are particularly influential in making those mental adjustments difficult, and both of them, as we shall see, converge in the theme of this study. One is the unusual acceleration of change. Concepts do have a certain elasticity, and when variation is slow and, above all, foreseeable, thought gradually brings them to function in a way that is adequate to the transformation taking place. At the end of a certain length of time, even when what I have called their "logical framework" has remained unaltered, their "significance function" [1] has varied sufficiently to make it possible to apprehend the new realities with which one is involved. This does not happen, however, when the situation changes so rapidly that the old concepts "come loose" from reality (if one may speak in this way), for their elasticity is not great enough for them to "catch up" with it. This danger is still greater when the change is *quantitative;* here the continuity of concepts serves no purpose but to mask the change that is taking place. It seems to the observer that what is involved is simply a matter of more or less, and he does not notice that beyond certain limits what is quantitative is converted into a *qualitative* change, so that it is now no longer a question of more or less, but of a *different* thing. When one tries to wake up to this fact, one has already been left too far behind—that is, a gulf has opened up between one's habitual ideas and the new reality one is trying to comprehend.

The other cause that makes it difficult to readjust concepts and bring them up to date is the unrelated source of those concepts that intervene in the comprehension of a reality or of a complex situation. I mean that when a form of thought utilizes, together with ideas that are habitual to it and within which it moves with ease and precision, other ideas originating in other fields and in other mental styles, in general it takes them from a tradition that is already outmoded, without being aware of the changes they have undergone in forms of thinking that are creative and completely contemporary and which are probably unknown to it. This is what happens, for example, when philosophical concepts are slipped into a scientific context, or vice versa. What is to be feared is that those concepts, which are what we might call "imported" into a different form of thought, are taken from a state of the other discipline at a more or less far-off time and do not correspond, except very imperfectly, to what those who are at present working in a creative way at the peak of that discipline now understand by those very same terms. It is most likely, for instance, that those who are not physicists, when they talk about atoms, are thinking of Bohr's model of the atom; that by space, undoubtedly and exclusively, Euclidean space is understood. Or that one who is not a philosopher pairs off space and time in accordance with a Kantian scheme; or if he talks about logic, he identifies it with Aristotelian logic.

These two causes, as I said before, converge in obscuring the real situation when one tries to determine with some exactness what has happened in our time with regard to energy and the relation between energy and the reality of the world. In the first place, since the beginning of the nineteenth century, the increase in the production and consumption of energy has been constantly accelerating and has now reached a level that excludes any comparison with previous epochs. This is what is essential, and what gives to energy a unique position among the factors that determine or condition the present period in history. All other factors have varied, of course, some in a decisive way; but there is a continuity in all of them that makes it possible to go without effort from one stage to another without change in the *meaning* of what one is involved with. In contrast, the utilization of energy has passed from one *order of magnitude* to another; probably the amount of energy utilized during any recent year surpasses that of several centuries prior to the nineteenth. "Quantitative" difference, when it is carried to extremes, is converted into a qualitative difference. And if one continues to think about this theme from the point of view of assumptions that were valid a hundred and fifty years ago (or, if one looks closely, fifty years ago), the unavoidable outcome is error and, what is more, general incomprehension of the situation that characterizes our times.

Then, too, we must consider that the word "world" is

usually understood in a way that conforms to the notion that was dominant in philosophy and science during the nineteenth century. At best, certain precisions concerning physical reality (or nature, if you prefer) that contemporary natural science has achieved may be brought into it. But the radical transformation that philosophy has introduced into the idea of *world* (precisely into this idea of world) during recent decades, and which represents one of the most profound and decisive advances in contemporary thought, is disregarded.

These are the two points of view that have to be kept in mind if one wishes, in 1960, to understand how energy affects nothing less than the reality of the world.

The confusion that has been produced in modern languages by the pair of Greek words *dýnamis* and *enérgeia* is not pure chance. While in Greek the first is opposed to the second in the way that "potentiality" is opposed to "activity" (that is, possibility and capacity belong to the first, while actuality and reality belong to the second), it has come about that *dýnamis* has given us "dynamic" and all its derivatives, and *enérgeia* "energy" and all its derivatives. "Force" and "potency" (*dýnamis*) are identified with "energy" (*enérgeia*), which in Greek would be opposed to them.

I believe that underneath such semantic transpositions lies the entanglement of *can* and *does* within the concept of energy. The increase of energy in the world signifies, first of all, an increase in *possibilities*, and so it has seemed from the beginning. To what degree is this decisive? I believe that we have to insist on the other aspect: the increase in *realities*. By this I mean that many things *could* have been done before now as well, but they were *not done*—that is, *many* were not done, only *some*. For example, prior to our century, and since the end of the fifteenth century, one could have crossed the Atlantic; the distinction of our times does not rest on that possibility, but on the corresponding reality, the realization of it. The fabulous increase in energy has brought about, not a situation in which one *can* cross the ocean, but in which one *does* cross it innumerable times. Energy thus appears as a factor of *realization*, which is what the physical notion of "work" means in a more restricted sense. There are two independent accounts that should not be confused: that of possibilities on the one side, that of the actualization of them on the other. When the *technological* evolution of the world is considered, there is the danger that attention will be concentrated on the first, with disregard for the other aspect of the question. In this way, for example, a technical reality is taken as existing from the time that it is invented; but if this were the case, the automobile would have been an artifact of the nineteenth century. Of course, it is not, but of the twentieth, which is when the automobile came to condition and transform human mobility. Because what is important from this point of view is not that one *can* travel in an automobile (that is, that "somebody" travels in that way), but that it is actually *done* (that is, that "anybody" does it, in principle everybody). Aviation, in this same context, did not exist prior to the First World War but following it. Analogously, atomic energy, which from the point of view of utilization is "already here," does not pertain to the present except as a possibility; and precisely what is going to define the epoch immediately following our own is its effective existence, once it has gone past what we might call the "threshold" of its realization as a constituent factor in the reality of the world.

The immensely different quantity (and thus the different significance) of the energy produced and utilized in the world today brings about an equivalent change in the image of its role, in the mental scheme by which its function is interpreted. The traditional image, by which I mean (and this, which is stupendous, is of the utmost significance) the one that was dominant *from prehistoric times until the beginning of the nineteenth century*, that is, through almost the whole history of humanity, would be this: energy acts *in the world*, it makes it possible to perform certain actions *within* it. The image of transition, prevailing approximately during the nineteenth century, would be already considerably different and might be expressed in this way: energy *transforms* the world, it *transfigures* it (that is, it changes and alters its form or configuration). The situation at present, which has an inceptive character (by which I mean that we are tending toward it and that it is going to be dominant in the very near future), would replace those images with a third: energy affects the *reality* of the world.

What does this mean? And the process of change, does it depend solely on what has been happening in the origination of new sources of energy, in their exploitation, utilization, and application? Or is it perhaps conditioned as well by a change in the *idea* of the world, which is, in its turn, an ingredient in the *reality* of the world? In other words, are we involved only with a technical matter of energy, or is there a convergence of technology and the thought of our time within the changing situation, a convergence of natural changes and changes that have taken place in human thought during our century?

The traditional idea of the world as a collection of things, when not considered false, has appeared to the eyes of the philosophy of our century as at least very secondary and deficient. First of all, the discovery of the "mundane" or "intramundane" character of things shows that, in any case, the world is not reducible to the *sum* of things, but that things are secondary with regard to the world. In other words, things are *in the world;* and it is only within it that their character as things is constituted and, in general, their reality. The world is prior to each thing and even to all of them (that is, to a series or sum of them), and thus it is not possible to derive the world from them or from their mode of being, but just the contrary. Being in the world of circumstantiality seems, on the other hand, to be the constitutive character of man or, said more exactly, of *human life.* Through the Heideggerian idea of *Dasein* or *In-der-Welt-Sein* this notion has been in circulation since 1927; but in a more radical and, if I am not wrong, more exact form, it was the central nerve of Ortega's philosophy from 1914 on, at which time it encountered its most concise and most fortunate expression in the famous formula: *I am myself and my circumstance.*[2]

Contemporary philosophers, with quite considerable differences among them proceeding from their distinct points of departure and from the developing personal positions which they have achieved, have, during recent decades, arrived at a much broader, more complex, and profounder conception of the world. Some of the predominant characteristics of this conception are the following:

(1) The world is always *somebody's* world. To speak of a "world" without qualification does not make sense or, rather, it is an ingenuous displacement, into which an "I" surreptitiously slips, for whom this world is a world—except that later on this indispensable factor is omitted. The fact that the world always pertains to somebody does not, of course, "subjectivize" the world, but acknowledges its genuine and concrete reality instead of replacing it

with an abstract scheme that, rigorously speaking, is only a theory and a hypothesis. Such an abstract scheme would be that reality with which and in which I find myself, removing from it the fact of my encountering it, which is precisely what defines it. The world appears in this way as the *horizon* of a human life, related to me but at the same time irreducible to me, precisely because it is that with which and in which I find myself, that with which I have to involve myself in order to live.

(2) The world understood in this way is, first of all, a repertory of *facilities* and *difficulties* by which to live. As a reality it is at one and the same time unitary and multiple. The world is always *the* world, that is, *one*, specifically, my circumstance, everything with which I find myself in my surroundings; but it consists in the offer to me of a multiplicity of ingredients toward which I am able to turn, which exert diverse pressures upon me, and among which I am able to choose in many different ways. That multiplicity of contents in the world surrounding me brings it about that my being in it is always a *situation*, which is necessarily *one among several* and thus involves at least a virtual multiplicity of situations. That world, proverse and adverse at the same time, in the presence of which I have to do something in order to live (that is, in order to go on living), and which, at the same time that it shelters and protects me and makes it possible for me to do what I have to do, exerts upon me a system of pressures and urgencies and itself responds to my actions that are provoked by them. Life thus appears as a dynamic dialogue between me and my environment or world, and in that dialogue both these irreducible and inseparable elements (namely, I and the world) are found at their roots.

(3) At a later stage that world appears to us as consisting of *possibilities*—and, correlatively, of impossibilities. These are not immediate, however. They are the result

of my *projects;* only through projecting my plans upon the mere facilities and difficulties that are given are these facilities and difficulties converted into possibilities, which are always such *for* those projects. In this sense I have said in another place that possibilities are the first *form* of my life and that this form is, like all the others, acquired.[3] That is, possibilities are not just "here," they are not mere "data"; but they are mine, something constituted within my life, what I do with the facilities and difficulties in order to make my life. Well, since my life consists essentially in projecting itself to itself and, consequently, in projecting upon the environment or circumstance, the world is actually and necessarily *a repertory of possibilities.* On the other hand, we have to distinguish (and for our theme this will be decisive) between *bare* possibilities and those for which the necessary resources are given. These resources are things seen from the point of view of possibilities, but naturally they do not coincide with possibilities. Neither do they coincide with *mere* things. Resources are everything to which one may resort in order to realize possibilities (possibilities that are, within themselves, imaginary), and without these possibilities they lose all the character of resources. This would lead us to distinguish between *actual* possibilities (for which there are available resources) and merely *potential* possibilities (for which resources are absent or simply nonexistent).

(4) What we call things are primarily *interpretations* of reality, projected upon it. To us, however, they seem to be reality itself, since we are not individually their creators, but instead we find them "here" and have them "injected" into us from childhood by our environment. That is, the *primary* meaning of world is not nature, but society, which gives us from the beginning an interpretation of what is real, with which we are required to make our lives.

(5) Those realities that we must take into account, with which we have to involve ourselves, whatever may be our response with regard to them, are the *prevailing* realities, the social pressures that are exerted upon us and that condition our conduct. They are beliefs, received ideas, customs, values and valuations, collective projects, patterns of behavior, institutions, industrial organizations, etc. The combination of them all makes up one of the most immediate strata of what we call the world.

(6) Finally, in a dynamic way, the world is constituted by the combination or repertory of human activities with regard to which we have to know what to be guided by, with which we have to reckon, since in one way or another, from a mere news item to physical coercion, they influence our life, they limit, condition, or foster it, they expand it, they give it content, perhaps they "fill" it.

Naturally, these brief notes do not constitute a theory of the world, nor even an adequate abbreviation of the image of it that contemporary thought has arrived at. They are, rather, a reminder of the perspective from which the world has come to be considered today, a summary explanation of the *present* significance of the word "world" (not that of fifty years ago). We can now ask ourselves with some exactness whether the fabulous increase in the production and utilization of energy in our times affects the *reality* of the world as thus understood, and how it does if it does.

Above all, the contents of the world have undergone a prodigious change, and this has taken place in several directions. We will first of all consider what might be called the "ingredients" of which it is composed. Taking "things" not by the mere fact of their being real (corporeal, for example), but by their "serviceability," by their aptness in fulfilling a function and thus assuming a role in our life, the number of things has multiplied fantastically. No doubt due to the existing raw materials, the world has been filled up with things, which have to be taken into account and which it is equally possible to count on in order to realize innumerable vital projects. The world of any other period in history appears "empty" to us if we compare it with our own. This change is one result of technology, but not primarily what this means in the way of "invention," but what it involves in the way of a process of actualization or production based on the findings of invention—that is, in the way of the intervention of unheard of quantities of energy. Food, clothing, means of transport, machinery of all kinds, today constitute man's primary horizon, beyond which, on a secondary plane, "nature" reveals itself somewhat hazily. A world defined by the opposite relationship (that is, the world that existed from prehistoric times right up to the contemporary period) seems a "primitive" world to us, no matter what its *qualities* may have been—that is, regardless of its qualitative values. The differences that are important to us here are quantitative: that the world be composed mainly of some things or of others.

Taken all together, what are those that compose our world? We would say, to employ a single word, that what is involved are *artificial* realities. However, this already implies a radical transformation. Remember that, throughout the whole of Western culture, the dominant idea by which men thought about things, the idea that for twenty-five hundred years has been identified with this notion, is the Aristotelian concept of substance (*ousía*). However, as everybody knows, for Aristotle only *natural* things were substances in the true sense of the word: animals, plants, or their parts, stones, water, etc.—but not, on the other hand, artificial objects (*apò tékhnes*), such as a statue, a table, a bed, a pitcher, a ship. These secondary things are genuine things (substances) only to the degree that they are "made out of" truly natural things—marble, stone, wood, iron. It is their *material*, always a natural material, that confers upon them a substantial character, which on account of their artificial form they do not possess. Artificial things are always "exceptional" and were isolated upon the vast expanse of nature, which their material always brought them back to anyway. A certain human effort (art or *tékhne*, "technique") precariously and temporarily imposed a form upon the underlying natural reality that constituted the primary and predominant horizon.

Today, on the contrary, man moves within a realm that is primarily artificial, in the background of which it is seen, or rather supposed, that there is a "nature"—of problematical interpretation and frequently interpreted so as to make it conform to a technical framework. But there is even more. The materials that were the point at which what is natural recovered its predominance, even in works of art, have lost their ancient significance. *Today the materials too are artificial.* In a great number of cases, artificial things are made out of something that is equally artificial—a metal that is not to be found in nature, a plastic material with its properties "invented" on purpose for the performance of a chosen function and of whose natural origin no one has the faintest notion, a cloth that has no relation to a sheep, to a field of flax or cotton, or to the silkworm, but to a mysterious world of factories, laboratories, and machinery, only at the far end of which one may perhaps make out a trace of coal or oil as its hypothetical "raw material." Art, technique, invades everything, even to the ultimate redoubt of matter. Artificial things made of materials that are equally artificial surround us from the cradle to the grave; we handle them day after day; they are the visage that the world presents to us.

If one were to enumerate the consequences that flow from this fact and that affect the reality of that very world, one could not possibly be brief. I will point out just two. The first is *complexity*. Contrast the relative "simplicity" of what is natural, the "few" things (I mean, of course, types of things) that make up the world of nature with the almost overwhelming and increasing variety of products of the technology of our times. Simply leafing through the famous Sears, Roebuck catalogue teaches more about what our world truly is than the reading of hundreds of books and almost all newspapers. However, this is hardly said when doubt begins to rise as to whether it is true or not. Is it true that the natural world is so simple? Can it be said that there are few natural things, or few types of things? Replace the vague word "types" with the word *species*, place beside the Sears catalogue a textbook on botany or zoology, more especially on ichthyology or entomology, and you will see that the number of known plant and animal species (leaving aside the innumerable ones not yet studied) is overwhelming. Thousands of species of algae or of coleoptera surround us on all sides, even to obsession. How then is it possible to speak of the complexity of the technical world and the simplicity of the natural world? Is it not just the reverse?

This conclusion does seem to be compelling, but it does not get its way without a certain reluctance on our part. In spite of everything, it seems to us that the natural world is poor and monotonous, that technology signifies an incredible enrichment and complication. Is there some way of getting out of this difficulty, of accepting the two extreme positions, both undoubtedly true, of that opposition? I believe that what is involved is an ambiguous use of the notion of "world." Is it true that the two hundred thousand species of coleoptera form part of the natural *world?* We have to say definitely not. They do, if you like, form a part of nature, which is nothing more than an interpretation of the real, performed by some men, that is, by the naturalists. Those species would be, perhaps, ingredients of the world of the naturalist, but not of the world of man as such. They are not, strictly speaking, component parts of the *world,* as are, in contrast, automobiles, telephones, ships, trains, medicines, movies, guns, cigarettes, hats, newspapers, airplanes, television, houses, furniture, pictures, cameras, watches, food. What do they lack that would give them this character? Precisely what I just got through indicating as the second consequence of the predominant artificiality of the world: its *functional* character.

The innumerable species of diatoms, pteridophytes, or coleoptera have no genuine function in my life. Their differences, no matter how notable they may seem in the eyes of the naturalist, are *irrelevant* from a vital point of view; they are not differences *to me.* They are not, for me, facilities or difficulties, or at most they are a vast facility or an elemental difficulty; but they are in no way possibilities of mine except when I project upon them a program as special and improbable as is the scientific one of studying and classifying them taxonomically. In contrast, artificial and technical realities have been made *with a purpose in mind,* and thus already pertaining to them is an intrinsic function; they are constituted by their "what for" and are thus, by definition, *relevant.* And in this sense, unexpectedly, we find that they are *more world* than the others. What does this mean?

We have already seen that the world is constituted by "things" that are, strictly speaking, *interpretations* of the real, which forces me to make such interpretations in order to know what to be guided by and to be able to handle things. In principle, and in accordance with a principle of vital economy, these interpretations are the necessary minimum. This is why they are usually extremely *vague*, with no more than the degree of precision necessary for that vital guidance. The interpretation "bug" is so vague that it is little less than useless (and, if anything, irritating) to the entomologist. But it is also true that as a *vital* interpretation it is much more important than all the species of the naturalist because it makes it possible for me to handle, with a degree of exactness that is sufficient for most situations in life, a vast portion of reality that would be literally overwhelming if I were to confront it provisioned with the conceptual scheme of the entomologist. Imagine what things would be like if, in order to expel the intruding bumblebee that is buzzing around my workroom, I had to deal with it in an exact way, that is, as an individual of a precisely determined species perfectly located in the taxonomy of insects. It is clear that my behavior would have to be subsequent to its identification and classification and, if I were not to commit a blunder, would have to differ according to which species the intruder belonged to, since otherwise that difference in behavior would have to be considered *irrelevant* and thus would be nullified and omitted at the same time that it was being affirmed. Hence the precious, inestimable value of vague and general interpretations that allow us to respond with the maximum *vital* exactness in the presence of reality, precisely by disregarding innumerable considerations in order to concentrate on what in each instance actually *counts*. And therefore, as well, the effective *poverty* and simplicity of the natural world. In contrast, *artificial things are interpretations by design*—that is, with them the interpretation is prior to their condition as things. Thus they are experienced in view of their corresponding function, *as* a telephone, pistol, typewriter, radio, cork-screw, lamp, pencil, or, in any case, in view of their general function as "gadgetry," and so on successively.

For this reason, the technical world is immediately sig-nificant, we might say *expressed*, related to man, and con-stituted as well by a system of cross-references in which some functions refer to others—in short, with all its con-nections clear and manifest, at least to a much greater de-gree than the natural world. Notice that this has always been the character of those portions of the world in which technics exceptionally predominates: in the city as op-posed to the country, in works of art, in "institutions" of whatever kind. However, the increase in what is artificial and technical has generalized this situation, has converted it into the predominant characteristic of the world as such, and has affected the precise form in which it has the char-acter of a world. The immediate consequence of this is that the world has been made more *intelligible*, since its "meanings" and the connections between them are obvious and out in the open, and thus one takes them into account immediately. But when this characteristic is carried too far, when it goes beyond the limits within which the ad-justment of the individual is easy, the situation *is inverted*, and a new form of unintelligibility unexpectedly descends upon it. It is clear that a present-day room with its furni-ture, lamps, telephones, radio and record player, typewriter, books, and vases is much more immediately intelligible than a part of nature, since the functions and connections of all its components are manifest and do not depend upon a conditional and haphazard interpretation that may be placed upon them. But if this structure be carried to its end, one arrives at the control panel of an airplane or of an electric powerstation, where everything is significant and con-nected, but its complexity goes beyond the possibility of its being apprehended by somebody not in possession of a diagram giving the technical (and not generally vital) interpretation of that whole layout. And the outcome is that the ordinary man no longer understands anything at all and falls again into the very simple and rough mental contrivance "machinery," without precise content and thus interchangeable among many things, at least in a way similar to the concept "bug."

We may conclude, in summary, that energy in its present forms has essentially altered the *ingredients* of the world: first, with regard to their quantity, that is, the number of relevant elements; second, with regard to its character, which from being predominantly "natural" has come to be above all "artificial"; third, by increasing the complexity of the vital world; fourth, by introducing into it a great number of explicit and purposeful functions, that is, of interpretations that are intrinsically assigned to the "things" that compose it, which consequently are things in a different sense of the word; fifth, by intensifying its characteristic of intelligibility, although with the danger of falling into a new and more profound incomprehensibility when interpretative schemes are inadequate.

The influence of energy on the *structure* of the world, disregarding now the character of its ingredients, is no less than this. First of all, let us consider its *spatial* structure. During the whole of the time that man had only his own energy, that of animals, or at most that of the wind at his disposal, the main and almost the only factor in the spatial organization of the world was *distance*. What was "near" or "far" *in a vital sense* was also what was at a lesser or a greater distance, respectively. At most, this was qualified only by whether land or sea was involved, or was modified by the contours of the terrain. For a restricted number of privileged points, technology already in ancient times introduced an essential modification, *roads,* which by diminishing the energy necessary for displacement or transportation multiplied their available resources. But the order of magnitude of this transformation did not substantially alter the general conditions of localization. The decisive change, the *dislocation* of the old structure of distances, has only come about as a result of technological discoveries and, above all, as a result of their application en masse due to the fabulous availability of energy during the nineteenth century and especially during our own lifetime.

The technical discoveries alone, in fact, would not have had that consequence. The airplane, for example, makes it possible in principle to go to any place on earth in a very short time. Only the energy level achieved during the twentieth century makes it possible, of course; but even with that the spatial structure would not have been altered. It is not the "airplane," but aviation—that is, the "air lines" —that have transformed it. It is the railroads, the highways, with their "substantivized" traffic (if one may use this expression), the sum of all the permanent possibilities of displacement taken in their actual realization, that bring it about that the system of human vital distances no longer coincides either with the geometric system or with what was the existing system of distances up to a few decades ago. Madrid is "close" to New York and "far" from a Galician village, not on account of the geometric distances between those points, nor because one "might" not go rapidly to the village in Galicia (one *can* go rapidly in a helicopter), but because one *does* go in a few hours to New York and not to that village.

But we have to ask ourselves what it means to say "one does go" in contrast to merely saying "one can go." Simply this: there are a few air lines in permanent service that tie many points on the globe together and "bring them close" together, but not other points. Thus, an air line means three things: a scientific and industrial technology (airplanes), a social and economic technology (the organization of the enterprise and its functioning services), and the consumption of enormous amounts of energy (the millions of tons of fuel consumed in *actually* taking the plane from one place to another). Only this last item gives reality to the others, and thus it is energy that brings about the passage from mere possibility to reality. The *real*, existing structure of terrestrial (and very soon extraterrestrial) space is different from what it used to be on account of the new reality of energy on the planet.

If, leaving space, we turn our eyes on time, we find that the *temporal* structure of life has been equally changed. But here things are not quite so simple, by which I mean that the effects produced by the new energy go in contrary directions, as least as far as their repercussions on the configuration of human life are concerned. The first consequence of the new forms of energy and of its technology of utilization has been, as we have just seen, the reduction of vital distances, their virtual elimination for many purposes—the transmission of news, for instance. From a temporal point of view, this signifies an extraordinary *enrichment*. Time has actually expanded. Man is able to do many more things than before, and what is more he does them. The distances covered by any average traveler of the present day would have taken up his lifetime forty or fifty years ago and would have been simply impossible a hundred and fifty years ago. Extremely long journeys are made in the time that a few years ago would have been expended simply in getting ready to go. Possibilities have been multiplied by an immense factor.

And yet man has never had less *leisure*. What we are most in need of is precisely time, and every past epoch seems to us fabulously wealthy in time, compared with our own indigence. Why is this? Once more it is energy that has brought us to this situation. Because, as we have seen time and again, what is involved are not possibilities but the realities in all orders of life that are produced by this situation. The world, which is full of things, besieges us with solicitations that ask for fulfillment. The old poverty of resources was bound up in an equilibrium with a scarcity of stimuli, the result of which was free time, including the monotony of empty time that it was necessary "to kill." *Skholé* in Greek, *otium* in Latin, *loisir* in French, *leisure* in English, *holgura* in Spanish (to choose the word that is least inexact)—this was the outcome of that situation. Today we feel ourselves besieged, sought after, attracted by possibilities that, by virtue of an immense consumption of energy, not only can be but *are being* realized —that is, socially and collectively, in our surroundings, and they drag us with them whether we wish it or not. An individual life of ease and idleness is hardly possible; at least it would coincide with a partial detachment from the world, which in its turn has other requirements that are very difficult to satisfy.

One of the reasons for this lack of temporal ease is the time that is *lost*, a fact that is directly derived from the abundance in all orders of life, which is the immediate product of energy. The world is *full* of objects, of persons, of activities and movements, and thus of *obstacles* that oblige us to wait—until the telephone is free, until the traffic lets up so we can cross the street, until those same cars or the pedestrians let us drive on in our own car, until the clerk is free to take care of us, until it comes our turn to enter the theater or the stadium, until the bureaucracy allows us to go ahead with our plans. In *The Revolt of the Masses* Ortega, thirty years ago,* pointed out "the

* [Now forty years ago; *La rebelión de las masas* was first published in book form in 1930—Trans.]

fact of overcrowding" as the primary characteristic of our times. Since then, the situation has been prodigiously intensified. At the bottom of it all are the rivers of oil, the infinite waterfalls, the electric powerstations, the tons of burning coal that liberate their calories upon the world.

A third structural aspect of this transformation is what might be called the *economization* of the world. I will explain what I mean. That "artificiality" that I previously pointed out, along with the employment of energy of an industrial origin in the immense majority of the activities that man performs, has brought it about that everything now may be immediately and explicitly "cost related." Almost everything today, object or service, has its price. The world is governed economically by means of payments. The fact that in many countries there is an infinity of machines that are made to operate by the insertion of coins is the immediately perceptible form of a very general situation. Before our times, many aspects of life were free: one walked on foot through the cities; one contemplated natural spectacles; one sat on public benches (or on a stone or a tree trunk); to some extent one consumed foods or goods of other kinds that came from one's own labors or from the work of others who were not directly remunerated; to a considerable proportion one profited from nature with hardly any human intervention.* Today the world is a vast machinery of economic structures that operate by means of money. And this has an unexpected but not contemptible consequence: the introduction of *quantification* into values that in other times appeared in a

---

* [Some elements in this enumeration may seem fantastic to present-day readers, especially the young; let me therefore explain (1) that one did not always have to pay a fee in order to sit down in a park in Europe, and (2) that not so long ago many items of food were gleaned from nature in an uncultivated state: berries, dandelions, watercress, herbs, mushrooms, rabbits, wildfowl, etc.—Trans.]

way characterized by hierarchy or intensity, but with a qualitative character. It is not easy to overestimate the influence that this process of economization has on the entire meaning of the world.

If again we change our point of view and abandon the transformations in the structure of the world in order to turn our attention to other internal aspects, we find a modification as profound as the previous ones in *forms of life* and especially in the ways in which people live together.

Available energy has been, in an ever-increasing way, a decisive factor in liberation from the localization characteristic of human life. Until a very short time ago (an almost negligible fraction of the course of history), man was a serf attached to the soil. It does not make any difference that during that time it may have been possible for a few individuals to go around the world; *man* in his generality remained assigned to one place, at least to a small district out of which in principle he would never venture. Not only sedentary peoples, but nomads too, plotted their movements within a relatively restricted area. What is now being produced, and is only at its beginnings, is a vast human mobility. There is a constant increase in the numbers of persons who displace themselves from their place of birth and customary residence, with greater frequency and to greater distances. In the space of a few years that liberation from circumstantiality has been produced for very large numbers of people, although the change remains restricted to a minority of the human race. Within a few decades, if things continue along the course that is foreseeable, those displacements will pass to a new order of magnitude, to include the majority of the population of a great number of countries, and in a future not so immediate, yet foreseeable and calculable, to human beings in their entirety, with very few exceptions.

Any Western man has consumed in his displacements (in overcoming his assignment to a locale) more energy than was consumed by any of his ancestors during the whole of his life; some individuals more than entire cities of former times. What this implies with regard to the expansion of the horizon of life, with regard to the widening of it, with regard to liberation from a servitude that has seemed to be the human condition, can be imagined, though with some difficulty. On the other hand, one may ask oneself whether there are not also some perils involved. A few lines prior to this I spoke about the place of "customary residence." Is not this distinguishing trait of man in danger? To what extent can it be said of many of our contemporaries that they have a customary place of residence? The two human possibilities, *to be at* and *to be passing by,** have always been enormously unequal, with an overwhelming superiority of the former. This is still the way things are for the majority of people; but the number of those who are less and less content "to be at," of those who have practically reached a condition of rootlessness, grows day by day. You will observe that, when things are considered from the point of view of one individual (that is, while preserving the relative "immobility" of all the others), things do not seem to be very serious, but as soon as that mobility is extended, then that of each individual will be multiplied by that of all his fellows and the forms of community life as they have existed

* [Both *estar* and *pasar* in Spanish, and my translation of them as well ("to be at" and "to be passing by"), imply what Marías calls "localization," reference to a place; perhaps a preferable translation of *pasar* in this context, one that attempts a "liberation" from locale, might be "to be in transit"—Trans.]

up to now would turn out to be impossible. Community life would be reduced to a series of fugitive, perhaps repeated, contacts, more like the encounters of molecules in a gas than like what, up to now, we have considered living together as human beings to be. This mobility, which seems to be (and is) a marvelous possibility for man, can easily turn into one of the most vexatious problems of the coming world, unless vital means of compensating for it are sought and found.

But if we follow this metaphor, this image of gas, we have to add that energy seems to have been employed in increasing its temperature. Consequent upon the immeasurable augmentation of the mobility of its molecules, their interrelations (the diverse forms of living together) have been multiplied and differentiated. The human horizon of each person, which was until a short time ago extremely restricted, has been enlarged much more than we would believe at first sight and includes persons in very distinct spheres with whom normally we would never have come into contact, except under exceptional circumstances. A few years ago it occurred to me to write down the names of the people with whom I had spent time on both sides of the Atlantic; in a few minutes I found myself with some two hundred names that had come to memory. I am sure that if today I were to repeat this notation, I would easily arrive at five hundred.

And this is not all. To the physical presence of persons today we have to add all the startling intermediate forms between presence and nonpresence: telephone, radio, television. Due precisely to the utilization of energy, especially electrical energy, the world has become full of *virtual* presences, independent of localization, which enrich and at the same time impoverish (in any event, which fundamentally change) our living in communities. Saint John of the Cross spoke of the "pain of love that is not to be cured except by the presence and the figure" of the beloved. But for him the sole alternative was absence, relieved only by imagination or a written letter. What is presence on the telephone, auditory but without figure, or that of television, with a ghostly, untouchable figure of only two dimensions? The fact that man actually *experiences* those forms of quasi presence, that he loves, converses, argues, murmurs, commands, conducts business, teaches, and learns through the telephone receiver or the television screen, is going to condition the very meaning of those activities, especially in the near future when they will have entirely lost whatever exceptional character they may now possess and, above all, when people perform them spontaneously with the same naturalness with which through millenia they have conversed face to face. One of the profoundest differences between countries in the world today is in the level of their utilization of energy, in the extent to which it has been translated into changes in those forms of community life. When one considers and conjectures with some degree of exactness just what the significance is of the fact that New York has many more telephones than the whole of Asia, this one statistical fact alone illuminates one whole side of the structure of the world in which we live.

Finally, all the factors that I have been enumerating, plus the establishment of a permanent system of communications, no longer human and personal, but "symbolic," of signals and reports, give a new social and vital "elasticity" to the world, absolutely unknown up to a little more than a century ago. In the same way that the "economization" of the world has been produced, one could consider its "electrification" as a superimposed structure that transforms all vital relations and functions. Consider, for example, the fact that night has been eliminated in great portions of the world due to electrical illumination. Electrical energy has made possible what we might call the conquest and colonization of the true "dark continent," that other "hemisphere" of the human world, which is night. That tremendous force, invincible through millenia after millenia, which imposed its silence, its interruption, and its articulation of vital time, has been vanquished, and the remains of its power are beating a retreat in those few places where it continues to dominate. And this, in a way similar to what I have called liberation from the assignment to a place, seems (and in a certain sense is) marvelous, but it raises delicate problems of adjustment in life.

One consequence of all these changes is the multiplication of "impacts" of all kinds that each individual receives today. During the whole of history (and I do not mention prehistory) man was restricted to what actually occurred around him, within his physical neighborhood, and only a very few distant happenings reached him, in the form of an effect or as information, impaired in addition by temporal distance, so that by the time they reached him they were already "old" and had lost a good part of their vitality. Today man is literally bombarded by everything that happens, whether near or far, and the techniques of transmission (energy, once again) accomplish this in a very brief time or even instantaneously, that is, while everything still possesses its full effectiveness. Few things have more profoundly modified human life than this incredible intensification of what I would call the "density of events." And not the least of its consequences has been the defensive reaction that the contemporary soul has spontaneously brought into play in order to resist and to adapt itself to this new vital "medium," a peculiar "callousing" that is the insensitivity and indifference with which the man of our times responds to the stimuli that come to him from all the points of the globe, and some from beyond it. It is obvious that if he were to preserve the sensitivity inherited from other times, it would literally be impossible for him to survive.

I should still add one more influence, perhaps the most important influence, of the energy that man has brought into being in the world: that which is exerted upon his own condition as man. In other writings,[4] I have used the term *the empirical structure of human life* to refer to that zone of reality which, without being an a priori requisite of human life, without being its "essence," such as is to be discovered by analyzing its analytical structure, is also not a mere de facto, accidental, and chance ingredient of life. The empirical structure is empirical, but a structure; it belongs in fact, but in a permanent and stable way, to the human lives that I empirically discover and encounter. Human life is essentially circumstantial, corporeal, sensitive, temporal, etc. Each one of our individual lives has singular empirical determinations of those dimensions; each one of us lives in a precise circumstance, has *this* unique body, with its corresponding sensory system, lives during a number of years within this (the twentieth) century, etc. Between one zone and another there is an intermediate zone, which is precisely the empirical structure. Not only is life being in a world, but its world is precisely *this* world and not some of those that are possible. Human corporeality is that which we do in fact encounter, and not that of the bird or that of the echinoderm or any other that we might imagine; the scheme of sensibility is that which we find to be characteristic of our species, practically stable and constant, but which could have been quite different. The duration of life is from seventy to a hundred years, approximately, and on this one counts, although *individually* it might be anything from a few hours to more than a century, but that duration could have been from a week to a millenium and then the empirical structure would have been different. The empirical structure, I have said, is the historical form of circumstantiality, which could vary and which, to some extent, does vary, without man ceasing to be man.

Well, the repercussions of energy upon the empirical structure are enormous; much of what I have previously considered affect it. But I wish only to point out the most important. What we call man's size, his "magnitude," does not consist in the dimensions of his body, but in the possibility of his operating within a certain order of magnitude. During the time that man is limited to his natural somatic possibilities, he moves within a very narrow margin of operation. This is what is usually called, with considerable myopia, the "human scale." But man at the present time, by means of present-day technology and, above all, by virtue of the availability of incalculable stores of energy, "operates" with separate magnitudes between which there are great gaps. Not only does he "observe" reality through the electron microscope and the telescopes of Mount Palomar, but he effectively *manipulates* reality from the particles of the nucleus of the atom to the rockets and satellites that travel through the spaces of the solar system millions of miles from earth. That is, the "magnitude" of man has become elastic without limit, not only in principle but in reality and in fact. The "human scale" is extended unbelievably in both directions and seems, paradoxically, and in contrast with that of animals, to be defined by its *indefiniteness*.

In these pages I have proposed doing no more than one thing: to call attention to the significance that the contemporary fact of energy has for the very reality of the world. And, of course, to emphasize that what we are dealing with is something completely new—for the changes realized during the whole of human history, from the time of primitive man to the nineteenth century, are of an order much less important than those that have recently taken place in a few decades. I have also pointed out that the pace of that transformation is *accelerated*, that is, that we are only at the beginning of a process that is going to carry us, very quickly, much further still. Now, in conclusion, I would like to take a glance at the prospects that the immediate future discloses to us.

The first thing that must be said is that we are on the threshold of a new era: nuclear energy, which already belongs to the realm of our *possibilities*, does not yet enter into the composition of the *reality* of our world, but this is going to happen in a very short time. That is, the future awaiting us is not so much a mere intensification or acceleration of the process of change, such as has been occurring for something more than a century, but the passage to a different *order of magnitude*, with respect to which our present situation will be like that of previous epochs compared with our own. In fact, even more than that. Once the increase of energy and its applications had been initiated, it would have been feasible, in the middle of the nineteenth century, to calculate what the situation around 1950 would be like; but the situation of the year 2000, *from this point of view* (let it be observed that this is true from this point of view but not from others), is unforeseeable.

The possibilities of change in the world that now appear likely are of such a scope that we are not able to "take charge" * of them nor, consequently, to confront them in-

* [The expression used here, *hacerse cargo,* may mean either "to take charge" or "to understand"—Trans.]

tellectually in an adequate way. And this is one of the most disturbing and urgent aspects of our situation. I am simply going to *mention*, without even trying to analyze them, three possibilities of change that appear on our horizon bearing the characteristic of imminence, and which are, each one of them, entire chapters of possible modifications in the whole repertory of our conditions of life.

(1) The alteration of the *somatic structure* of man (and secondarily of plant and animal species). It is believed that atomic energy and, above all, the effects of radiation could be determining factors in certain *mutations* whose exact nature is unforeseeable, which does not necessarily have to be dreadful, but which is far from excluding this eventuality.

(2) The alteration of the boundaries of the *world*. In other words, the possibility that man's living space may not be limited to the planet and, therefore, that the identification of "world" and "terrestrial world" may be insupportable in a future not too far away. This would be the radical and extreme form of what I have called "liberation from circumstantiality," raising it too to a new order of magnitude.

(3) The very *existence* of man. For the first time in history it seems perfectly possible that the species may exterminate itself through its own actions, as a consequence of strictly human behavior. This situation is absolutely novel and places a sinister shadow upon the human future. But let us not forget that, at the same time, nuclear energy represents the possibility that mankind may be able to exist in the numbers that are going to be reached in a very short time if different and decisive factors do not intervene. Only through prodigious intensification of the production of foods, goods, and services of all kinds can there be any expectation that mankind may go on growing and

living on the surface of the globe—and eventually beyond it. As are all things human, energy is ambiguous. It has two sides, heads and tails, and reveals to us two faces—one benevolent, the other hostile.

What conclusions may be drawn from this brief glance at our situation? The power to do all these things is in man's hands, but what is not in his hands is the choice of doing or not doing them, as he may wish. The power is in his hands, but not the direction of that power. And the most serious reason for this lies in the ambiguity of the expression that I just got through using, "as he may wish." We have to ask ourselves: as *who* may wish?

A few individual men? To think in this way would be a deceptive illusion. Those who are called the masses? Presumably not, since as such they do not wish. Society? Or perhaps societies, "those great bodies that are the nations," as Descartes said, or their equivalent, in short, the social units? But this last solution, more plausible, brings us to new problems. What and how do societies "wish"? To what extent is it possible to determine, regulate, modify, or simply foresee their behavior? These are our most serious and compelling problems, spurring on the man of our times. Contemporary man possesses all the techniques, except one: that of the management of techniques—in other words, the technique of managing himself. What he lacks is an adequate sociology and, in particular, one of its decisive pieces: a contemporary and efficacious *rhetoric*. That is, what is missing is the technique of words. Because it has not been sufficiently observed that man lives in a world that is not *primarily* either matter or energy, but *words*—or, if you prefer, personal energy.

The extreme situation to which we have been brought by the origination and utilization of energy in proportions incomparable with the whole of the human past confronts man with the evidence of the condition that is will have to return with precision to this problem. It will be enough here to give a few indications of the direction in which one might look for a solution.

I said before that the experience of life is acquired in solitude, but that one arrives at this solitude precisely by withdrawing from life in the company of others. When it is said that we are *within* life, this is obviously true, but it is necessary to make a distinction. I am within *my life*, as the radical reality, but it presents itself to me as *my* life because *within it* I find other realities that are irreducible, in relation to which I am necessarily "outside." The experience of *life* is not in the last analysis experience of *my* life, although we might be inclined to think so. It may be that, in the rigorous sense of the word, no experience of my life is possible. In any case, looking at things now from the other side, it is precisely the presence of other lives, which are not mine, that pours out that pure experience of *life*.

But we have to continue asking what it consists of. Those other lives appear and are constituted *within* my life, and to that degree they seem to be accessible to my experience. But, is that what we are involved with then, a new experience *of things?* Are other lives no more than things that I find within the realm of my life, located within them? Whatever degree of caution we exercise here will be too little. They are, certainly, rooted realities * within the radical reality that is *my* life, but they are never things;

* [The term Marías uses here, *realidades radicadas*, is of course complementary to *realidad radical*, "radical reality"; the adjective *radicadas* is derived from the verb *radicar*, which originally meant "to put down roots," but now is most commonly used to mean "to situate or establish"; thus, *realidades radicadas* would be "established or rooted realities"; a little further on I have translated *radicación*, which refers to the action or effect of putting down roots or of establishing (oneself), as "rootedness"; perhaps something as far-fetched as "radicularity" would be more precise—Trans.]

most characteristic of him: unlimited, moldable, destitute, insecure, deluded, expectant, and full of hope.

NOTES

1. See my *Introducción a la filosofía* (Madrid, 1947) [*Obras*, III], in English translation as *Reason and Life* (Yale University Press, 1956), chapters V and VII.
2. *Meditaciones del Quijote*, comentario de Julián Marías (Río Piedras, Puerto Rico, 1957). [Translated into English as *Meditations on Quixote* (New York, 1961)—Trans.]
3. *Introducción a la filosofía* [*Reason and Life*], chapter IX.
4. See "La vida humana y su estructura empírica" and "La psiquiatría vista desde la filosofía," in *Ensayos de teoría* (Barcelona, 1954) [*Obras*, IV]. [Both these essays appear in translation in the present volume—Trans.]

CHAPTER FOURTEEN

THE EXPERIENCE OF LIFE

This essay consists of the two contributions Marías wrote for the collective volume *La experiencia de la vida:* the introduction to that volume and his own comprehensive study of its theme.

INTRODUCTION

Through the whole of his life, from the very moment of his birth, man is continually having experiences. What the value of these may be is an important question, and answers to it have oscillated incredibly throughout history—from those that have *forgotten* all about experience when explaining what man knows and what he can do, to those that have made *everything* of it. Consider for a moment the expression I have just used, for the fact is that *denial* of the significance of experience is exceedingly rare and difficult to justify, while *forgetfulness* of it is quite frequent. That is, experience is something that commands respect and acquires notable proportions if one pays attention to it, but that by its very nature can be forgotten. And this characteristic seems to me so significant that I would like to hold onto it from the beginning.

But it is not experience that interests us here, by which I mean not just any experience. At a certain age, sooner or later (with immense variations in this sooner or later), at one time or another, a strange impression befalls many men and (let us not forget) women, the impression that they are possessed of a certain *experience of life*. This experience is not to be reduced to those they have gradually been accumulating day by day, nor confused with the sum of them either. Nor does it have much relation to the quantity or intensity of those experiences. Some people have had "a great deal of experience," perhaps on account of having sought it and having made of it their principal occupation. Others, in contrast, are to be found with a rather scant measure of experience; if they were to be questioned, they would have little to tell. And yet it might very well happen that their "experience of life" stands in inverse relation to their "experience"—that the "experience of life" of the latter may be exceptionally rich and dense, while that of the former may seem uncertain, schematic, and bloodless. How is it possible? By which I mean: How is that relative independence of "experience" and "experience of life" possible? How is it that "experience" may decidedly prejudice what comes to pass with the "experience of life"?

The experience of life is a superior kind of knowledge that can be placed beside the highest and most radical. That *can* be, but which at times is not. A second anomaly, this brings us back to consider again the strange phenomenon of the possible forgetfulness of the function of experience in general. There have been societies and historical periods in which, in fact, the experience of life has been thought of as the highest and most valuable kind of knowledge, compared with which all other knowledge was considered extremely frivolous and incoherent. On the other hand, in other times (such as our own, perhaps) hardly anybody thinks about it at all, and naturally nobody gives it any credibility. We do not know very well what to make of the experience of life; we do not dare disregard it, but at the same time we do not feel inclined to acknowledge it. In fact, we do not know very well what it consists of, how it is acquired, what security it offers, what it is to be used for, what its claims to legitimacy are. That extraordinary knowledge—not on account of what it is in itself, but because of what I would call its *context*, on account of the perplexity concerning its conditions, role, and place in the hierarchy among other forms of knowledge—comes to be converted into something just the opposite of knowledge, into a *problem*. Throughout long ages the experience of life has been the radical way of knowing what to be guided by; but it has turned out, for extrinsic reasons having nothing to do with the experience of life itself, that this has become questionable, so that today we do not know what to be guided by *with regard to it*.

This is why we make it the object of our questions. We can neither spurn nor renounce it; nor can we trust in it, because it seems to us an obscure and unverifiable kind of knowledge, of dubious legitimacy, difficult to justify, problematical in articulation with those other forms of knowledge which orient and direct our lives. What are we to do with it, along with science, philosophy, art, religion, opinions? How are we to evaluate it, in ourselves and in others? How have we acquired it, and how can we be certain that it has been, that we actually do possess it? Is it possible to authenticate it or put it to the test? If it comes into conflict with other aspects of our knowledge or with similar experience in others, how are we to decide the issue? To what extent and with what techniques would we be able to communicate it? And what would be the use of it? More than that: this experience of ours, what good is it to us? *Si jeunesse savait, si vieillesse pouvait!* This gloomy opinion is traditional and seems to suggest, precisely as a precipitate of the experience of life itself, that it is a patrimony of age and that, at such a stage in life, it turns out to be useless. Are both things true? Supposing both of them were—will they be always true, will they be invariable?

One can understand why, faced with such a cloud of questions, the rationalist, who is the proud possessor of other kinds of knowledge that are not so shy or problematical, that have a very clear and unmistakable outline, should have chosen to disregard that disquieting, embarrassing "experience of life." We do not have a very clear idea of the price that has been paid for this disregard, for this already old forgetfulness, but the fear begins to assail us that we may have paid very dearly. We are not certain about this, but our doubts are enough to make it impossible for us to remain at ease. There is no way out in any direction. "Neither with you nor without you," we might say to our Sphinx of the moment, the experience of life. We are able neither to trust and have confidence in it nor to turn our backs on it, for we do not know what it is we would be leaving behind.

What are we to do? Perhaps, as Unamuno would have advised, not to count the hairs on its tail but to look it in the eyes. To ask ourselves peremptorily, what is the *experience of life?* Because we have to confess that, even at this late date, we do not know. Even supposing that we knew what *experience* is (perhaps it is only at the present time that this is beginning to be known), we have already seen that the experience of life is irreducible to the experiences that are deposited in our soul with the passage of time. We might suspect that we are not even dealing with the same thing. When we say experience *of life*, it could be that this possessive substantially modifies the meaning of experience. The experience of *things*, no matter what they may be, is not the same as the experience of *life*, which is not a thing of any kind, even though without things it would have no reality.

We have to ask ourselves, from many different angles, what the experience of life is. From the point of view of the life that possesses it: trying to discover when and how one arrives at it, what relation it may have to the acts, events, and adventures one has gone through or the tranquillity or peacefulness one has been in, what its true role is in the economy of daily life, whether it is due (and how it may be) to one's relations with one's fellow human beings or comes from the depths of one's own self, whether one achieves it once and for all or achieves it and loses it, how subsequent experiences affect it once one has come to exist or to believe oneself to be existing in that great basic experience. From the point of view of the life that does not have it, of one that is without it (or that feels itself deprived of it, which is not the same thing): how one may try to acquire it, whether it is possible for one to acquire it, or whether it may not be an elusive reality that dodges whoever may be looking for it. From the point of view of the life that proclaims it and anticipates it, like a melon ripening on the vine. From the point of view of the life that is always looking outside itself, into other lives, which it is able or not able to share.

Each person, from the point of view of his own vital experience, has to question himself about the experience of life. The sum of those endeavors, if they are authentic, would perhaps make it possible to decipher the enigma. For, let there be no doubt about it, we are involved with a reality that is enigmatic, obscure as few are. If this could be accomplished, perhaps the result would be well worth the trouble. Because it would be nothing less than the conquest of an essential discipline in the humanities, the theoretical possession (and with a new and subtle mode of theory, corresponding to such a fleeting and unmanageable object) of one of the great resources that humanity has had available through long millenia as a means of orienting itself, as a means by which to search for a way out of the entanglements that, instant by instant, the drama that is living consists of. Beside religion, magic, drugs, customs, law, technics, philosophy, science, art, fiction, and in addition intermingled with them all, another of the great potentialities advances questioningly, another of the great resources that are of some help in man's constitutive destitution—the experience of life.

PERSPECTIVE ON THE EXPERIENCE OF LIFE

The fact of having written the introduction to this volume on "the experience of life"—that is, having posed the problem and enumerated the questions about this subject that seem to me most urgent and important—places me in a delicate position at the moment when I begin to write on this theme. For it would seem that the fact of having asked those questions obliges me to respond in such a way that this questionnaire is binding on me, since I am the one who is "responsible" for it. But nothing is further from what is possible for me. And the reason why this is so is that my questions were not at all rhetorical, by which I mean that they were actual questions that I was proposing to myself, not at the moment within the solitude of the mind but out in the open and, above all, in the open forum of the intellectual community. I do not possess the answers to my questions in advance. Not only do I not have the answers, but I would not be *able* to be in possession of them, for if I were they would then be false. Why?

I will try to explain. Adequate answers about the experience of life cannot be individual—rather, what they cannot be is *singular*, from one person only. Life is, in and of itself, living together; the experience that is achieved of it is also founded on community life. And this means that its own contents include other people. It includes them in the sense that they are *irreducible*, that is, that they exist beyond my knowledge of them, that they are not exhausted in my knowledge of them. From the point of view of the experience of life, the experience I achieve involves a reference to that of others, going beyond my own. In other words, it is part of one's knowing oneself to be limited, one among others, conditioned by a particular horizon, which is only one of the possible horizons. This finitude, partiality, and limitation is the first constitutive element in the experience of life, which comes to cure certain absolutist or solipsist illusions into which the person who has only "experiences" may fall. And this characteristic affects of course all theoretical reflection upon life, since that reflection has to begin with the presence of its object, and that meditation, in addition, cannot be anything other than an intensification and purification of that very experience and is, consequently, subject to the requisites and conditions of that experience.

This obliges one, if one wishes to raise questions seriously and not in a utopian and abstract way, to choose a point of view, a concrete perspective, which is not exactly the same as that from which one has acquired personal experience of life (this has always been acquired from a multiplicity of perspectives), but that from which one has *organized* oneself and which, consequently, represents the guidelines for one's own interpretation of the experience of life. All reality as it is lived, and this is even more true of this experience, has to be interpreted, experienced as the reality it is—that is, with a definite function within the totality that is life. In other words, reflection on the experience of life is possible only within a concrete *perspective* upon it, a perspective that is related to others postulated by this one. And this condition is from the beginning a primary positive condition of that experience.

What experience itself is, is not such a clear thing as might appear at first sight. We now have available to us a text that (unless I am wrong), more than anything else up to the present, clarifies what experience is, precisely by virtue of having brought historical reason into play in the clarification of experience, in the most exact study of etymology and semantic history. Both are, needless to say, directed by philosophy, which *makes* the linguistic data speak what they carry within, but which, left to themselves, they would never say anything about. I am referring to a passage in Chapter 19, "Ensayo sobre lo que pasó a Aristóteles con los principios," in Ortega's *La idea de principio en Leibnitz y la evolución de la teoría deductiva.*[1] I am not going to summarize what is said there. It will be enough to recall that for Ortega this word "experience," *empeiría*, takes its life from the root *per* (in Germanic languages, *fahr*), combined in *peligro*, "risk," "danger," and on the other side in *poros, portus*, "departure," "passage." It is the idea of a journey, of being on the road, and of the danger of walking where there are no roads. This, originally and radically, is what experience consists of; and for this reason empiricism is quite literally "thinking with one's feet."

But here what matters to us is not experience, but the experience *of life*. Not many experiences, not the experience of many things, but the unitary experience of life itself, which is not a thing. This necessitates, first of all, so it would seem, finding ourselves at a certain "height of life"—if you prefer, returning to the meaning of the root *per*, with a certain distance traveled. How far? The meaning of that "how far" is already a fundamental question. What is involved is not exclusively, nor even primarily, a matter of quantity, but, rather, a form of life, its configuration. This only appears after one has gone through the length of it. For this reason, looking closely, we see that only the old can talk about life in a way that would be other than by "hearsay," that only the old have *been there* through it—and not only through smaller or larger fragments of it. This is the reason that in all primitive cultures the old have a relevant role, the reason that justifies the existence of "senates," or assemblies of elders. And I have shown in other places that *fiction*, by giving an "abbreviation" of life, to a certain extent provides that real presence in life and makes possible a kind of "virtual" experience that is of increasing importance.

One possesses the experience of life when, in some way, one has already looked upon the back of things. Does this necessarily mean "to be coming back"? I believe that at bottom there is no greater naïveté, no greater lack of experience, than to believe that one is coming back; for while one lives one is *always going away*. Life, while it lasts, consists precisely in this, in going on, and for this reason it is, at one and the same time, futurity, unforeseeability, irrevocability. It is possible to be coming back *from each thing*. Life is a movement of coming and going, toward things and away from them again, toward life itself, and since life is lived toward the future, this "coming back" is a paradoxical "coming back by advancing." In other words, individual experiences are being poured out pure into a common fund. Thus there is a double operation that engenders the experience of life: the fulfillment of the many singular experiences that I call experiences of things and the pure pouring of them into those still backwaters where they acquire configuration and significance.

At times those two modes of operation obstruct one another; on occasion one of them is resolutely predominant. The impression of profound experience that is at times produced in us by people who are "elemental" and not very complicated corresponds to this mechanism. The peasant, the half-literate woman, show at times a surprising accumulation of experience *of life*, combined with tremendous poverty in "experiences." They are people who have always done the same thing, people to whom nothing much has happened. What is almost always involved, in addition, in the case of the peasant, is immersion in a living tradition, in transpersonal experiences, in a virtuality different from that of fiction but with an affinity to it. The woman usually has the immediate and effective experience of the child, an elemental form of human life that is much more profound and closer to the reality of life than is usually believed. And the *presence* of the mother who is somewhat aware of the life of her children has an immediacy and intensity about it that take the place of great complexities. In contrast, in forms of life that are more complicated and restless, filled up with more "experiences," there is usually a lack of time or leisure to carry out those "retreats" or comparative judgments to a degree that would be adequate. The experience of life in fact requires *withdrawal*, since, as we have seen, it consists in withdrawing from involvement with things to life itself, where the meaning and significance of all things resides.

How do we come to know about the experience of life? We talk about it, perhaps, because we know that we possess it, or we miss it, or we observe it in others. Can we have the experience of life and not know it? Not know it in a complete way—of course. But a certain knowledge of itself pertains to the experience of life; it consists of a certain transparency and reflection. Its discovery in ourselves, at a certain level of life, is usually translated into what I would call the experience of *"I have already been through this."* * This implies a strange apriorism with regard to *each* new experience, at least with regard to its fulfillment and complete performance—that is, as soon as each singular experience is initiated, this sense of "I have already been through this" is unleashed (if that is the

---

* [Once again, I have tried to give the exact meaning, not a literal transposition of the Spanish words: here, *ya sé*, which literally means no more than "already I know"—Trans.]

proper expression). The consequence is that *at the limit* (and this emphasis should not be disregarded) experiences are unnecessary. For this reason, the man or woman with experience of life knows what to be guided by practically in advance, as soon as concrete experiences are initiated. The Spanish idiom *estar al cabo de la calle* expresses this in an excellent way;* one who possesses experience of life is "at the head of the street," meaning, of course, the street he is actually on, which he does not have to run through from one end to the other. From the time he steps onto it, he is "at the head" of it; he anticipates the whole of it in a virtual and condensed experience.

This leads to an extraordinary "rapidity" that is not always taken in its true sense. The man with experience of life is never a "hurried" man; on the contrary, he requires a certain calm and tranquillity. He is, however, possessed of the celerity of one who does not have to go to the end of everything, going through the complete circuit each time. Another Spanish idiom, taken from a card game (that fountain of human experience), speaks of one who *las ve venir.†* Just like *estar al cabo de la calle*, this too expresses anticipation, the relative apriorism *cum fundamento in re*. In the first case, one who has begun to walk on a street anticipates his arrival at the end of it; in the other case, one sees from the beginning something that actually is already coming.

The experience of life is acquired in the solitude of one who withdraws—understanding, of course, out of living together with others. The main factor is attendance to the lives of others, which are always interpreted and in that way made transparent, or at least translucent. For that

* [An equivalent English idiom is "to know the ropes"—Trans.]
† [Literally, "watches them (the cards) come," referring to one who is an astute observer—Trans.]

reason, longevity seems a necessary condition for sufficient experience. But here a curious ambiguity arises that it is necessary to pursue. Longevity? Whose?

Obviously the longevity of the subject of the experience, so it seems. However, I am not certain. The longevity *of others* augments the experience *of the young*. When a society is normally long-lived, a man may, without waiting to grow old, go through the experiences of many generations and thus of different modulations and varieties of human life. When people normally had short lives, ordinary experience was of three generations, except for the old—that is, the exceptionally long-lived who received a bonus of experience, like the old Nestor. As I am writing these pages I have not yet reached forty-five. However, I have gone through the vivid and effective experiences of some men of the generation of 1856, at least in their public activities, men such as Palacio Valdés, Ortega Munilla, a few politicians; in a full and saturated way, of the generation of 1871 (that of '98, as it is usually called), that of 1886, that of 1901, that of 1916 (which is my own), that of 1931, and even of older generations (or let us say less young), of the incipient generation of 1946, to which those born since 1939 belong, and who are already beginning "to count." Thus, here are *seven* generations that in one form or another I am already "witness" to. Will our experience of life not be incomparably greater, at least in this sense? It is possible for us to acknowledge "environmental" or communal longevity as a factor in experience. If to this we add the purely virtual, but no less important, experience of fiction, which has a role in our world that is enormous, the outcome is a *possible* precocity in the acquisition of the experience of life, characteristic of our times and perhaps compensated for by other factors with opposing tendencies.

I would not like to make things deceptively simple.

There have always been "old people" whom the young man has encountered "already" in his world, frequently with more prestige and influence than they have now. What does the present dominance of longevity concretely add? And, in the second place, how can that form of acquiring the experience of life be verified?

Above all, in periods when death occurred at a *statistically* earlier age, old people were few; however, this is not what is most interesting, but that, being few, they were exceptions. They seemed to be privileged individuals, survivors from age groups already exterminated. Now, no. Now those groups, although decimated by death, endure as such. What is involved is not only that there are "more" of them, but that, now that they appear as a group, their attributes no longer function simply in an individual, singular, accidental, haphazard way. It is not that John Doe has to be this way through being John Doe (or perhaps only on account of his being old), but that with his generation he brings a *way of life* into being. And as there are not only "old people," but various "graduating classes" of old people and others not so old, those ways of life appear stratified into various *levels*, which taken all together, in their turn, compose a *form*, that is, a way of life of a different order, namely, a *historical* way of life in which the *variation* of human life is made immediately accessible and experienceable. Each man experiences things and problems from the point of view of his age level and his historical level—that is, from the point of view of his generation. Life thus presents itself from the beginning as something that is modulated in very different ways. And specific attitudes are not identified with old age as such, but with a certain precise generation, since the old age of other generations do not share them. To our eyes, "old," like Aristotelian "being," may mean many things. And, analogously, when it is seen that each generation passes through successive ages or (if you prefer) that each age comes to the various generations, the behavior patterns of "age" are distinguished from those of "history" in the same way that experiencing things that are cold and dry and other things that are hot and moist has taught us to distinguish cold from moisture.

In a certain sense, however, this would seem to make the experience of life difficult, since the man of our times is not as ready as men of former times were to accept placidly the decree that there is one category of "things of the old" and another of "things of the young," since he knows that what is involved is not a simple automatic distinction of age. The experience of "I have already been through this," in which I found the consciousness of the experience of life to consist, is thus foreign to him. This is true, but what was involved was, rather, a deceptive experience; now an experience other than "I have already been through this" is poured into the soul of man, an experience with a different content—"I have already found out that life is unforeseeable"—which is never wholly "given" and which is not, therefore, a simple datum. The presence of history in a real and "experiential" (not merely theoretical) way dissipates the deceitful illusion of "human nature." It was the pretended knowledge of "human nature" that *dispensed* precisely with the possession of the experience of life, gave it up as unnecessary, and replaced it with an abstract knowledge frequently composed of commonplaces.

The second issue I raised is that of the communicability of the experience of life. By its very nature it is not communicable in a theoretical form, by which I mean in the form of "statements." That is why, when an old person tries to share his experience by "expounding" it, he always fails. In general, when one is installed in it and seeks to bring it into play, he is immediately successful. It is conduct itself that makes the experience "visible." Does this mean, for example, that an old man behaves in a "more experienced" way, in the sense that he is more prudent and cautious than a middle-aged person or a person belonging to what in other days (though not now—why?) was usually called "wild youth"? I do not believe this is the case. Nor do I think that old people are especially prudent or that old age assures experience *of life*—and this is what I am trying to show. Nor is the experience of life, assuming that it exists, made visible in an act of wisdom or good sense, for example. No. The experience of life is manifested in conduct as the "argument" or "plot" of the life that possesses it. It is the trajectory, the configuration of life, not its isolated acts, that discloses "where" one is experiencing from, that going away and coming back from things to life and back again, of which I previously spoke.

For this reason, if that experience has to be made visible in words, these words cannot take the form of statements or explanations, but *narration*. In a narrative form, yes, the experience of life is communicable, for narration is a way of *being virtually present* in life itself. Let us not forget (and I have recalled it many times) that for the Greeks the supreme form of *paideia*, of education in the radical sense of the word, was close to the meaning of *Bildung* in German; it was not a science, not even a philosophy at the beginning, but poetry: Hesiod's *Theogony*, the Homeric epics, tragedy—*fiction*, in short. This is the form in which wisdom is made accessible, in which, by contagion perhaps, that experience is shared which seems to be, by its very nature, incommunicable.

We encounter the experience of life in an "assimilable," communicable form (that is why I say we "encounter" it, not that we infer that the author has it, not that we suppose him to have it on account of his "regard for the social graces," as all too frequently occurs) in a few works of literature: in the *Celestina*, even though its author was a young man and hardly more than a student; in Cervantes almost always; in Quevedo when we least expect it, and thus in his amorous verse, hardly ever in his treatises; in Montaigne; in Shakespeare; and hardly ever in Calderón. It is difficult to find it in those who make a profession of it, in the moralists and ascetics. A false "lucidity" that pretends to be doing the impossible, "to be coming back from life," such as occurs in Sartre, nullifies it. Much greater experience of life is communicated by Simenon or Thornton Wilder or Antonio Machado (except when he is trying to explain it in prose or to versify it in aphorisms) or Unamuno (when he leaves off "opinionating" for a moment—in *San Manuel Bueno*, in a few of his poems, in the "innocent" articles he sometimes wrote). Those who are "clever" usually are radically lacking in the experience of life, for they do not let it come to birth, especially those who try to avoid "playing the fool," *être dupe*. The politician is frequently possessed of the experience of life (when and where there is a political life, something rather unusual these days), on condition that he not be entirely "of this world." Or the priest, when he does not believe that he has all the answers.

But, however that may be, we can ask ourselves *what* the experience of life is good for. The dominant conviction is that it takes a lot of time to acquire it and that when it has been achieved then there is nothing left to be done and it turns out to be useless. *Si jeunesse savait, si vieillesse pouvait!* If things were like this, it would be an always untimely and inopportune kind of knowledge, literally out of season, almost a sarcasm.

Even if this is the way things were, it would still be

possible to oppose such a precipitous judgment with a few considerations. The first would be whether the temporal limits of life are actually those they are believed to be, those that statistics reflect—at least until a few years ago. I mean by this that perhaps man's old age and death are *biographically premature.* I am thinking of something extremely simple. At each moment man has the immediate impression of being at a certain height in life, in a definite phase of his vital trajectory; he feels that he is just beginning his life and has "everything in front of him," or that he stands in the middle of it, or that it is declining, or that he has outlived it. It is not possible to deprive this basic sensation of its value, since it conditions the temper of our life and is the main factor in shaping its configuration. All men know that they may die at any moment, that nothing is certain, but they experience all this from the point of view of their installation at a precise height of that trajectory. The two meanings of the expression *to count on,* one of which points toward "security," the other toward "availability," are to some extent opposed, but in this ambivalent situation they converge. Man "counts on" such and such a span of life, even though he is very well aware that he cannot "count on" it. Thus, *in our times* (I am not saying that things have always happened or happen in this way—far from it), the man of around fifty usually has the impression that he is "in the first half of life," at most *nel mezzo del cammin.* He knows of course that it is unlikely that this is so, that probably there is not much time left to him; but this awareness does not make any difference because what is involved is a "configuration," and an earlier death would be experienced more or less as accidental and, I repeat, biographically premature. And, looking at things from a perspective adequate to them, it seems quite likely that it may actually be premature and that within a very short time life will "come into its own," it will have all that we feel rightly belongs to it, and that it will no longer have much to do with biological deterioration but with its "plot," with its biographical trajectory. Then, perhaps, *de jure* there will belong to life a zone of utilization and enjoyment of its experience, and the presumed futility of this experience will not mean anything more than the fact that, except in rare instances, man has still not reached the point at which he is able to "take possession" of it in an adequate way.

A second consideration would lead us along a very different path. Let us suppose, in fact, that there is no such zone, that the experience of life would be reached not long before it is overtaken by death and would thus be practically useless. Would that deprive it of its value? The effort man has been engaged in for something like a century to empty death of all content (a startling *evacuatio mortis*) would lead one to believe so. But it is more than questionable whether this position is acceptable. If, instead, death is seen as something positive, as the culmination of life and an intrinsic part of it, the experience of life would make possible the perfection of death and, consequently, of life itself. The man with the experience of life would be the only one who, when dying, "would know what he was *himself* doing." The *himself* is essential here: what he was himself doing, he himself and with himself, at least what he was himself doing inside himself. What, then, would be the function of the experience of life?

It would help in the possession of life as such. It is that which does not allow us *to leave ourselves in things*, lost among them, but makes it possible for us to return from each thing back to life. Ortega has made it known that the organ of comprehension is life itself; *instrumentum reddendi rationem*, I have said on occasion. And I have defined reason as "the apprehension of reality in its connectedness." This is the idea of *vital reason*. Well, when things are seen from this perspective, we unexpectedly find that the experience of life is the *alveolus* of vital reason, where vital reason is lodged and functions, where it fulfills its role of apprehending reality in *its* coherence, bringing the systematic unity of life itself into play.

Perhaps things would turn out to be clearer if, for a moment, we were to leave individual life, which is the life to which in a strict sense the experience of life belongs, and introduce some historical considerations. It is obvious that the experience of life has not always had the same reality. That is, the functions it performs vary in different forms of collective life. I am going to consider only one example. My example is liberalism. This is so close to us—there was a time, very recently, when it was so much taken for granted—that we are inclined to accept as natural what is really one of the strangest and most surprising of all historical phenomena, and one of the most marvelous too: the state of the liberal soul and, what is more, its collective prevalence. The fact that the problem of liberalism has almost always been posed in political terms, which are secondary, has created a situation in which almost everybody disregards what is essential to the theme, which is the *attitude*, the way of life from which it springs.

Liberalism came into being following the eighteenth century and Romanticism. By this I mean that it was the *consummation* of those two that made it possible. The eighteenth century was not yet liberal; some men of that time were, as individuals: Jovellanos, perhaps at times Rousseau, precisely the "pre-Romantics." In general, and taken as a whole, the men of the eighteenth century were too confident to be liberal. On occasion I have defined the liberal as "one who is not certain about what one cannot be certain about." In order for the men of the 1700's to have been liberals, they would have had to have a certain failure, at least partial, of the kind that consists in the consciousness of limitation—that is, to look at rationalism from the back, but still without irrationalism. This is what Romanticism added, when it was observed that beyond rationalism, irreducible and indomitable, are the passions and emotions. The result, however, was not skepticism but just the reverse: *enthusiasm*. A living belief in freedom, united to consciousness of the limitations of rationalism, of the irreducibility of real things (individuals, traditions, opinions, emotions, ways of life, local color, inwardness), led to the liberal attitude. When one believes that everything can be set right, ordered and disposed once and for all in conformity with a model, one is not a liberal; one is authoritarian and probably despotic, although it may be with an enlightened and benevolent despotism (the enlightenment and the benevolence usually last hardly any time at all, leaving only the despotism). Liberalism presupposes a certain essential, although partial, failure; for this reason, it is abnormally human and carries with it a certain sadness, perceptible to all. I would define the fundamental temperament of liberalism as *enthusiastic melancholy*. Precisely that which permeates one of García Lorca's works that is not very highly regarded, but which seems to me, for that reason and for others, admirable: *Mariana Pineda*. It is the temper of mature Romanticism, that of Byron, the July Revolution of 1830, *Notre Dame de Paris*, *El estudiante de Salamanca*, that of Spanish life between 1820 and the end of the first Carlist war.* Liberalism is the politics of an era with *collective experience of life*. Precisely because within the span of an individual lifetime, within forty years, the "backs of many things" had been

---

* [Some items on this list may not be familiar to American readers: the July Revolution occurred in France as a liberal opposition to the despotic decrees of Charles X; *Notre Dame de Paris* is of course Victor Hugo's novel, published in 1831; *El estudiante de Salamanca* ("The Student of Salamanca") is a verse legend by José de Esproceda, a Spanish poet who lived (1808–1842) what Marías once called "a typically Romantic life"; the first of the Carlist wars in Spain ended in 1839—Trans.]

seen: rationalism, the revolutionary spirit, the *ancien régime* and the divine right of kings, abstract violence, militarism, the empire.

As that experience has been lost and has become no longer familiar (it would take us too far afield to tell how and why), liberalism has disappeared and been replaced by all the other things. I would like to point out only that the *juvenilism* of recent European political movements signifies a negation of the experience of life and thus of liberalism. Which is not to say that young people cannot be liberals, but rather something quite different—that they cannot be *juvenilists*, just as before them Romantic youth was not, but just the contrary. What is proper to the young is youth, not an *ism* that replaces it. And maybe even to put on years, to fall in love with a mature woman and, instead of singing *Giovinezza*, to use this youth in singing of the autumn and the fallen leaves.

Upon arriving at this point we have to ask ourselves, a little closer up, *what* the experience of life is. And we are assailed by an unexpected uneasiness: if we take things seriously, might it not be a contradiction? Let us recall Kant's objections to metaphysics. Of its traditional objects —the world, the soul, God—no experience was possible because they are "infinite syntheses." In other words, since (for example) we are *in the world*, we cannot have an experience of it, but only of the things it contains. Are we not "within" life? Will it be possible to have experience of life?

The difficulty is considerable, and it would not be wise to put this problem aside too hastily. The day that one attacks the theme of the experience of life in a direct way (for it is practically untouched), that is the day that one and to the degree that they appear as things they are de-based, altered, converted into something other than what they are—that is, they are no longer present as lives. The irreducibility that defines other lives is twofold: they are irreducible with regard to my life; they are also irreducible to any thing. For that reason, while they are rooted re-alities, they appear as centers of rootedness, with regard to which I myself and my life are, in our turn, rooted realities.

This is one of the most difficult problems in the whole metaphysical theory of human life, the clarification of which would be an indispensable step for one who wishes to arrive at an adequate doctrine of the experience of life. I believe that the path toward it would consist of the ex-ploration of a concept that I introduced many years ago in *Introducción a la filosofía,** that of the *communicability of circumstances*. Thanks to this communicability, I find other lives in my circumstance that are not wholly alien to me, since their circumstances "communicate" with mine, and I have access to them not only as "things" but as "lives." This is the basis of the possibility of love, of friend-ship, and of all relations that are characteristically human —that is, personal.

And this also makes possible the experience of the *selfness* of my neighbor or, if you prefer, of my neighbor *him-self*. As an expression this is almost redundant, since if he is not "himself" he is not "neighbor"; and his neighborliness is not, of course, spatial or physical, but precisely that of his *self-identity*. The uncovering of this self-identity has not been easy, neither in a theoretical, nor in a literary, nor in a real sense. Probably it has been fully realized only in Chris-tianity, and later persistently forgotten within it. An ex-ample from literature will serve as an illustration. Only very lately have characters in fiction come to be irreduc-

* [In English as *Reason and Life* (Yale University Press, 1956)— Trans.]

ible, irreplaceable, genuine *persons*, and not "cases." [2]
Types that are more or less restricted, and in principle inter-changeable, in time give way to persons "themselves." Not
to speak of medieval epics or romances, consider that even
in the Spanish baroque drama—Lope almost always, Calderón perhaps always (*El médico de su honra, La vida es
sueño*)—lovers change partners with extraordinary
facility, whenever the fortunes of the drama or the will of
the sovereign compels them to do so. But this would not
happen in *Romeo and Juliet* nor, long before that, in the
Celestina, the work in which, in Spanish literature (and I
am not sure that it is only in Spanish literature), the mature discovery of the irreplaceable character in fiction
takes place. Calisto loves Melibea and Melibea loves Calisto,
with a singular and unique love; they love one another,
"themselves," in their irreducible self-identity, without
possibility of substitution. This is, I believe, the meaning of
Calisto's blasphemous endearments: "I am Melibean and
I adore Melibea, I believe in Melibea and I love Melibea,"
and so on, intermingled precisely with religious references
and thanks to God for that very Melibea—that is, in a
context that *excludes* lack of faith and requires one to ask
about the significance of those expressions. Calisto, upon
falling in love, has made the discovery of the *absolute* of
the person, of the person in her radical self-identity, and
this leads him to a "divinization" of her, since that is the
only way of expressing, and of acknowledging to himself,
the absolute and unique character revealed by his love for
Melibea.

This would not be a bad criterion, in our dealings with the
other, for distinguishing whether we look upon him as a
thing or as a person. In the first case, I may be obtaining

some utility, service, or pleasure from him, and he is more or less easily replaceable. In the second case, what I derive from the other is happiness, and then he is a neighbor—irreplaceable and unique. It has become customary, when some great man dies, to say that he leaves an unfillable vacuum; but one who is schooled by experience knows that before very long he will be replaced and that "nothing has happened." We are dealing, of course, with society and a social vacuum; and society is impersonal. But if one takes a different perspective, a personal perspective this time, one sees that many men are in fact irreplaceable. Who could we possibly put in place of Cervantes or El Greco or Saint John of the Cross or the genial Cadalso or Galdós or Azorín? Each one of them, with his unmistakeable voice, represents an aspect of our life, of our Spanish reality, that cannot be repudiated—and analogously in each society, and for all of them, there are some privileged men. And the profound (and consoling) reason that when one of those men disappears "nothing happens" is that in reality and from a personal perspective that man has *not passed on.*

Human life is made present in an adequate way only when, beyond its contents, it manifests its *form.* This is already revealed in the details of its internal movement, in what might be called, improperly, its "mechanism." Human life consists at each instant of a free decision, in a choice among the possibilities that constitute it. The past and the future are *present* in the act of decision, which for that reason is not an unextended "instant," but a temporal environment. Motives and ends are ingredients of each vital act. In other words, one's past history and one's vital program, intention, or vocation—that is, the temporal extension of which life consists and, with this extension, life's trajectory and its form—are at work in each one of those acts. Biographical *life* is not to be identified with its trajectory, but includes it as one of its contents. To such a

degree is this identification impossible that several trajectories pertain to life, not only the real and accomplished
one, but also those possible and unrealized ones in their
vitally true connections. That is, it is life *as a reality* that
decides among its trajectories and gives different degrees
of authenticity, and thus of "reality," to them.

And if life be considered in the act, not life concluded
and seen from the outside, under conditions where it is
possible to look upon its "precipitate" as a trajectory, a
biography, without regard for the fact that the radical
reality is not a biography but a *life* that is biographical—
if life be considered in the act, consequently with its
essential dimension of future intact, two important things
appear. First, different possible dimensions belong to its
"form," and with them an essential *multiplicity*. Second,
the experience of life formally *excludes* completeness or,
what is the same thing, it is "open." *Das Leben ist eben
mehrseitig*, Dilthey used to say: "Life is exactly many-
sided." Very different flavors belong to life, Ortega taught.
Through the years man gradually comes to know life by
savoring it in many different ways. The experience of life,
as this is distinguished from things and from its particular
contents and becomes transparent or translucent, gradually
discovers its abundance and its limitation, its destitute condition and its abundance beyond all fable, the impossibility
of happiness and at the same time its unquestionable, frag-
ile, and imperiled existence. One of its precipitates is the
acceptance, at one and the same time, of reality and its
limits—what is usually called contentment in limitation.
And it would not be excessive to interpret charity as the
supernatural form of the experience of life; or, if you
prefer, the experience of life would be the natural human
substrate of charity in the sense in which Saint John uses
this term.

Human life is *systematic;* regardless of the point at which it is touched, it is life itself that is touched. For that reason, all real contact with life discovers it in its self-identity, which does not imply that it is grasped as a whole. This is decisive for the comprehension of how the experience of life is possible and what it signifies. When a man "withdraws" into himself, when he retreats from things to the drama of which he himself consists, then he is creating the experience of life out of his own life. But, understand this well, far from having it "in his hand" and thus "given," it presents itself to him open and completely outspread, unfinished and in some ways unforeseeable—that is, he is creating experience in its inexhaustible reality. He feels an aftertaste of eternity, but it belongs to the very experience that is produced in him by the disenchantment he carries within him, for life is never complete, but means inexorably falling again into time, for future, the project without which it does not exist.

This is why the experience of life consists in *not being able* to be coming back from life. Whoever says that he is has "thingified" it, and this means that he radically lacks the experience *of life*, which is not a thing at all, but the realm in which all things are given, and which is not to be confused with any thing nor with them all together. For this reason, even granting all the experiences of things it is possible to imagine, even so the experience of life would not even have begun.

In a certain sense, life is "prior" to all its contents, and thus to everything, even though without them it would have no reality. It now becomes clear why one cannot be "coming back" from life, but always going on, although this going, at a certain level, may be at the same time a staying, a staying within oneself. What happens is that life is something that one cannot "take for granted." And also, literally, that it has no back.

Now, at the end of this circuit, we are assailed by one

final perplexity. This relates to the meaning of the expression we have been using constantly throughout these pages: "the experience *of* life." What does this mean? What is the meaning of that possessive, ambiguous in so many ways? A first meaning would be: experience *concerning* life. Evidently this is involved, and we do have to retain this meaning. But a second meaning would be: experience *characteristic* of life, experience that life itself possesses or acquires. But if not, then who? Whose experience can it be, any experience?

It could be said that ordinary experiences, experiences of things, of events, of happenings, are experiences of man, or perhaps only of his mind. They come down to a definite object and, as their subject, affect the psychophysical reality of the man who has them. But something else happens in that situation in which life becomes transparent to itself, in which (beyond the individual items of knowledge and experience) it accepts *the actual organization of reality,* which is *my life* itself, since the genuine encounter with reality (not merely in a mental or theoretical way) takes place by *experiencing* it. Thus it is life that is affected by experience, life as a whole, as a *drama* that includes the world, not simply the mind or psychophysical reality. It is life, then, that organizes and reorganizes itself in relation to that experience, which comes to form a part of its reality, not as a mere item of knowledge, not as contents of the mind, but as an ingredient of its reality, and thus as a decisive factor in the conduct of life. To such a degree is the experience of life not mental *alone* that it conditions mentality and itself becomes an instrument of intellection.

Both rationalism and irrationalism destroy the experience of life. For that reason, the experience of life is in crisis in our times, is disqualified (and, in parentheses, lost in a context that, regardless of its contents, makes it problematical). Rationalism, because it is all too sure of things and believes itself in possession beforehand of the knowledge of how things are—namely, rational. And this is why it is inclined toward abstraction, toward inert thought, toward a condition contrary to the *ultimate* concretion in which the experience of life consists. Irrationalism (which, unfortunately, has replaced rationalism in great regions of Western thought), because it too is sure of the irrationality of the real, of the inability of reason to apprehend it, and still more because, being impossible (life cannot exist except while reasoning), it obscures its own condition with arbitrariness and a different form of abstraction.

The experience of life is, unless I am in error, the nontheoretical form of vital reason, when it is applied to the whole of what is real and not to things. We might say that it is the nontheoretical homologue of vital reason, the "alveolus" within which vital reason functions. In this sense, it could be thought of as the *subsoil of philosophy*. Only from the point of view of the experience of life, upon this itself, and as a theoretical realization of it, would an authentic philosophy be possible—which does not, of course, mean that the function of the experience of life is to make philosophy possible. This might be the authentic and most profound meaning of the old observation that the owl of Minerva flies only at twilight.

NOTES

1. (Buenos Aires, 1958), pp. 190–194.
2. See Julián Marías, *Miguel de Unamuno* (Madrid, 1943); also in English (Harvard University Press, 1966).